THE PLAY'S THE THING

The Play's the Thing explains how analysing and working with plays can be central to the way dramatherapists think about their work, and highlights the use of plays in clinical, educational and performance settings. Discussion of plays from a wide variety of periods and cultures provides the context for exploration of theory and practice throughout the book.

Dramatherapy theory is revisited through the playwright's attention to plot, character and language; psychoanalytic concepts relevant to the dramatherapist, in particular the ideas of Winnicott and Melanie Klein, are illustrated by means of close analysis of dramatic text and discussion of practice. Exploration of several plays in depth invites the reader to return to take a fresh look at such different playwrights as Shakespeare, Ibsen and Caryl Churchill, and to become acquainted with new writing from India and Britain. Drawing on her wide experience of working with plays, Marina Jenkyns presents her own methods while defining her theoretical framework for the specialist and non-specialist alike. *The Play's the Thing* shows a dramatherapist at work as the reader is invited to share the author's personal response to the plays, including her feelings and inner thoughts as she prepares for her work, engages in the therapeutic relationship and reflects on the process.

A refreshingly original book, *The Play's the Thing* draws together different theoretical perspectives into a form which will stimulate the practising dramatherapist while also providing a crucial perspective for the student of dramatherapy. Marina Jenkyns's treatment of her subject makes fascinating reading for anyone interested in the ways that plays illuminate our lives.

Marina Jenkyns is a freelance dramatherapist, lecturer, trainer and director. She also has a private therapy and supervision practice.

To Julian

If we do meet again, why, we shall smile;
If not, why, then, this parting was well made.

Julius Caesar Act V, Scene 1

THE PLAY'S THE THING

Exploring text in drama
and therapy

Marina Jenkyns

London and New York

First published 1996
by Routledge
11 New Fetter Lane, London EC4P 4EE

Simultaneously published in the USA and Canada
by Routledge
29 West 35th Street, New York, NY 10001

Typeset in Times by
Datix International Limited, Bungay, Suffolk
Printed and bound in Great Britain by
Biddles Ltd, Guildford and King's Lynn

British Library Cataloguing in Publication Data

A catalogue record for this book is available from the British Library

Library of Congress Cataloguing in Publication Data

Jenkyns, Marina.
The play's the thing: exploring text in drama and therapy / Marina Jenkyns.
p. cm.
Includes bibliographical references and index.
1. Drama – Therapeutic use. I. Title.
RC489.P7J445 1996
616.89'1523–dc20

ISBN 0–415–11497–7
0–415–11498–5 (pbk)

CONTENTS

ACKNOWLEDGEMENTS

As this book is a distillation of many things in my life there are many people to thank. Though they are too numerous to name here I want to record my own gratitude to all those whose lives and work have touched mine and in doing so have their own place in the pages that follow. Some of them are here in direct reference, albeit anonymous and with identifying details disguised as is my practice when writing about people I work with. Others are here indirectly through the influence they have had upon my thinking and development at many stages. I thank them all.

For their direct help in getting *The Play's the Thing* started and completed I thank the following people. First Dr Sue Jennings for suggesting I write it in the first place and second Edwina Welham, my editor at Routledge, for inviting me to write it and her lively interest in the manuscript in which I found much encouragement at times when I particularly needed it. To the staff at Routledge whose personal response to the book and style of communication to me during the process have been bonuses I had not foreseen. To all those who responded to my invitation to send me feedback on some of my workshops; I am sorry not to have been able to include everyone's contribution. To Claire Tarjan, Vikki Gardiner and John Whitelock for reading some of the chapters at first draft stage and for their astute and helpful comments. To the following people for giving me permission to quote their words and/or experience in various chapters: Jan Addison, Mary Brunning, Nicole Buijsse, Helen Chambers, Pam Corti, Roger Grainger, Jenny McMahon, Flo Maitland, Jo Osborn, Bill Radmall, Gill Spendlove.

To members of the East Anglian Regional Dramatherapy Group who attended two workshops and provided me with valuable feedback. To Sudha Buchar and Christine Landon-Smith of Tashama Theatre Company for introducing me to 'A Shaft of Sunlight' and giving me permission to include this play in the book; to Naz Sienkiewicz for her helpful discussion of this text; to Arti Prashar for her help with the workshop on the play and to Surjit Bharij, Nena Kelley, Surjit Nazran, Geli Welzel and Bridie Woodburn for their contributions to it. To Daphne Thomas for creating such a rich text as 'Thursday's Child' as well as for her permission to quote from it here and to

ACKNOWLEDGEMENTS

Jessica Williams-Saunders for her important written contribution to Chapter 6, as well as what I learned from her in our work on this play. To Peter Gannon for his calm presence, good humour and systematic practical help with the bibliography and the vagaries of my computer in the hectic days before the delivery of the manuscript.

For permission to quote from the following copyright works: *Our Country's Good*, copyright © 1988 by Timberlake Wertenbaker based on the novel *The Playmaker* by Thomas Keneally © The Serpentine Publishing Company Pty, published by Hodder & Stoughton and Sceptre, by permission of Michael Imison Playwrights Ltd, 28 Almeida Street, London N1 1TD; *A Shaft of Sunlight* by permission of Tamasha Theatre Company and Birmingham Repertory Company; *Under Milk Wood* by Dylan Thomas, by permission of J. M. Dent; *Mary Barnes* by David Edgar, by permission of Methuen Publishers; *Saved* by Edward Bond, by permission of Methuen Publishers; *Cloud Nine* by Caryl Churchill (Pluto Press, Joint Stock Theatre Group, London, 1980), reproduced by permission of Pluto Press; *Roots* from *The Wesker Trilogy Volume 1* by Arnold Wesker (Penguin Books 1964, first published by Jonathan Cape 1960), copyright © Arnold Wesker, 1959, 1960, reproduced by permission of Penguin Books Ltd and Arnold Wesker; 'Mushrooms' from *The Colossus and Other Poems* by Sylvia Plath. Copyright © 1960 by Sylvia Plath, reprinted by permission of Alfred A. Knopf Inc. and of the publishers Faber and Faber Ltd; 'Little Gidding' from *Collected Poems 1909–1962* by T. S. Eliot, by permission of the publishers Faber and Faber Ltd and Harcourt Brace and Company; 'Burnt Norton' by T. S. Eliot, by permission of the publishers Faber and Faber Ltd and Harcourt Brace and Company; *Ghosts* from *Ibsen: Plays Volume 1*, translated by Michael Meyer, published by Methuen and Rupert Hart Davies, by permission of David Higham Associates.

During the whole process of writing this book I have received other invaluable gifts. Two in particular I wish to acknowledge here. I thank Joy for her quiet wisdom, and for her incredible patience and support which was manifest in many different ways, particularly in the final stages of writing when she managed to combine making sure I ate with providing most helpful critical response to pages waved at her hot off the printer at often inconvenient times. And finally I thank my own psychotherapist, Ohja Khaleelee, who has been both a guide and a follower in the landscape of my inner world; to her skills, humanity and faith I owe much.

AUTHOR'S NOTE

1 With some considerable reservations I have used the word 'clients' to represent the people with whom dramatherapists work. There are many complex issues to which my dilemma of language relate, such as power, status, difference, etc. (Therapists themselves are often clients in one context and therapists in another.) My own unresolved difficulties over terminology are dealt with in this book by the word 'client' often being used interchangeably with the word 'participant' or 'group member'. While describing drama or dramatherapy sessions the word 'actor' is frequently used to denote the participant/client engaged in the work.

2 The spelling of 'phantasy' and 'fantasy' is as far as possible in accordance with Susan Isaacs's definition: fantasy to denote 'conscious daydreams, fictions and so on', and phantasy 'the primary content of unconscious mental processes'. *International Journal of Psycho-Analysis*, XXIX, 73–97.1948. (Note also Laplanche and Pontalis's reservations about this distinction in *The Language of Psycho-analysis*, p. 318.)

PROLOGUE

While setting about writing this book I visited a new theatre to discuss a play I was about to direct. The artistic director was refreshingly flexible about his space and excited by the possibility of a play which explored the relationship between process and product, theatre and therapy. Words like Grotowski, Brecht, experimental theatre, the Off-Off Broadway plays of the 1960s, filled me with nostalgia for the days when financial constraints, box office success, and conservatism were not the hallmarks of much of British theatre. The days when Peter Brook still worked in Britain. This artistic director had lived in England for only three years and for him the questions about what theatre was about had not been asked in a society characterized by a decade and a half of Thatcher and post-Thatcher mediocrity.

Then I reflected on what had been happening in the field of drama during these years in Britain in areas other than that of the professional theatre. One of these was the development of educational drama and the other the development of dramatherapy. So now I write at a time when dramatherapy seems to have 'arrived' in Britain. Like Sylvia Plath's 'Mushrooms'

> Overnight, very
> Whitely, discreetly,
> Very quietly
>
> Our toes, our noses
> Take hold on the loam,
> Acquire the air.

Since the mid-1960s this growth has been taking place. Quietly pushing itself into visibility, growing in apparent darkness. When I trained we had to look to the USA for literature and articles. Still relevant writings in French, German, Dutch and Russian remain untranslated and therefore inaccessible to many practitioners. Now there are books on dramatherapy coming out every year in Britain.

This book is part of that growth. My own love of plays, forged in me from childhood, nurtured at university, and honed throughout my teaching career with both children and adults, found an unexpected development in drama-therapy. At all those stages of my life my engagement with dramatic text included practical work of one kind or another – acting, directing, teaching experientially, etc. – then as a dramatherapist I realized I was reading texts differently. Old and familiar plays informed my life in a different way and I began to realize the potential for the use of dramatic text in the areas of self-knowledge and healing that were different from those which already existed for me when I read them as actor, director or teacher. I also found myself being a different kind of audience member. Side by side with these new in-sights another influence 'crept by me upon the waters'; my own experience of psychoanalytic psychotherapy and my study of aspects of psychoanalytic theory, particularly that of object relations, further enhanced my life and my work.

The purpose of the book is therefore to share something of how I read and work with dramatic literature. I do not presume to say to the reader, 'This is how to use text as a dramatherapist'; rather to invite you to consider if there are ways in which you might wish to work with text to enhance your own work, whether it be that of therapist, theatre practitioner or educationalist. Quite unashamedly I also want to indulge myself in writing about plays which I find stimulating, moving and exciting, plays which have influenced me both personally and professionally and new plays which I am just getting to know. As a teacher I was convinced that if I felt passionately about the ma-terial my enthusiasm was infectious – I engaged the students; they did not have to end up thinking as I did, God forbid! I would not have been much of a teacher if they did, but they got involved and it stimulated them to make their own explorations, wherever that text might lead them. Maybe I am still a teacher, for that is my hope in writing this book, that by sharing the way I read, think about and work with dramatic text, you too, whilst you might dis-agree with my interpretation, will be stimulated to make connections which will take you into hitherto unexplored regions of your own interests.

In order to do this I first set the context of dramatherapy, familiar ground for some readers, new for others. I do this through exploring relevant theories in the light of a dramatic text which raises many important issues about theatre, about the nature and function of drama in society and as a means of healing and growth. The play I have chosen for this is *Our Country's Good* by Timberlake Wertenbaker.

This is followed by setting out a parallel context, that of psychodynamics, focusing particularly on the work of Winnicott and Melanie Klein. Again drama and plays provide the framework for this and I refer to several plays as well as focusing in more detail on one, Edward Bond's *Saved*. Here I shall look at some of the relationships which I find between some of the basic tenets of psychoanalytic theory, dramatic texts and dramatherapy practice. The first part of the book concludes with a chapter describing the ways in which I think about practical application of theory; this I think of as a kind of 'nuts and bolts' chapter. Reference is made here to a variety of texts, in particular Beckett's *Waiting for Godot*.

There follows an exploration of five plays combining a personal analysis of the text with a consideration of some of the implications for practice for both participants and dramatherapist. Of the examples from sessions several are taken from training contexts, because much of my dramatherapy work on text has been in that area to date. Dramatherapist readers may wish to consider the possibilities of how this way of working can apply to their own fields and client groups, for I explore some of the life themes which are most common to us when working in dramatherapy through focusing on individual texts from a variety of periods and cultures. Since dramatherapy only highlights the essential concerns, difficulties and pains of ordinary human living, these themes are also those with which the theatre concerns itself and which educational drama can, perhaps more easily than many other areas of the curriculum, tackle – disturbing, sensitive and painful though they may be. To describe this section of the book let me borrow Dylan Thomas's lines from *Under Milk Wood*,

> Only you can hear and see, behind the eyes of the sleepers, the movements and mazes and colours and dismays and rainbows and tunes and wishes and flight and fall and despairs and big seas of their dreams.
>
> (Thomas 1954)

The characters and life of any text opens to us the moment we open the book. They sleep till we come. They can waken to us over and over and over again. Each time we encounter a text we bring to it our own 'movements and mazes and colours and dismays and rainbows and tunes and wishes and flight and fall and despairs and big seas' of not only our conscious but also our unconscious life. So we do in dramatherapy. As the child in the drama class does. As the actor does. As the audience does.

The speech from which I have just quoted begins with words which hold in their hand the utter darkness of the night and the fact that it is Spring, the time of growth.

> It is Spring, moonless night in the small town, starless and Bible-black. . . . And all the people of the lulled and dumbfound town are sleeping now.
>
> (Thomas 1954)

In dramatherapy we are concerned with growth. The working world, as that of any dynamically orientated therapy, is the unconscious, the darkness. What I endeavour to do is to move through the mazes of some of the life experiences which bring people to therapy, choosing plays which seem to me to present these issues challengingly and with depth and compassion. In these six chapters I attempt to explore some of this richness.

The book ends with looking at the Epilogue from Shakespeare's *The*

Tempest. This to my mind echoes the therapeutic process when the aim of the therapy has been accomplished and client and indeed therapist move on. Just as the lights coming on in the auditorium or the students walking away from their final drama lesson signal the carrying away of the theatre form within, we can, through internalizing this art-form through dramatherapy, continue life enhanced. And so I hope it will be with this book.

1

DRAMATHERAPY
Through the lens of the play

INTRODUCTION

The play's the thing
Wherein I'll catch the conscience of the king.
(*Hamlet* Act II, Scene 2: 616)

When Hamlet lays a trap for his uncle Claudius to check if he really has killed his father as the Ghost has suggested, he chooses the device of the theatre. When the players arrive at Elsinore he asks the Player King to put on the *Murder of Gonzago*:

We'll ha't to-morrow night. You could, for a need, study a speech of some dozen or sixteen lines, which I would set down and insert in't, could you not?

(ibid.: 550)

It is the text which will touch Claudius; it will act like a truth drug giving Hamlet the evidence he needs. And indeed it does.

I have heard
That guilty creatures, sitting at a play,
Have by the very cunning of the scene
Been struck so to the soul that presently
They have proclaimed their malefactions.
(ibid.: 661)

Hamlet's image of the power of the play is shocking. It is as though the text can be a kind of thought-police from Orwell's *Nineteen Eighty-Four*. But there are other ways in which this power identified by Hamlet can be used; the play can be a powerful mirror of human experience, not only to catch out the guilty, which is Hamlet's focus here, but also to show us who we are, to mirror our lives to us.

Aristotle in *The Poetics*, writing of Tragedy and the tragic poet, says,

1

The poet's function is to describe, not the thing that has happened but a kind of thing that might happen i.e. what is possible as being probable or necessary.... Poetry is something more philosophic and of graver import than history, since its statements are of the nature rather of universals whereas those of history are singulars. By a universal statement I mean one as to what such or such a kind of man will probably or necessarily do – which is the aim of poetry.

(Bywater 1920: 43)

This word 'universal' is extremely important when we consider the use of a dramatic text, for it is that ability of the playwright to present a text 'to which every bosom returns an echo' which draws us to the theatre. If in the theatre we can watch fellow human beings doing what we might do, we can tap into the universal community of human experience. Such doing need not, of course, be literal. Theatre is in itself a metaphor for life and its function symbolic. We do not have to have literally killed to understand Claudius' feelings when he sees his crimes enacted on the stage; we can identify with our own murderous thoughts. Claudius gives them 'a local habitation and a name' and thus helps to make the unbearable bearable, the unspeakable spoken. The connection can be actual as well as metaphoric; the actor Brian Cox reports that after he had played King Lear at Broadmoor, the British secure psychiatric hospital,

A consultant came and told me that three of her patients . . . came quite separately to her and said, 'I did so envy the ability of Cordelia and her father to have a farewell . . . it made me think about my own situation, particularly before I murdered my parents.'

(M. Cox 1992: 56)

Claudius has the reality of himself mirrored to him by being audience of a representation of himself, his situation and his deeds. The patients at Broadmoor similarly. They were, in a sense, both actors and audience. Sitting and watching they were members of an audience, but they were, through empathic identification, actors reliving their own situation as it was, like Claudius, or as it might have been, like the patients.

The idea of a play within a play is a frequently found theatrical device. Its popularity with dramatists may lie in the fact that it is a language in which characters explore their world in a way that cannot be done by any other means. By this method playwrights underscore the value of plays themselves as means of communication. I want to invite the reader of this book to look at them with me because I believe that the reading of, the thinking about, the experiencing of plays are vital ways of deepening the dramatherapist's awareness. Jones, responding to Landy's concerns about the ways in which dramatherapy theory needs to be defined in 'theory derived from drama' (Landy 1986) finds the problem as 'one of defining a language that is meaningful for dramatherapy' (Payne 1993: 42).

In defining a language we also define our thoughts and the very process of defining our thoughts depends on the language we already have. The way we think about a play is different from the way in which we read either a theoretical study or exposition, different from the way we learn from reading case studies and clinical material, different from understanding our own work through recordings or the supervision process, different from practical work we may do in improvisation or being a participant in a dramatherapy group. In reading dramatic text we can develop the language of metaphor in the way we think about dramatherapy.

In the reference with which I began this chapter, Hamlet asks the Player King to 'study a speech of some dozen or sixteen lines', in other words dramatic text. At the moment of 'action suiting the words and the words to the action' Claudius reacts to his secret laid out before him. When watching the play Claudius rises, unable to endure it. He has survived the dumb show which wordlessly tells the story of the usurper poisoning the king, wooing the widowed queen and gaining her. He has seen his own actions mirrored precisely. But he does not apparently react. It is only when the words are suited to the action and the action to the words, when the scripted version is enacted before him, that he experiences the full impact of the meaning of the play as it applies directly to himself. We do not know precisely when 'the king rises' but we do know the last words the usurper has spoken. Referring to the poison which he is about to pour into the sleeping king's ears he says,

> Thy natural magic and dire property
> On wholesome life usurp immediately.
> [*Pours the poison into the sleeper's ears*]
> (*Hamlet* Act III, Scene 2: 265)

It is the brilliant placing of the word 'usurp' which causes the reverberation in the depths of Claudius' being. He himself not only had usurped the crown, his brother, but also has, in doing so, blasted the 'wholesome life' of Denmark. The famous line 'Something is rotten in the state of Denmark' complements this: what is wholesome has become rotten. And not gradually but immediately. 'The funeral meats did coldly furnish forth the marriage feast', as Hamlet puts it, corroborated by Horatio, 'Indeed my lord it followed hard upon.' All Claudius' crimes are therefore in that one line. The use of the word 'usurp' to personify the poison mirrors Claudius to himself, not only as a usurper and poisoner but also as poison itself. It dehumanizes him and makes him one with his deed. Claudius experiences the power of the drama both to mirror his life to him and in doing so to present him with alternatives for his future action.

This moment illustrates the powerful ways in which metaphoric language coupled with dramatic action can speak to us. However much it might be described, elucidated, analysed, it can have its full impact only in its context, played on the stage at best, at second best read with the reader's imagination supplying the theatre. Take the example of 'All the world's a stage'; the precise meaning of this sentence which may be used by many people who do not know where it originates, lies in its metaphoric value. (For an illuminating and entertaining example of the extent of Shakespearian usage in everyday English see Levin (1986) quoted in Cox and and Theilgaard (1987), p. 44.) As in all poetry it is multi-layered and gives expression to something the speaker wants to express at that precise moment for which no other words will do. Let us look at what has just happened. Automatically, when faced with the use of metaphoric language, images and associations reverberate at both a conscious and unconscious level; our perceptions are expanded cognitively, emotionally, psychically and maybe spiritually at the same time. This is what happens to Claudius. He does not stop to think, he acts. The action may be an externally visible one, as in Claudius' rising. It may also be an inner shifting of feeling and perception, not visible externally. We find this when Hamlet witnesses the Player King's acting and prompts Polonius' comments on the actor's pallor and tears. The effect of the acting on Hamlet is to create shifts of feeling and perception within himself which find their voice only when he is on his own; marvelling at the actor's ability to feel emotion for things and people so far removed from himself causes Hamlet to say,

> What would he do
> Had he the motive and the cue for passion
> That I have?
> (*Hamlet* Act II, Scene 2: 570)

Then action follows – the action of deciding to use the performance of a play to mirror Claudius' crime.

Responding to a dramatic text, therefore, is one way of helping us not only to think but also to perceive dramatically. A dramatherapist needs to perceive dramatically for drama is at the heart of our work; we need to allow the characters, plot, dialogue, form, language and structure of a play into our repertoire of thought mechanisms and perceptions. Such perceiving, not just thinking, is, I believe, integral to the development of the dramatherapist's practice. It is neither more nor less important than those other ways in which dramatherapists develop their art. It is simply different – and to my mind equally important. It is part of the language in which dramatherapy must be defined.

OUR COUNTRY'S GOOD AND DRAMATHERAPY: WORLDS WITHIN WORLDS

In this chapter I shall be discussing some of the central concepts of dramatherapy through reference to a single dramatic text. It is not my intention to present a definition of dramatherapy or to go over ground already

4

well-worked by other writers (e.g. Landy 1986; 1993; Jennings 1990; 1992; Grainger 1990). It is, rather, to draw attention to ways in which we can read those concepts in the text and read the text in them.The text provides us with a framework for thinking about dramatherapy, what it is and how it works, whether we are familiar or unfamiliar with it.

The play which provides my framework is *Our Country's Good* by Timberlake Wertenbaker. It is a play which revels in the theatre. Seeing it on stage one is drawn in by the many levels of theatrical metaphor at which it operates; it creates a theatrical hall of mirrors. Some of the reflections in those mirrors have relevance for the dramatherapist. It has already sharpened and honed the dramatherapist I am, as I believe dramatic text should. Some of what I have written already was developed by my engagement with this text – by the events, the characters and the world of the play, both as it is lived out in the play and as a metaphor for life. It takes a singular historical experience, which combined with the dramatic art form reflects a universal one – a combination of Aristotle's opposites.

The play is based on the novel, *The Playmaker*, by Thomas Keneally (1987), which in turn is based on the historical fact that a group of deported convicts staged a play in New South Wales in 1788.

> A play is a world in itself, a tiny colony we could almost say.
>
> (Act II, Scene 2)

The Governor's words are a neat inversion of Shakespeare's 'All the world's a stage'. This kind of tightness of metaphor, echoing, and multi-layered allusion are typical of Wertenbaker's writing and are why it is exciting as a text. It triggers off image, memory, half-forgotten, half-remembered moments of theatre and life. Indeed I suspect that it relies on this kind of audience response for its success. So what is it about?

Basically its story is simple. A lieutenant eager for promotion directs a group of convicts in the rehearsal and performance of Farquhar's *The Recruiting Officer*. The performing of a play is born of the fabric of the social unit which is this colony and weaves itself into it. One of the important questions it raises is: can new cloth be made from old to clothe this community in garments which are not the same as those of the old world? Can this colony become indeed a New World? And if so what place has theatre in this transformation?

These are also the questions that face the dramatherapist working with a group of people which will become a 'tiny colony' called a dramatherapy group.

Let's look at Wertenbaker and see who are the 'group members' of her tiny colony.

In the dark hold of the convict ship the convicts 'huddle together in the semi-darkness' while one of their number is being flogged. The officer monotonously counts the lashes. From the silence a convict speaks into the hushed and darkened theatre. Thus John Wisehammer:

> At night? The sea cracks against the ship. Fear whispers, screams, falls silent, hushed. Spewed from our country, forgotten, bound to the dark edge of the earth, at night what is there to do but seek English cunt, warm, moist, soft, oh the comfort of the lick, the thrust into the nooks, the crannies of the crooks of England. Alone, frightened, nameless in this stinking hole of hell, take me, take me inside you, whoever you are. Take me my confort and we'll remember England together.
>
> (Act I, Scene 1)

Let's juxapose this passage with another. In Act I, Scene 6 we find the officers arguing like true eighteenth-century gentlemen; their subject? The theatre. The Governor, Arthur Phillip, is encouraging Lieutenant Ralph Clark in his proposal to produce a play with the convicts. Ralph struggles to articulate his ideas in the face of some strong opposition from his superiors.

> RALPH: ... in a small way this could affect all the convicts and even ourselves, we could forget our worries about the supplies, the hangings, the floggings, and think of ourselves at the theatre, in London, with our wives and children, that is, we could, euh –
> PHILLIP: Transcend –
> RALPH: Transcend the darker, euh – transcend the –
> JOHNSTON: Brutal –
> RALPH: The brutality – remember our better nature and remember –
> COLLINS: England.
> RALPH: England.
>
> *A moment*
>
> (Act I, Scene 6)

Both groups have one very obvious thing in common, which is their isolation from their homeland. From England. They deal with it in different ways but both ways are aspects of the whole, though at this stage they are polarized. The feelings of rejection by both convicts and officers, equally at the mercy of the hostile land and climatic conditions, are common to both. Here they are all ill-adapted. In King Lear's words they are all 'unaccommodated man' subjected to the environment and dependent on a supply ship which might or might not arrive. All are vulnerable. And they are interdependent.

The two groups represent to us, the audience, two facets of the wider society of any human group and these are important to understand if we are to fully appreciate the significance which the performing of a play in this colony has.

The convicts have escaped death by being sentenced to transportation. They have in a sense come up from the bottom. They have nothing to lose and perhaps something to gain, if – but only if – this community can be different from the one they have left. All their lives they have been victims of a harsh and unequal society, abused, exploited and brutally punished. The officers are in some ways therefore, in terms of the shock to their system, in a worse state than the convicts. They have everything to lose and little to gain in terms of the privileged life they are used to.

But maybe they do have something to gain.

> PHILLIP: ... we, this colony of a few hundred will be watching this together, for a few hours we will no longer be despised prisoners and hated gaolers. We will laugh, we may be moved, we may even think a little.
>
> (Act I, Scene 6)

What they may gain is a sense of integration, a glimpse of a more equal society, less split, less polarized, more humane. A state of being unintegrated is not one conducive to thought. The fact the Governor says, 'we may even think a little' indicates his belief in the play's ability to effect change.

What is important to be aware of here is the level at which these two different groups experience commonality. The splits mean nothing if the two groups are not part of the same whole. I believe they are. In the text there is much to support the view that both share the rejection and sense of abandonment, and both groups are deeply vulnerable, needy and afraid. Both groups find ways of expressing their feelings and experience and both find ways of dealing with it. In the passages quoted both groups talk of fear, darkness, the need for comfort, the need to somehow retain the memory of England. Let us look at these passages in a little more detail and explore some of the psychological and emotional sub-text, the meaning held by the metaphor.

In his opening lines Wisehammer gives us a picture of the experience of these convicts and an understanding of their need for both escape and containment. It is a male vision and the female is both mother and mistress, the Oedipal dream enacted, the punishing father banished. (See also the last lines of *Greek* by Steven Berkhoff (1988).)

> Take me, take me inside you.
> (Act I, Scene 1)

In the play this place of comfort is represented, for these English convicts, by England and English women, the brilliant play on words of the 'nooks, the crannies of the crooks of England' suggests the merging of mother, mistress and mother-land in the desire for both comfort and relief. Wisehammer eloquently describes the need to escape from all the pain. In the outcome of sexual coupling there is a fantasy for a new beginning and new birth, salvation, continuity not annihilation. That something should be born is implicit in the sexual imagery of these lines, simultaneously with the need to crawl back into mother for security in a frightening world. Here he speaks meta-phorically for the whole convict community, women and men as well.

In Scene 6, from which the second passage is taken, it is the officers who are aware of their own vulnerability, who are tired of the strain of their new ex-istence and who want some form of escape. Ralph expresses this through the metaphor of the theatre. In the theatre they can forget their troubles, he poses, and in forgetting remember the comforting image of home.

In their different ways both groups are expressing something fundamental to the well-being of this society – the acknowledgement of vulnerability, the need for human contact and for respite, and the ability to come through. Both groups need hope, the possibility of transcending the unbearable.

What is so interesting for the dramatherapist is the particular combination of elements which comprise this 'tiny colony'. The officers, the educated men, have at their disposal a model from the culture from which they come, that of the dramatic art-form which they can exploit for the good. The aesthetic principle is produced in this unlikely setting as a means of bearing with the unbearable. There is by no means unanimous support amongst the officers for the idea of a play being produced but it is what is eventually decided. The governor holds firm to it even when Ralph himself feels too daunted to con-tinue, in Act II.

In these early scenes the mouthpiece for raw human experience is held by the convicts and the possibility of the healing power of the art-form by the officers. The fact that the balance will change and these roles become less rigid is part of the change that begins to be wrought in this society. The vital thing is that both elements are present in the community; the possibility for growth, change, even healing, is inherent.

We have hardly begun to look at the play and yet already it can help us to focus on dramatherapy and on the social and psychological function of drama.

Before coming to the dramatherapy group the client will have received many metaphorical, or all too often actual, lashes at the hands of family, husband, wife, partner, mother, father, sibling, friend or foe; at the hands of that amoeba-like creature society which has power without responsibility be-cause it is composed of all of us. The beginning of *Our Country's Good* counts out those lashes. 'Forty-four, forty-five, forty-six, forty-seven, forty-eight, forty-nine, fifty' (Act I, Scene 1).

The vulnerability which we have seen in both convicts and officers is there in the group. Group members may experience themselves as 'spewed from [their] country, forgotten, bound to the dark edge of the earth'. Some may cover this with defensive mechanisms such as Tench's sarcasm: 'perhaps we should build an opera house for the convicts'. However they may present, all may wish to transcend the brutality and find some comfort.

In the dramatherapy group, just as in the play, there is a need for contain-ment, for safety, for the mother who will provide not oblivion but keep in mind the wider context of society. Wisehammer's words mirror the therapy group where the need for regression in a safe environment co-exists with the hope for re-birth.

The desperation with which many come to therapy, the desperation of the unhappy child in the drama class, the 'quiet desperation' of many human beings who witness the theatre in the desert villages of Rajasthan or from the most expensive seats in the West End theatres of London is voiced here, 'Alone, frightened, nameless in this stinking hole of hell'.

With such inner (or indeed outer) pain, containment is vital if it is to be faced. It is for us the audience and it is for those in the dramatherapy group. So what is it that provides the containment? Here we link up with one of the most useful things a dramatic text has to offer the dramatherapist. It is a container for the chaos of the community and like all effective containers it provides the conditions for growth. (For more extensive discussion of 'container' and 'containment' see Chapters 2 and 3.) The other container is the Governor, Arthur Phillip. He resembles the banished Duke in the Forest of Arden (*As You Like It*), a man who craves for a better society and dreams of establishing it outside the confines of the realm from which he comes and indeed to which he owes allegiance. It is Phillip who puts forward the value of the experience of theatre.

> TENCH: There is much excitement in the colony about the hangings.
>   It's their theatre, Governor, you cannot change that.
> PHILLIP: I would prefer them to see real plays, fine language, sentiment.
> (Act 1, Scene 3)

It is his vision which is realized in this play as the convicts eventually perform Farquhar's *The Recruiting Officer*. It is he who has to hold on to the idea in spite of opposition when it seems as though the negative forces will prevail. Like the dramatherapist he must hold on to the aims. In this Phillip is helped by the questions which already concern him: 'Was it necessary to cross fifteen thousand miles of ocean to erect another Tyburn?' (ibid.).

These are his opening lines. They encapsulate questions which are at the heart of this play. What is crime and what is punishment? What possibilities are there for a community from an old world to find, and indeed found, a new one for itself? What are theatre and spectacle and ritual? What are the implications for new beginnings, education, change, the social order? He is a thinker and his thinking is about change.

Already this little community in its infancy is taking the realm of the theatre to define itself. The juxtaposition of the hangings and the debate of educated men about the theatre mirror the juxtaposition of the two parts of this society, crudely and cruelly satirized by Tench's quip about Garrick. It also reveals the need of these men to retain the familiar at least in their minds, in order to cope with their outcast state. It reveals their fears, their defences and their vulnerabilities. On the ship the convicts are like children, huddled together for comfort, coping with abuse and deprivation as best they know how. On land the officers are like parents trying to work out how to survive and contain, uprooted from all that is known and familiar; they struggle to enable the family to survive and they provide a stark representation of 'good' and 'bad' parenting.

In the context of this 'family' we can explore how *Our Country's Good* exemplifies some of the key concepts in dramatherapy. The rehearsal work in the colony helps us to focus on some of these within the larger concept of enactment. *Enactment* is at the heart of dramatherapy and within the concept of enactment lie the functions of *role, aesthetic distance* and *audience/actor relationship*. In understanding the ways in which these contribute to the phenomenon of enactment we can understand the very heart of dramatherapy itself.

ROLE AND ENACTMENT

While much has been written about roles both on and offstage, for the dramatherapist no more exhaustive study of role and its use in dramatherapy has been made than that by Robert Landy (1993). He points out the paradox which is 'at the heart of the dramatic experience' with the actor 'living simultaneously in two realities'. He suggests that taking on a role and taking off a role is a kind of living and dying.

> The actor's dilemma is not to choose between life or death but to find a way to emerge into a state of being that holds life and death together, accepting the inevitable shifts in and out and among several roles. The paradox of drama is to be and not to be simultaneously.
>
> (Landy 1993: 12)

Our Country's Good shows us how this process happens. With the characters we enter into the experience of what being in role actually means and highlights the confusion and the working through of this.

Once the play has been decided upon Ralph Clark has the difficult job of defining his cast. And they have the equally difficult job of understanding what being in a play actually means.

> MARY: How can I play Silvia? She's brave and strong. She couldn't have done what I've done.
> DABBY: She didn't spend eight months and one week on a convict ship. Anyway, you can pretend you're her.
> MARY: No, I have to be her.
> DABBY: Why?
> MARY: Because that's acting.
> DABBY: No way I'm being Rose, she's an idiot.
>
> (Act I, Scene 8)

Let's look first at the character of Mary Brenham and see what it means to her to be involved in a play. The first time we see her is in Act I, Scene 1. In this first encounter we see that it is her literacy which speaks for her, otherwise she has hardly a voice at all. Apart from one 'yes' and one 'no' she says nothing other than the lines from *The Recruiting Officer* which Ralph asks her to read. All other questions put to her are answered by Dabby. She appears totally unconfident. When we next meet her in Act I, Scene 8 her commitment to the play is clear. She is trying to keep Dabby on task in learning her lines whereas Dabby is totally absorbed in thinking about how she might get back to England. Mary is in the present, Dabby in the past and the future. The character of Mary is congruent with the prerequisite for role work; the 'being present-ness' without which it is impossible to be engaged in the two realities of actor and character simultaneously. Wertenbaker reveals her as a woman for whom the transformational properties of role enactment are within reach. Her attitude could be likened to that of a professional actor or a member of a dramatherapy group committed to the task of the play or enactment. She defines her responsibility as an actor to identify completely with the character.

At this point it is important to note the starting point at which Mary comes to the role. She considers she is not brave like the heroine she is to play. Although she has endured the rigours and shame of the convict ship she is totally unaware of the irony of Dabby's words referring to this. In other words she projects on to Silvia her own bravery. This is crucial to note if we are to see how an exploration of Mary reveals the process of dramatherapy role and text work. Although we shall look at this concept and this example of projection more fully in the next chapter here we can see how Mary allows herself to relate to the play within the boundaries of the text, what the text requires and what the text allows. She debates the meanings of her part that she does not understand, she helps others with their parts and at one point is substitute director. In other words she allows the world of the play as it is written to be the context for her exploration of her own world of feelings, behaviour and thoughts.

MARY: If I had been Silvia, I would have trusted Plume.

(Act II, Scene 7)

This, and indeed the scene from which it comes, which is entitled 'The Meaning of Plays', shows the role-taking at work as a force of development and change. Through playing the role Mary is able to consider an aspect of her own personality. She can compare herself with the character and in doing so the character can act as a catalyst to her developing thoughts. This is one of the ways in which the taking on of a role functions in dramatherapy and where the script is all-important. The script is written; it already exists. Had Mary been working through improvisation she might have played Silvia as trusting Plume, but the script does not allow this. Instead it allows Mary to consider her own feelings which the role has put her in touch with; she can

11

pace her responses and so be given time to focus on them. The timing is all-important, for of course eventually Silvia does trust Plume. The fact that Mary is falling in love with Ralph is therefore 'held' by the pace at which the role works in the script. In other words Mary is given time to move into a position where the relationship is one in which her feelings are in accord with his. She has time to develop her own place in relationship with him so that she enters freely into it rather than being reactive to the man, or abused in the fashion of the convict's usual life. She has time to develop her confidence by acting the role of the confident Silvia.

As the play and the rehearsals for the play-within-the-play proceed, Mary reveals her ability to think about what being in a play actually means, to debate the issues. She discusses the intricacies of role and adopts her own stances on the possibilities and limitations of enactment.

> DABBY: You're playing a man: Jack Wilful.
> MARY: Yes, but in the play, I know I'm a woman, whereas if you played
> Kite, you would have to think you were a man.
>
> (Act II, Scene 7)

But at the same time she is not exempt from the struggle which all the convicts are having about the nature of the theatre and its relation to 'reality'. While she attempts only a few lines after this to stay within the task of the rehearsal, she finds herself unable to work with Ketch, the convict who is to be the colony's hangman; here the reality of her life-context overshadows the reality of the play. The rehearsal breaks down in chaos because the play-within-the-play at this point fails to support the characters against the onslaught of the hostile environment encroaching across its boundary.

The next time we see Mary she is practising her lines alone on the beach. Ralph enters and joins in, playing the part of Plume to her Silvia. The two realities come together here. It is as though each part of the paradox is put under a microscope and in slow motion; both Mary and Ralph know that they are acting and that within the acting they are declaring their love for one another. After they kiss Ralph says, 'Don't lower your head. Silvia wouldn't.' He invokes the role to enable Mary to take her equal place with him. He asks to see her naked and she in return claims her right to see him. The dialogue is simple and moving. The language is balanced and harmonious. How different from the initial meeting of Ralph and Mary when she could only speak, head bowed, through the reading of Silvia's lines. Here Mary's submission is not to Ralph, but to her own feelings. She is in control of her own destiny here, unlike the Mary of the ship who submitted to Dabby's procuring in order to eat and who carries the disabling shame of that abuse.

The play has given Mary a power of her own. She restores herself through the role. She allows the role to work for her. By projecting herself into the part of the independently minded, adventurous Silvia who knows what she wants and how to work to get it, Mary can get in touch with those aspects of herself.

12

What do we learn from Mary about the value of being in a role where the words are prescribed? The role provides her with a context, the text with a language in which she can grow, finding her own language, her own assertion of personality from what is, to start off with, a very unpromising situation. Being a convict with no rights she has little going for her. Being Silvia in *The Recruiting Officer* she has everything going for her. By holding the paradox of being both self and other simultaneously she can enlarge herself through the engagement with the role. She can project aspects of herself onto Silvia, bravery, for example, and by playing the role discover her own bravery which was there unrecognized all the time. Silvia gives Mary a chance to find it. She can therefore begin to truly enlarge her way of being in the world by taking on those unrecognized aspects of her own personality.

If we return to the dialogue between Mary and Dabby we find a contrast in how the two women let the role work for them, as Mary does, or not, like Dabby. Here we see in action, embodied by two dramatic characters, the separate components of Landy's paradox. Mary has to 'be' the character if she is to act her. Dabby, on the other hand, is very clear about the 'let's pretend' aspect of acting. At the same time she understands the game which she is being asked to play and turns the play to her advantage. It suits her to go along with Mary's argument once she is presented with it as a way of holding on to her own identity, that is to refuse to play a part she does not want to. She is reminiscent of the adolescent in the dramatherapy group who uses every advantage for resistance. It is not as though she 'breaks the rules', it is more that she does not acknowledge them in the first place. In this case the rules are that of the conventions of the theatre, of the holding of Landy's two realities at once. In Act II, Scene 7, Ralph reminds her of the character she is playing:

RALPH: You have to say these lines with charm and – euh, blushes.
DABBY: I don't blush.

Shortly after this she says

DABBY: If Wisehammer can think he's a big country lad, I can think I'm a man.

(Act II, Scene 7)

From the two opposite positions which these quotations reveal, and her earlier conversation with Mary, we know that though Dabby might not acknowledge it, she understands the paradox of being in role, the holding of two realities simultaneously. But Dabby is a classic player of the system and here her willingness or refusal to allow herself into the process of the theatre convention is exactly that. The effect of this is that she, as it were, plays the system of the play, exploiting it for her fixed ends. In this way she can preserve her identity intact by not allowing the transforming power of the drama to operate for her. At the end of the play Dabby uses the cover of the theatre performance to attempt to escape from the colony and find her way back to

13

England. She is not interested in change but in returning to what is familiar. The refusal to work with the transforming power of the drama is a turning away from renewal and regeneration.

If we agree with Landy that taking on a role implies life and taking off a role or de-roling implies death then it is as though the actor lives many lives. There is a constant process of regeneration that takes place. But this can happen only if a role is let go of in order for a new one to be played. The goal of therapy is ultimately to enable an individual or a group to move on into new life, widely speaking; to be 'en-roled' into a fuller existence where more choice is possible. Much living, engaging and dying of aspects of the self must therefore be engaged in. Unhelpful defences may be replaced by more healthy, enabling structures. But new life, transformation, can happen only if there is a dying of the old. Where Dabby represents the resistance to change through her standing outside the risks involved in the role-taking process, other characters in the play illustrate superbly the possibility for transformation afforded by role-taking. In doing so they also illustrate the paradox involved in acting a role. Engaging with this paradox is the means whereby the taking on of roles facilitates change.

In dramatherapy it is helpful to remember Peter Slade's terms that he first coined back in the 1950s to explain his theory of *Child Drama* (1954). These were *projected play* and *personal play* out of which, according to Slade, dramatic play evolved. Projected play, as its name suggests, is concerned with the child focusing on the tools of the play activity, the toy, the musical instrument, the board game, etc. This develops the quality of absorption. Personal play involves the activity within the self, I am the train/ witch/ rabbit, etc. These two forms of play I believe develop the ability to be in role.

> Thus projected play is mainly responsible for the growing quality of *Absorption* and, by absolute faith in the part portrayed, personal play develops the quality of *Sincerity*.
>
> (Slade 1954: 36)

Slade adds that by 5 years old,

> the two qualities combined . . . should be strong enough for even the somewhat unobservant to perceive moments of unmistakable acting.
>
> (ibid.)

The idea of absorption can be related to the taking on of the role, the 'being another'. The idea of sincerity is a helpful way of holding on to the 'real self' which must work with the 'other' to retain the paradox inherent in role work. If the role-player is not sincere then there is no real engagement with the self. These positions are illustrated by Dabby and by Mary. Dabby is unable or refuses to let the role work for her. She uses it more like a projected play mechanism, retaining her distance from it, coming out of role to comment on it and generally treating it like a toy which sometimes she enjoys playing with

14

and sometimes wants to throw out. Mary, on the other hand, brings the qualities of personal and projected play together in sincerity and with absorption, exemplifying Landy's statement that

> The healing potential of role is to be found as it positions the role-taker or role-player within the dramatic paradox of 'me' and 'not me'.
>
> (Landy 1993: 46)

This leads us on to look at the concept which can help us to understand how that healing potential is realized.

AESTHETIC DISTANCE

The notion of *aesthetic distance* also requires the attribute of sincerity in order to come into existence. Aesthetic distance is a concept central to existing dramatherapy theory and can be briefly summed up as the moment when the tensions of an emotional paradox are felt simultaneously and catharsis occurs. Landy (1986) draws his theory of aesthetic distance in dramatherapy largely from the work of Scheff (1979) on catharsis. While it would be helpful for the reader unfamiliar with this notion to read Landy (1986: 98–104), I would outline the concept of distancing as follows. In a state of underdistance the individual is overwhelmed by feeling and conversely when in a state of overdistance is cut off from feeling. In therapy when this applies to painful feelings of past experience neither the state of overdistance nor underdistance can facilitate a change in the relationship to those painful past experiences. At the moment of aesthetic distance, however, there is a state of balance and the past and present are brought together in a new relationship. This means that the painful moments of the past can be relived in a way which enables a new relationship to be formed with those events or experiences. My own way of understanding and describing aesthetic distance through the language of dramatic text leads me, in *Our Country's Good*, to the character of the convict Robert Sideway. In order to see how aesthetic distance works in this example we need to follow Sideway's stages towards arriving at operating within the mode of aesthetic distance.

We need to look first at how the 'theatre', which he loves, functions for him, and at his relationship with Ralph. The play opens with Sideway being flogged while Ralph, as his officer, counts the lashes. We next meet Sideway in the scene entitled 'The Audition' (Act I, Scene 5). It is in this scene that we begin to see a partnership being tentatively established. Here the two men are struggling to find a meeting ground and both are backing off from confronting the truth which might get in the way of what they want. Ralph wants to get a cast together and Sideway wants to be in the play; they have a mutual interest in finding a way through. How do they negotiate the reality of the flogged and the flogger? How do they find a partnership which is crucial to enabling the theatre to be more than a place for Sideway to escape the awful reality of his convict life and become a place where he can engage with that reality differently? Ralph's job is to hold on to the task of the play. Only by doing so can he help the convicts to believe in it as a thing of importance. (In this way he is like a therapist, holding to task, maintaining faith in the process, and struggling to hold the boundaries of commitment even in difficult circumstances.) At first the subject of the theatre itself, and both men's experience of it, provides a safe bridge over otherwise treacherous waters:

> SIDEWAY: Ah, Mr Clark. (*He does a flourish*) I am calling you Mr Clark as one calls Mr Garrick Mr Garrick, we have not had the pleasure of meeting before.
> RALPH: I've seen you on the ship.
> SIDEWAY: Different circumstances Mr Clark, best forgotten. I was once a gentleman. My wheel of fortune has turned. The wheel. . . . You are doing a play, I hear, ah, Drury Lane, Mr Garrick, the lovely Peg Woffington. (*Conspiratorially*) He was so cruel to her. She was so pale –
> CLARK: You say you were a gentleman, Sideway?
> SIDEWAY: Top of my profession, Mr Clark, pickpocket, born and bred in Bermondsey.

At first Ralph tries to catch at the straw of familiarity, of the boundaries of his own known world, 'You say you were a gentleman, Sideway?' The reply which comes shows how removed Ralph is from the language of Sideway and his experience. Yet the familiarity is there between both of them and it is Ralph who presents the reality of that. 'I've seen you on the ship.' The words are ambiguous for we do not know if Ralph is registering Sideway as the man whose lashes he counted or not. In its begging of this question the sense of the alienation of officer and prisoner is presented to the audience. However, Sideway picks up the allusion to their relationship as it exists so far in what seems to be an unconscious way. He uses their experience of the theatre to convey to Ralph the reality of that relationship: 'He was so cruel to her. She was so pale'. Sideway surely cannot ignore the reality of their relationship of flogged convict and flogging officer which Ralph brings to mind by his non-committal allusion. Sideway, while apparently brushing off the allusion – 'Different circumstances, Mr Clark, best forgotten' – in fact finds a metaphor to speak feelingly of the reality of that relationship through a metaphor taken from their joint interest in the theatre. It hits home so that Clark cuts across him, trying to deny the true nature of their relationship where he is the cruel tyrant and Sideway 'pale' from the beating which had left him unconscious. Ralph flounders to try to find another point of contact where he feels safe and perhaps where such raw truths are not expressed, 'You say you were a gentleman . . .?', only to find that the ground slips from under his feet again as Sideway's definition of a gentleman is that of a top pickpocket.

I suggest that although Sideway uses the reference to Woffington and

Garrick to mirror his own situation in relation to Clark, he does this unconsciously for he must maintain the theatre as a place of escape, unrelated to life. Later, accepted into the play, Ralph endeavours to get Sideway to be 'more natural' (Act I, Scene 11), to which Sideway's reply is, 'Natural! On the stage! But Mr Clark!' Sideway's concept of theatre at this stage of his involvement with the play is one which can offer only the solace of escapism. But because he loves the theatre and is moved and excited by it it can start to work for him at a deeper level. Unconsciously he is already able to draw on this as we have just seen. We are now moving into a position where we can see how the rehearsal process of the play within the play illustrates the concept of aesthetic distance as an active agent for change.

In Act II, Scene 5, the cast is rehearsing. They are interrupted by the officers Ross and Campbell. Ralph protests that rehearsals are a private affair: 'Major, there is a modesty attached to the process of creation which must be respected.'

The senior officers' response is to proceed to taunt the players, abuse and degrade them. Sideway is picked on first and is ordered to take off his shirt and expose his back to the assembled company. They refer to his flogging:

> ROSS: I have seen the white of this animal's bones, his wretched blood and reeky convict urine have spilled on my boots and he's feeling modest? Are you feeling modest Sideway?

They continue in this vein to Dabby and then to Mary. Sideway can stand it no longer but instead of shouting back at the officers – answering back was the original crime for which he received those fifty lashes – he finds another way.

> ROSS: Where's your tattoo, Brenham? Show us. I can't see it. Show us. I can't see it. Show us. (*Mary tries to obey, lifting her skirt a little.*) If you can't manage I'll help you. (*Mary lifts her skirt a little higher.*) I can't see it. (*But Sideway turns to Liz and starts acting boldly, across the room, across everyone.*)
>
> SIDEWAY: What pleasures I may receive abroad are indeed uncertain; but this I am sure of, I shall meet with less cruelty among the most barbarous nations than I have found at home.
>
> (Act II, Scene 5)

Sideway rescues the situation by utilizing the task of rehearsal in which they are engaged and which has been interrupted. He stays within the boundary of the play and in doing so finds a way of preventing his companions from suffering further degradation. The text he speaks gives him words with which to express his feelings, providing him with another way of articulating the truth of his and their situations.

He speaks with the authority of the text and the authority of his own feelings. Although Ross and Campbell give the order to begin the punishment of

17

Arscott, whose cries offstage eventually bring the rehearsal to a halt in depressed sympathy for his situation, these officers do leave the cast and its director and make no more attempt to take over the rehearsal. Sideway has found another way to stand up to them. Answering back brought cruel beating; the play lends him its words and he is empowered by it. The language of the play which they are rehearsing is tellingly appropriate to their situation; the pain of continued ill-treatment is reflected in the England in which they are still captive though abroad, the appalling 'home from home'. And the hope with which they came, that perhaps things would be different 'across the herring pond', lies in those lines too. The tension between their own real-life situation and the very different situation of the play and its characters provides an extraordinarily moving moment of theatre. The authority with which they speak contrasts with the brutish authority of the officers, Campbell and Ross. This tension invokes the moral universe and takes the audience along with it.

Here is an example of aesthetic distance at work in the theatre. In this rehearsal we witness Sideway engaged in aesthetic distance. The distance provided by speaking the text of the play within the play makes the unbearable bearable; Sideway finds a way both to be in the role and be in his real-life situation at once. All his flourishes, such as imitating Garrick 'establishing [Hamlet's] melancholy', are gone and what we experience is a superb fugue being played between text and life. In turn it is there, for us the audience, to feel upon the blood. There is such disparity between the good fortune of the characters they are playing and the convicts' own lives, and yet the fact that the characters' words somehow manage to echo their own situation deepens our own response, as we are faced with the many layers at which drama can operate in returning an echo of our own lives and our own responsibility as members of the human race. Here again Aristotle's singular and universal come together.

Sideway in his earlier flourishing mode is overdistanced. He does not feel the part. His attempt to imitate Garrick by dropping to his knees and 'sobbing in a pose of total sorrow' only brings from Ralph the response 'What are you doing down there Sideway?' Ralph has to educate him into drawing life and art together:

SIDEWAY: A greeting. Yes. A greeting looks like this. (*He extends his arms high and wide.*) . . . I'm not quite sure how to do 'Welcome'.
RALPH: I think if you just say the line.

(Act I, Scene 11)

How different is this from the Sideway of the other passage I have just explored, where he finds within his text and himself a relationship of balance which is the very point of aesthetic distance. At that point he can take his own authority. And in doing so he can take it for us the audience. He is truly 'standing in' (Wilshire 1982) for all human beings oppressed and in an exiled

relationship to their own land. He also speaks to our ability to oppress ourselves by his very taking of his own authority in the use of the role and the
text. He challenges us to find the metaphor of creative expression for his example is one of freedom within captivity. 'Man is born free but everywhere he
is in chains', wrote Rousseau. The ending of this scene holds that tension for
us and we meet it with a quality of feeling which can allow a movement inside
us. Too much distance would have left us unmoved, maybe even ridiculing,
like Ralph's challenge to Sideway's posturing earlier. Too little would have
had the effect of distancing us in response to being perhaps overwhelmed.
This scene is beautifully crafted and takes us, the audience, to a place where
we too experience the moment of aesthetic distance at which something
shifts.

Once, when I was asked about the concepts of role and aesthetic distance,
someone said to me, 'Then it's there that the magic happens?' I almost started
explaining again but stopped myself. 'Yes,' I replied, 'it's there that the magic
happens.' And in the theatre you can feel it. And in the dramatherapy group
you can feel it. It is that moment of perfect tension between two realities in a
moment of absolute sincerity and absorption.

AUDIENCE/ACTOR RELATIONSHIP

In considering aesthetic distance I have begun to bring together the audience
and the actor. A vital component of enactment is that very relationship. In
Our Country's Good the bond between actor and audience is established not
only by Ralph's work with the convicts. It exists within the framework of the
colony. The convicts 'act' – they work, and the officers 'watch', keep guard
while they do so. Even in personal relationships this dynamic exists. Duck-
ling, the convict who is the lover of the Marine, Midshipman Harry Brewer,
protests to Harry:

> DUCKLING: I don't want to be watched all the time. I wake up in the
> middle of the night and you're watching me. What do you think I'm
> going to do in my sleep, Harry? Watching, watching, watching. JUST
> STOP WATCHING ME.

> (Act I, Scene 7)

However, the play within the play provides a very different model of watching
from that of oppressor and oppressed. It provides the opportunity for the
convicts' creativity to be seen, heard, – witnessed. It gives them the opportunity to be the ones who are powerful, who have the audience in 'thrall', in captivity. And with the tables turned, a different dynamic can be present. One of
the interesting things about the discussions which take place in *Our Country's
Good* is the amount of attention that putting on a play in a convict settlement
receives. It is not that the idea of a play is unimportant, a 'frippery frittering
play' as Major Ross calls it; it is rather that it is threatening, that it can change

the status quo, that it has enough status in itself to do that. The opposing views are hotly debated, as hotly as the debates which took place in Ancient Greece, where the notion of drama was taken seriously by philosophers and where the good of society was reckoned to be enhanced or damaged by this art-form. At no time in this play is there the suggestion that the play can be performed without an audience. The concept of actor and audience are inextricably linked.

> PHILLIP: And we, this colony of a few hundred will be watching this together, for a few hours we will no longer be despised prisoners and hated gaolers. We will laugh, we may be moved, we may even think a little. Can you think of something that would provide such an evening, Watkin?
>
> (Act I, Scene 6)

Here there is the notion of the theatre as social equalizer. The theatre can draw all together, bound simply by the ties of common humanity.

This partnership, this bond between actor and audience, is at the centre of dramatherapy. Dramatic engagement involves the taking on of a role in the presence of another. It cannot be done alone, there must be an 'other' who receives, witnesses and provides the containment necessary for the self to act, that is to take action in role, wearing, as it were, another self; living out Landy's paradox in the presence of another. As such the audience acts as *witness* to the actor. This term has grown into dramatherapy parlance, but as yet I have found no satisfactory integration of it within dramatherapy theory. What does it really mean? In order to discover we need to look more closely at the idea of audience and actor.

> The act of witnessing in dramatherapy is that of being an audience to others or to oneself within a context of personal insight or development.
>
> (Jones 1991)

Throughout Jones's discussion the fine nuance of the word 'witnessing' is missing. The idea of active witnessing is synonymous with audience, varying only in the delineation of more functions than the 'conventional' theatre allows. Corti in her article entitled 'Bearing Witness' (1993/4) comes nearer to focusing on this when she considers the function of the dramatherapist and group members as one of testifying to the experience of others. Wilshire (1982) sees the relationship between actor and audience as one of mutual authorization. The actor, wearing the role, is authorized by the audience to 'stand in' for their feelings, to portray them through the role. The actor, by the very portrayal of those feelings, authorizes the experience of the members of the audience via the character. There is an affirmation of self in what Wilshire defines. Both actor and audience are part of the same world, that of human experience. Both, from their different positions, affirm the commonality of that human experience to one another.

> Together the audience and actors engage in incarnated imaginative variation on the meaning of human being and doing. Together they experiment on the nature and extent of mimetic involvement, identification, and sympathy – and on how these relate to the individual's identity.
>
> (Wilshire 1982: 24)

To explore this further let us go back to Act II, Scene 5, and look at the processes which are happening in this part of the rehearsal. Sideway is playing Mr Worthy and Liz Morden Melinda:

SIDEWAY: What pleasures I may receive abroad are indeed uncertain but this I am sure of, I shall meet with less cruelty among the most barbarous nations than I have found at home.

LIZ: Come, Sir, you and I have been jangling a great while; I fancy if we made up our accounts, we should the sooner come to an agreement.

SIDEWAY: Sure, Madam, you won't dispute your being in my debt – my fears, sighs, vows, promises, assiduities, anxieties, jealousies, have run on for a whole year, without any payment.

(Act II, Scene 5)

When Sideway steps in to rescue the rehearsal, which is being sadistically demolished by the officers Ross and Campbell, he is authorized to do so by the other cast members and his director by the very fact of being in a rehearsal. The context gives him the authority to play the role. Sideway as actor can then, through the role, authorize his audience, which comprises the other members of the cast. He validates their condition through the words of the character: 'I shall meet with less cruelty among the most barbarous nations than I have found at home.' He therefore validates the authority of their experience as human beings.

They, as audience, have a role too in this context. Though not actually role-playing at the time they are active *as authorizing witnesses*, though in a *passive mode*.

When Liz joins in she moves from being in the *actively passive audience mode* to the *actively active audience mode*. This happens when she takes on her character to respond to the words spoken by Sideway's character. In role she is the *audience* to Sideway's character. Now they can mutually authorize each other and intensify the authorization of the audience's experience.

Every actor needs to have access to these functions if they are to allow the dialogue between the 'me' and the 'not me' parts of the self in role. Every actor also needs to be able to be witness to a fellow actor while still being in

21

role if the enactment is to enable the actors to let the roles work for them through the means of aesthetic distance. This is when the action on stage feels truthful and the actors provide a mirror for the audience. In both theatre and dramatherapy group audiences we can see the functions of *passively active audience* and in each actor the function of *actively active audience*. The role-player uses the active engagement with the role to provide him or herself with a framework in which to bear witness to his or her own experience. There must be an ability both to play the role and be present as the self who is witnessing the life of the role. Both realities must be held together. For those people who do not have the inner structure to enable them to do this, role work is not suitable. Here the dramatherapist will exercise professional judgement and use assessment procedures which will help them to determine the suitability and helpfulness of role work for individuals. As Sue Jennings points out (Jennings *et al.* 1994: 107), with very vulnerable clients with serious mental health problems, direct involvement in role could 'further reduce their fragile defences'. It must therefore be used judiciously. There must be a strong enough ego to enable the individual in role to come out of role knowing the difference between the two states of playing and reality. For, as Wilshire puts it, the demands of being in role mean that

> We must endeavour to reflect from the body as we find ourselves springing into action on the stage, and as we find ourselves identifying empathetically with the performers. We must endeavour to reflect while in action.
>
> (Wilshire 1982: 54)

Reflecting while in action is the essence of the dynamic of theatre. This is true of both the actor and of the audience member in the actively passive role. The actor presents a character to us, the audience, by breathing life into it by the means of taking on a role. Wilshire's use of the words 'standing in' as opposed to 'represent', conveys the reality of the fact that the actor physically embodies the role in enactment. The character represents an aspect of life to us. As audience we are invited to be open and receptive, to accept the life which is being lived out on stage and empathetically to enter into it as witness.

To testify is to make a statement to the world. Both Sideway and Liz testify to the reality of their oppression through the language of their characters. Here the function of drama is unique in that the members of the audience and the actors mutually testify to the validity of their common humanity. It is interesting to note that Campbell, an opposer of the play, begins to get drawn into the spirit of the convicts' endeavour after Sideway and Liz begin to act: 'Mmhem, good, that. Sighs, vows, promises, hehem, mmm. Anxieties.' It is fascinating to see the power of the play working on an audience member who appears not to possess the witnessing, testifying function. The play is speaking to Campbell, to his anxieties as a member of this colony. Here the actors are witnesses to the issues of the audience, here they validate the audience without conscious intention, for that is the power of the theatre. It may even be that Ross's response to Campbell, 'Captain Campbell, start Arscott's punishment', is provoked by his feeling threatened by the play. Like Claudius in *Hamlet* it touches Ross too nearly and he must fight its message.

In dramatherapy the act of bearing witness is, I believe, present in the very role-play itself. It is here that both the concept of audience – one who hears – and that of testifying, which is inherent in the concept of witnessing, must come together. The individual role-player is supported by the passively active or actively active witnessing of the audience who provide a holding function for the role-player to explore. Similarly the audience provide the holding function for the actor in the theatre. In turn the audience receive a mirror of their own experience.

When the relationship between audience and actor is truthful everyone knows it. It is the moment at which the players and the audience know that the stone has been thrown imperceptibly into the pond. The ripples touch all in their circular net which both contains and releases the waters of the unconscious from which the poetry of drama is formed. It is so often felt in the theatre through a charged silence, the 'still point of the turning world'.

Let Liz Morden have the last word. Liz is presented as one of the most abused and wretched women, with a reputation for coarseness and foul language. A classic scapegoat. In Act II, Scene 10, accused of stealing biscuits from the stores, she refuses to escape hanging by speaking the truth and declaring her innocence. On both occasions that I was fortunate enough to see *Our Country's Good*, this scene and especially its culmination produced a catharis which was experienced by a whole audience as an exquisite moment of tears and laughter. It was a moment in the theatre when human vulnerability and human achievement came together in an extraordinary meeting of extreme pathos and high comedy. Truly a moment when role, enactment, aesthetic distance and the relationship between the audience and the actors affirmed triumphantly that, as Hamlet says, 'the play is' indeed 'the thing'.

> RALPH: Morden, you must speak.
> COLLINS: For the good of the colony.
> PHILLIP: And of the play.
> (*A long silence*)
> LIZ: I didn't steal the food.
> . . .
> PHILLIP: Why wouldn't you say any of this before?
> LIZ: Because it wouldn't have mattered.
> PHILLIP: Speaking the truth?
> LIZ: Speaking.
> . . .

ROSS: You are taking the word of a convict against the word of a soldier –

. . . you will have a revolt on your hands, Governor.

PHILLIP: I'm sure I will, but let us see the play first. Liz, I hope you are good in your part.

RALPH: She will be, Your Excellency, promise that.

LIZ: Your Excellency, I will endeavour to speak Mr Farquhar's lines with the elegance and clarity their own worth commands.

2

PLAYING WHERE TWO WORLDS MEET

INTRODUCTION

In *Our Country's Good* we saw a group of people in a situation of oppression engaging in a creative dramatic task. The play is one of the funniest and one of the most moving I have seen. One of its characteristics is its balance of the tragic and the comic. It illustrates that attention to pain and attention to laughter are inherent in the processes of both survival and healing. It illustrates integration, where the apparently disparate parts of an individual or a community can begin to relate to one another.

Working towards integration is the aim of dramatherapy, achieved through the creative symbolic process which enactment provides. Sometimes all one can do as a dramatherapist is to help people to survive. At others we have the satisfaction of witnessing the work of healing. Either way we need help. If we are to structure the therapeutic process (Cox 1978a) we need dramatic and theoretical structures to help us to bring reason and emotion together as Boal suggests when writing about training actors (Boal 1992: 48). The famous phrase in therapy, 'stay with the chaos', doesn't mean stay there forever, but encourages us to allow unconscious processes to take their own time, rather than prematurely worry them into submission by reason. The implication of the phrase is that, having stayed with the chaos, we can begin to make sense of it. In order to help our clients find their own order hidden in their own chaos we need help in becoming acquainted with the landscape.

An analogy to finding one's way in the country of therapy is to think of the kinds of books that come with suggestions for country walks. They are not Ordnance Survey maps which tell you exactly where everything is. They give you a framework for a walk and you get used to using the particular ways of describing the walk and the particular symbols and suggestions of the accompanying maps. You get used to the style of a particular author and the house style of the series in which they are published. But you do the walk yourself, no one can do it for you and you pay attention to different features of the landscape according to who you are. You go at the pace which feels comfortable for you. Every therapist will have their own favourite 'walk book' which will help them have the kind of walk they best enjoy. My favourites happen to be those which come from the 'house' of psychoanalysis. Here certain concepts draw me to look at the landscape of dramatherapy in a particular way and help me to structure my work, like my walk, not rigidly but in a way which allows me to recognize aspects of the landscape when I see them.

In this chapter I want first to look at some of the ideas developed by practitioners working within the broad school of psychoanalysis, considering them from the standpoint of a dramatherapist who has a particular interest in plays. Firstly I explore Winnicott's concepts of *potential space* and *the transitional object*, then consider aspects of some of the essential ideas of Melanie Klein, moving on to discuss the concepts of *container*, *containment* and *holding* and conclude by paying some attention to *transference* and *countertransference*.

POTENTIAL SPACE

When Winnicott (1971) talked of potential space he spoke of a place which was in between 'behaviour' and 'contemplation'. He considered it to be the place where cultural experience begins and proposed that play and the capacity to play were the essential ingredients of creativity.

Let us look at this picture. Under the table two adults are crouched. They look out at their audience. They are children, wide-eyed, conspiratorial in their play. They whisper these words:

> Can this cockpit hold
> The vasty fields of France? Or may we cram
> Within this wooden O the very casques
> That did affright the air at Agincourt?
> (*Henry V* Act I, Scene 1)

and we, the small audience in this dramatherapy workshop, are taken into the world of Shakespeare, the world of the theatre and the world of a great historic battle, all in an instant. How? Because at this point both actors and audience are sharing 'potential space'. Slowly, wonderingly, these 'children' speak these well-known lines as though they have never been spoken before and, as I am caught up in their wonderment, I experience the questions, 'Is it possible that these two realities can exist together in the mind, in the imagination? Is it possible that we can be here and somewhere else at the same time? Is it possible that we can be "me" and "not-me" at the same time, here and elsewhere?' And even as the questions are evoked, every breath and gesture of the actors affirms that all these things are indeed possible.

Dramatherapy affords adults as well as children the opportunity to play. If we explore the example of this work with the chorus of *Henry V*, we see playing taking place on several levels simultaneously. First, the adults are symbolizing the play activity of children as well as playing in their own right as

26

adults. Shakespeare is also playing with the audience; he is asking us to imagine that the theatre can represent 'the vasty fields of France'; the two workshop participants play with the text by representing the stage as the 'under-the-table play' of children and can create this particular play only because there is an audience with whom they can create shared meaning. This parallels Shakespeare's need of his audience in order for meaning to be given to his metaphor of the wooden stage standing in for 'the vasty fields of France'. Here in these layers we can discern potential space, the space where things become possible, where there is 'potential'. In potential space there is the potential for 'potency', for creativity and growth. At this point we can link up with Slade's notion of child drama being an art-form (Slade 1954). Both Winnicott's perception of potential space being the place of play which itself forms the basis for cultural experience and Slade's that the play of children developed into drama becomes an art-form, are integral to understanding the dramatherapy context. It is here that the functions of the audience and the mother or therapist as active witness come together in the potential space of the dramatic enactment. If we look at this more closely we can see how the relationship between the two 'players' – child/client and mother/therapist – can operate within the potential space of dramatic enactment and the context in which it happens.

The art-form of drama implies an audience. Whilst a child can play alone, frequently the presence of the adult is there as witness, providing the child with the experience of his or her perceived and enacted world being validated. Winnicott talks of the experience of the potential space as being the place between the 'me' and 'not-me'; it is therefore a place where the child can learn to be separate, to grow and discover his or her own identity. Winnicott places the potential space at the time when the infant begins to cease being merged with the mother (1971:128). It is the space in between merger and separation where what he calls 'intermediate living' can take place. He emphasizes the importance of the safe and consistent environment provided by the 'good-enough mother' which can enable the child to be in this area of intermediate living. This becomes extended to the good-enough therapist who can provide a holding environment. By holding he means a condition of safety which allows for the infant, or the client, to experiment, to grow, to learn about what is me and what is not-me, to creatively use the potential space. Such conditions allow separation which is not experienced as threatening but rather as a healthy possibility. The dramatherapy group echoes this place where the individual can literally play. Indeed the group itself can also provide the good-enough mother and the space can become a potential space where the individual can explore self in relation to other (as we shall see in Chapter 3).

An example of how such a space operates outside the actual condition either of infancy or of adult therapy comes from a teaching context long before I knew dramatherapy even existed (indeed, as we know it now in England it did not exist at that time). A class of 12-year-olds was improvising a story in groups. In one group was Susan, a large, physically mature and angry girl who spent much of her time outside classrooms rather than in them. During the first lesson with this new class Susan warned me, arms folded across her chest, face red with fury, that she would never consent to doing drama. She did her best to disrupt everyone else's work, terrorized boys half her size and remained intractable for most part of most of the lessons. About halfway through the first term of my working with this class, Susan announced that she wanted to be the baby in her group's story. The rest of her group were trying to get her to play the mother, presumably (ostensibly at any rate) because she seemed the eldest, the biggest. She was adamant that she wanted to be 2 years old, and I concurred, saying that no member of the group should play a part they did not want to. No one in the group wanted to be mother. Suddenly Susan said, 'You be mother, Miss!' and they took up the cry with one accord. My instant reaction was that it was, in some way which I did not instantly understand, important for me to take this role. Working in role with one group meant that I would therefore not have the outside eye for the whole class. Quickly looking round and checking everyone seemed absorbed and working, I agreed.

In the basic storyline common to the whole class, Susan was a child who had taken a dangerous poison from her father's home laboratory and was in danger of death, and, the children speculated, of punishment. In their story she was saved and not punished. This was the children's decision. Susan was the star part, totally absorbed as the child aged 2 (in the other groups no one elected to be as young as 2). 'Cor that was good, Miss!' she said when the enactment was over, and she was glowing, not with her customary belligerence and fury, but with excitement and pleasure. They wanted to do it again, but I told them I needed to see how other groups were getting on. No one wanted to play mother so they said they would quietly watch what the others were doing. Part of me expected the usual mayhem and yet part of me was not surprised that it did not come. Instinctively I realized that something significant had happened for Susan though I did not know what. I just knew that it had been important that I had responded to her need to be 2 years old and for me to be mother for this ten minutes of her life. As I left to go to the other groups, she found a way of solving the problem of the transition for herself by saying, 'Mum's gone shopping' and added as I walked away, 'Don't forget the chocolate biscuits!' When I got to my classroom the next morning, written on large letters on the board, was, 'Don't forget the chocolate biscuits.' In successive drama lessons Susan was enthusiastic, not difficult or disruptive. Drama was one of the few lessons she either stayed in out of choice or was not evicted from. Susan, it turned out, was the eldest of several children, whose parents both worked, and whose mother had to work for part of the evening cleaning. Susan was frequently required to be mother – no wonder she did not want that role in the drama, and no wonder she wanted the chance to be 2 years old, to be the centre of attention and to enact being near to death, being saved and to be given expressions of love and care within the dramatic context.

This story is, although not an example of work done expressly within a therapy contract and environment, evidence of Winnicott's potential space. Both Susan and I played at the level of the unconscious and of symbolic play. Her unconscious knew what she wanted, and I responded intuitively to that. Together we played in that intermediate area. Susan was, in a symbolic way, as a little individual of 2 years old with mother, practising being separate, getting into serious, life-threatening trouble and finding Mum and Dad still there, and all the siblings concerned about her too. Having expressed her unconscious fears and needs she could then let the symbolic mother go. She did this by finding her own metaphor to link the real world of the drama lesson with the symbolic world which had just nourished her. In order to cope with my coming out of role and attending to other responsibilities and other children she invented the idea of shopping. Susan was extending her own potential space in relation to me in my wider role of teacher to both her and her classmates. The fact that I thanked her for her message on my blackboard rather than told her off further supported her in her testing out of whether or not her world, her concerns and needs, could be tolerated and contained by me. (The biscuits I see as a message to me about her anxiety as to whether or not I would go on 'feeding her'.) I believe this gave her the confidence to use the subsequent drama lessons to try a variety of roles and behaviours, to work well with other children and nourish herself through allowing the drama lesson to work for her rather than rejecting it.

In this example we can see how the potential space was the area of creativity in which Susan, the other children and the teacher played. They suspended their disbelief and together created an environment in which, amongst many other things perhaps, feelings and anxieties about separation and survival could be symbolized and played out. Within the context of the play reassurance could be found and the child strengthened. She could then use the external world or 'reality' – the lesson, the drama context, the school – more constructively. This was, in my view, the use of potential space.

Winnicott calls it an intermediate area because it is neither in fantasy nor in reality. If we can beg the shorthand of equating 'inner' with fantasy and 'outer' with reality we can say that the child's inner experience found an external form and that form was created by the taking on of roles in the context of the story. The story was the text, or script. It had a clearly defined storyline not invented by the children. It was a 'given', just as a dramatic text is a 'given'. What Susan did with it was discover it and use it as a vehicle to express some of her inner concerns and to find a way of having those heard and met symbolically. Winnicott is clear that in the shared experience of potential space both the mother and the child, the therapist and the client, play. In this example we see at least two clear aspects of this playing. One is the potential space of the drama itself, where being in role and playing out a story which is not literally true but which stands in, to use Wilshire's term again, for a literal truth of the emotional and psychic life of the child. Here as the drama unfolds and the children and teacher improvise together the drama represents aspects of unconscious or inner life and gives it expression; the teacher is both in role and active witness at the same time. But, in my example, before this took place something else had already taken place which had enabled the dramatic play to happen. This was the moment of relationship when Susan had said, 'You be mother' and I had followed my hunch and said yes. At this point both Susan and I were playing in the sense that Winnicott speaks of therapist and client playing. We were not then in role within the context of dramatic enactment but we were both spontaneously reaching out to find the meeting ground which would provide Susan with what she needed at that point. Together we were exploring possibilities without knowing where they would lead, letting our own unconscious take the initiative.

But this is not the end of the story for I have often puzzled over the 'chocolate biscuits' epilogue to the drama. Here Winnicott helps me out again. Susan was trying to deal with the fact that I would be leaving the drama and in doing so I would also be leaving her as 'mother' of her 2-year-old self as externalized in the role. I believe that she had found the dramatic play nourishing enough not to need to slip into her usual attention-seeking, needy and destructive self the minute the drama was over. But she had to find a way of separating from me and find the separation tolerable. She did this by means of inventing a role for me so that she could keep that part of me which had nourished her in the playing. This could help her to tolerate living in what Winnicott calls the actual world (1971: 113), in this case the actual world of the drama lesson. She was continuing the game; though no longer in the drama 'script' she was finding a way to continue playing. When I reinforced it by smiling at her inventiveness and saying, 'O.K. Mum's gone shopping', I knew and she knew that I was actually leaving her to attend to the other children, which, given her family situation, could easily have been intolerable and coped with only by a burst of her usual 'acting out'. I believe that both she and I held the potential space, or rather extended it into another dimension by the device she invented and my validation of it. This 'held' her through the lesson. She was able to be separate, having acted out the threat of the ultimate separation of death in fantasy provided by the play. In the drama she had not died but been rescued and recovered her loving parents rather than being persecuted, punished or abandoned. Winnicott locates potential space in the dimension of the separating away from mother. In relation to Susan it is worth looking at these words.

The potential space happens only in relation to a feeling of confidence on the part of the baby, that is, confidence related to the dependability of the mother-figure or environmental elements, confidence being the evidence of dependability that is becoming introjected.

(Winnicott 1971: 118)

There was the relative safety of the school environment; the consistency of the social holding environment. (Susan's rebellion against it does not invalidate its consistency and parental role.) Then there was the environment of the drama lesson which happened regularly with the same children and the same teacher in the same place every week. Once Susan had found something for herself in the potential space of the context of dramatic enactment she was able to extend her own creativity, which is, after all, what potential space is for. She was able to initiate another playing area for herself and me in which she could still use fantasy to let me know her needs, 'Don't forget the chocolate biscuits!' Whatever else it meant to Susan I feel that she was asking me not to forget that she was still hungry and needed the nourishing which she had allowed this context to give her. She therefore extended the potential space into the wider context of the school by finding my classroom the next day, located in a different part of the school building, and putting her message on my board. Here she was using the potential space which she had created to extend into the wider environment and still be connected to me. The drama in which I had responded to her need was now connected to the system, 'school', in which the relationship between her and myself and the drama were rooted. This seems to me to illustrate the point which Winnicott makes that potential space is related to the experience of separating, where the child can safely grow into separation while not being separated because the potential space holds the parent and child in the gentle fabric of creative playing. She was the client playing, I was the therapist noticing and accepting at this point. I believe there was some connection between Susan's increased ability to act out less in the school generally and 'feed' herself by being able to co-operate more as she began to use the drama lessons to play out her unmet needs.

Both in the play of the dramatic enactment and in the playing between Susan and myself, outside the actual enactment but within the context of our relationship as drama teacher and pupil, there are echoes of Winnicott's therapeutic imperative, *'psychotherapy is done in the overlap of the two play areas, that of the patient and that of the therapist'* (Winnicott 1971: 63, original italics). Indeed I would go further and say that whilst the encounter was not, as I have already said, within a therapy contract and context, the essential elements of Winnicott's potential space were operating and to a therapeutic effect.

THE TRANSITIONAL OBJECT

Dramatherapists frequently use objects. Often, but not always, this use of objects will echo the function of what Winnicott famously called the 'transitional object' or the child's first 'not-me possession' (Winnicott 1971: 1) which the child relates to as other than him or herself. Yet, the crucial aspect of the transitional object is paradoxical; the infant experiences this object as both created by itself and simultaneously existing out there in the world. It belongs, 'Between the thumb and the teddy bear' (ibid.: 2). It is, therefore, not the infant as denoted by the infant's own body and it is not entirely other-than-infant either, in the infant's experience.

This quality of intermediateness is crucial to Winnicott's theory because it is this aspect of it which allows the baby the first sense of the world of illusion and therefore opens the door to the ability to symbolize and play and create; to begin the process which leads to the use of the potential space with another in relationship. It is the beginning of discovering the concept of 'as if' upon which drama itself essentially depends.

As an 'objective object subjectively perceived' it marks the beginnings of independence and the possibility of being separate from the mother, of moving eventually to a place where objects can be objectively perceived. Out of all the objects an infant might have at its disposal it is one which it endows with meaning – or cathects – and as such must be respected by the adult who must not attempt to alter or interfere with it; it is under the child's near-omnipotent control. The transitional object itself has certain characteristics; it is usually soft, capable of giving warmth and comfort, of having some re-sponsiveness. It is frequently used as a comforter and to allay anxiety. Whilst it is a reminder of the mother's breast, Winnicott is clear that its being the infant's possession and not part of the mother is an essential characteristic (1971: 11). It can tolerate the child's varied treatment of it, of both love and hate and those in excess if need be. Eventually it is forgotten, loses meaning and is not mourned.

> I really enjoyed the soothing and tactile reassurance of literally holding onto a chosen object . . . a transitional object makes it easier to venture into the unknown.

wrote a dramatherapist who had attended two workshops that I had held where objects were used. The word 'chosen' is significant here, for it echoes the idea of the infant creating the object which is there to be created. In both instances to which this participant is referring the object was intended to re-flect some of the qualities of the transitional object; in one it was used to help the group begin the work and in the other to end it. Both times are 'entries into the unknown', and as such are usually attended by some anxiety. They are also transition times marking the boundary between the group members' creation of their own world through enactment and the outside world. I find it a helpful way of enabling the group to manage that boundary.

There is much to consider about dramatherapy and transitional objects and some of these aspects will be found in other parts of this book; here I simply want to introduce the idea that a dramatic text can take on the func-tion of the transitional object when these infant experiences are being re-worked as we revisit these stages in the therapeutic process. We have already seen how Susan used the storyline of her group play in a similar way. If we now think of an actor preparing for a performance, working with a text, we could say that he or she is playing with the 'object' which helps that actor to get to know the world of the play. In this instance it is the world of the play which is the 'world out there' to which he or she must relate and must join in with. A foray into the unknown must be made and the actor must move from his or her own subjective experience of life to discover the objectivity of the world created by the writer. The text is something which exists out there already and yet is created by the actor; it therefore has an essential ingredient of the transitional object. It can also give the actor a certain omnipotence in relation to it; it can be loved and hated, pulled about or 'affectionately cuddled', as Winnicott puts it. It can be forgotten about and resurrected. It will probably eventually lose meaning; the actor de-cathects from it, ceases to relate to it. There are many actors who say they forget the lines of a play after the run is completed.

After the rehearsal period the sequence is repeated. This time the subjective world is the play as written by the writer and internalized by the actor and company. The 'world-out-there' is that of the audience. The actors are creating the play; for them it is a 'me' object, yet it is also being created by the audience, so it is also a 'not-me' object. And for the audience this is also true the other way round – members of the audience and the collective audience bring their subjective realities to the object on stage; they create it and it is created by them. Winnicott himself uses precisely this phenomenon as an example when discussing the reality principle (which is what I have been calling 'the world out there') in relation to the transitional object.

> This is the exciting thing about the curtain in a theatre. When it goes up each one of us will create the play that is going to be enacted.
> (C. Winnicott *et al*. 1986: 133)

In dramatherapy this transitional phenomenon is called into being when we work on a play. What we are doing here is using the text to help the members of the group to explore the relationship between subjectivity and objectivity and thus strengthen the individual's sense of 'I am' and 'This is me in relation to another.' This means that text and the group process go hand in hand; issues brought up by the text affect the relationships in the group and the relationships can be taken back into the text. Working on a text we live in an illusory world which is paradoxically intensely real, just as Winnicott describes the transitional object. From this work, connections can then be made to the 'world out there' as individuals find, for example, the father they have been playing in the play has re-worked either an aspect of their own internalized father or the relationship with their actual father or a father figure in their own lives. The audience to their lives, we could say, comes into the picture at this stage.

33

MELANIE KLEIN: ASPECTS OF OBJECT RELATING

Fundamental to dramatherapy is the practice of playing roles, using objects such as toys – which may or may not have the function of the transitional object – and of using the body and voice to externalize inner experience and conflict and work towards a more integrated state. In working in drama-therapy the individual can get to know the unacceptable parts of the self safely through the use of potential space, face the monster within which has been previously either repressed or placed 'out there', that is, projected on to another person, group, or object. To see how we can work in dramatherapy utilizing the potential space as a good-enough environment, I want to look at some aspects of the work developed by Melanie Klein. My main emphases are the concepts described by the terms *projection, introjection, splitting* within the context of *object relations*. I shall make some reference to *denial* and *idealization*, concluding with paying attention to *projective identification*. These concepts are particularly relevant to the mechanisms through which role and enactment work. When seen within the context of Klein's view of early infant development, particularly the *paranoid-schizoid* and *depressive positions*, they can be extremely useful as a way of thinking about those group processes which form an integral part of most dramatherapists' practice.

Projection and introjection

The opportunity for integration which enactment can provide is possible be-cause one is projecting part of oneself out on to the role (or other object). In the last chapter we saw how Mary Brenham projected the part of herself, her confidence in herself, which she was not in touch with, on to the role of Silvia, the part she was playing in the colony's production of *The Recruiting Officer*. By rehearsing this role over several months she began to introject it, that is she was able to take in aspects of Silvia's character and begin to find her own authority.

In dramatherapy the concepts of projection and introjection are particu-larly relevant for they relate directly to the therapeutic effectiveness of role work. Mary, playing the role of a confident young woman who gets her man in the end, is not two people, but there is a discrepancy between how she sees herself and therefore behaves, and how she could be and could behave. She is *split off* from that part of herself. In role she is able to contact and represent it; Silvia can 'stand in' for it. Gradually she can get to know it and introject it, almost without realizing that she is doing so. Thus we see that the process of dramatic role-playing involves a kind of dialogue between two parts of the personality – what is being sent out, or projected, is then able to be brought back in and reassimilated through the process of introjection.

We also saw how Liz Morden, through the process of being able to be in the play and therefore be creative, and through receiving the faith and support of her fellow convicts and Ralph, was able to introject enough goodness from the environment to be able to say 'yes' to life rather than to despair, which would have been to collude with the anti-life aspect of that environment. Both Mary's and Liz's experience originates, we could say, in the mechanisms at work which, according to Klein, are common to us all and are part of what has become known as object relations theory.

Object relations

If we bear in mind the phrase 'the object of my love/hate/admiration/ affections/envy, etc.', this implies an 'other' who is on the receiving end of my feelings; it very clearly represents a person. The phrase *object relations* implies a relationship with such an object – another human being to whom and with whom I relate. For Melanie Klein the phrase did indeed mean that – the infant's relationship to the mother for example. However, her theories extended that relation with the 'other' into an emphasis on the internal world. For the baby creates what she calls 'internal objects', as a part of the development of its own self. These internal objects are created through the relationship to those human beings outside itself, in other words the 'external objects'. Always we must bear in mind, however, that we are not involved in an arid desert of terminology but in a living relationship which, when applied to therapy, forms the therapeutic alliance. (See Sandler *et al.* 1973 on the treatment alliance.)

From the beginning infants are dependent on the environment which can either nurture them or neglect them. Sometimes it supports and sometimes it fails. Most normal experience will be a combination of the two which the infant learns to cope with. At best the infant will thrive and be happy and content and form a good sense of self, at worst the infant will be unhappy, disturbed or die. It is in this context of the battle-ground between life and death that the baby experiences being fed at the breast. The breast is a source of both nourishment – therefore death-defying – and pleasure, therefore life-enhancing. This is the 'good' breast, which gratifies the baby's needs. However, the breast is not always there when it is desired. Now the baby is prey to what it experiences as life-threatening anxiety. In order to cope with these overwhelming feelings the baby phantasizes the existence of two 'breasts', one which is the source of goodness and one which is the absence or withdrawal of goodness. This is called the 'bad breast' on to which the infant projects all its hatred and fury aroused by being plunged into the abyss. At this stage the infant is involved in what Klein called *'part-object' relations*; before a sense of the whole mother emerges the infant responds to a part of the mother's body.

> And she was weaned (I never shall forget it)
> . . . For I had lain the wormwood to my dug,

> . . . And when it did taste the wormwood on the nipple
> Of my dug and felt it bitter, pretty fool,
> To see it tetchy and fall out with the dug.
>
> (*Romeo and Juliet* Act I, Scene 3: 24)

Implicit in Shakespeare's words is the *relationship* between the infant Juliet and the breast; she fell out with it, had an argument, got angry with it as though it were a real person who was deliberately being cruel. At this early stage the infant relates to a part-object as Juliet does.

The feelings of shock and anger as described by Shakespeare really convey the sense that to Juliet it must have felt like a completely different breast she was relating to. It also puts the infant's experience in the context of the whole object relationship, for the Nurse speaks with amusement at the infant's dilemma, and thus emphasizes the vulnerability and lack of understanding to which the infant can be subjected by the adult world. The words help us to understand the powerful and intolerable feelings therefore in the face of the absence of food and the responses and reactions of adults which are harsh, cruel or neglectful. It is truly a struggle for life over death. It is the effects of these feelings which Klein, 400 years later, puts thus:

> The baby reacts to unpleasant stimuli, and to the frustration of his pleasure, with feelings of hatred and aggression. These feelings of hatred are directed towards the same objects as are pleasurable ones, namely the breasts of the mother.
>
> (Klein [1936] 1988a: 290)

Splitting

In order to cope with the conflict of life versus death, good experiences versus bad experiences, a defence mechanism comes into being which Klein came to call *splitting*. To deal with the intense anxiety that the lack of the breast evokes, the infant, through its unconscious fantasy mechanisms, divides or splits the object of its pleasure from the object of its frustration.

Already the mechanisms of *projection* and *introjection* are at work. They successfully ensure that the infant can take in, or introject, the good (i.e. life) and push away, or project, the bad (i.e. death). In an inadequate environment, however, the infant may take in more bad than good, which leads to distortion and even to psychosis. The infant has no choice in the matter. If 'bad' is all there is then 'bad' is all that can be introjected.

> From the beginning the ego introjects objects good and bad, for both of which the mother's breast is the prototype – for good objects when the child obtains it, for bad ones when it fails him.
>
> (Klein [1935] 1988a: 262)

The infant's intolerable feelings are disowned and attributed to the breast

itself and later to the mother. This is the essence of projection where unwanted parts of the self are attributed to another. This tendency remains with
us throughout life, as is evident in observation of ordinary human behaviour
from the infant school child – 'I'm a good girl aren't I and she's bad' – to the
daily slanging matches of politicians in which such a projective mechanism is
institutionalized. In the adult world we all continue to carry our internal
world, or objects, with us. In this sense we could be said to structure our own
environment. It is the re-structuring of this world which is possible in therapy.

If we move on to look at these mechanisms further we can see that there is
a price to pay for this convenient system of splitting, projecting and introjecting. Klein goes on to explain,

> *But it is because the baby projects its own aggression onto these objects
> that it feels them to be 'bad' and not only in that they frustrate its de-*
> sires: the child conceives them as actually dangerous.

(ibid., my italics)

For the implications of splitting off one's own unwanted agression and attributing it to the 'other' we need to look at the overall framework for this
aspect of object-relating.

The paranoid-schizoid position

Because the infant is dependent, 'mewling and puking in the nurse's arms', as
Jaques in *As You Like It* graphically reminds us, the rage which it has projected outwards is phantasized as being destructive, only to return as a per-
secutor. This persecutory aspect is reflected in the use of the term 'paranoid'.
The infant's own destructive impulses extend to extreme sadism and therefore
the terror of retaliation by the object of these attacks, namely the mother's
breast or the mother herself, must be defended against at all costs. The splitting, or schizoid, mechanism ensures that the goodness can be introjected to
sustain and nurture the ego so that the infant is not too endangered by a persecutory return of the rageful sadism which it has directed to the 'bad' breast.
The infant's worst phantasy is aptly described in an image from Webster's *The
Duchess of Malfi*:

> When I look into the fish-ponds in my garden,
> Methinks I see a thing armed with a rake,
> That seems to strike at me.
> (*The Duchess of Malfi* Act V, Scene 5)

The sadistic Cardinal who has destroyed his sister and her husband senses his
death is near in this graphic image where his sadism comes back to haunt him
and indeed heralds his imminent death.

37

Denial and idealization

Destructive instincts and internal persecutors are defended against by two other mechanisms, often existing in relation to one another, *denial* and *idealization*. When Othello realizes he has killed Desdemona on false accusation he says that he has 'loved not wisely but too well' (Act V, Scene 2: 345). In other words he has idealized her, not seen her as a whole person, denied himself the fullness of her personality. And she has done this too:

> my heart's subdued
> Even to the utmost pleasure of my lord:
> I saw Othello's visage in my mind,
> And to his honours, and his valiant parts
> Did I my soul and fortunes consecrate.
> (*Othello* Act I, Scene 3: 250)

The state of falling in love is one of idealization, but lasting relationship necessitates seeing the person 'warts and all'. What happens to Othello and Desdemona is that they fall in love with what they want to see, what they need from each other and therefore idealize in the other:

> She loved me for the dangers I had passed,
> And I lov'd her that she did pity them.
> (*Othello* Act I, Scene 3: 167)

This involves denying whole aspects of each other. The dangers of idealization are starkly illustrated in this play, which ends in Othello's murdering of Desdemona and subsequent killing of himself when he realizes she has been faithful to him and that he has wrongly believed her to be the opposite. Had their relationship been based on a fuller sense of who the other person actually was, Desdemona might have become aware of Othello's irrational tendency to jealousy and murderous rage and Othello to an appreciation of Desdemona's likely fidelity. As it is Desdemona acts naively in relation to Othello. She puts forward another man's case for promotion and Othello's response is to make two plus two equal five. Because of idealization and denial both end up with a very lopsided view of the other. The result is tragedy. I have deliberately taken an extreme example to make the point. Whilst this can be a factor in murder it has its echoes in less dramatic human behaviour which is, nonetheless, damaging. Hinshelwood points to

> the impossibility of the ideal object remaining perfect. Any imperfection that occurs . . . leads to an abrupt switch to a bad object.
> (Hinshelwood 1989)

Part of the function of idealization is to protect the other from one's bad internal objects. This is another aspect of denial – denying parts of oneself.

This is frequently seen in a therapy group where the therapist is idealized in order to be protected from the envy or aggression of the group members. I have quoted elsewhere (Jennings 1995) the example of a dramatherapy group I ran at a centre where the women needed a lot of support. The work had a built-in break because of a prior work commitment on my part. In the session before this break one member said, being invited to share how they felt about there not being a group the following week, how nice it was that I was going to give something to some other people. I had to be idealized and her own real feelings denied. The only way she could express her unconscious feelings of aggression against me, and her envy of the people I would be working with, was to act out these feelings by not attending the session after the break.

Before we leave outlining splitting and its mechanisms, we need to note the related concept of projective identification.

Projective identification

Klein formulated her theory of projective identification in her paper entitled 'Notes on Some Schizoid Mechanisms' in 1942. Since then much has been written about this concept as it would seem that it is of sufficient clinical usefulness to arouse the wish to continually extend or redefine it. In terms of dramatic text and dramatherapy it is a particularly helpful concept for its basic property is that it is a mechanism whereby the individual can get another person to feel his or her unwanted feelings. These feelings are not just projected *onto* the other person, rather they are projected *into* them. Kernberg (Sandler 1987: 94) defines projective identification as a four-fold phenomenon which consists of projecting unwanted aspects of the self *onto* another person while maintaining an empathy with those parts; also involved are the need to control the recipient so that the intolerable feelings continue to be kept at bay, and finally 'inducing in the object' the experience of the projected feelings. This last of the four processes he defines clearly implies '*into*' which Sandler himself uses when he describes what he calls the third stage of projective identification, 'the externalization of parts of the self or of the internal object occurs directly *into* the external object' (Sandler 1987: 18, my italics).

This process is crucial to our understanding of how projection takes place in relation to both character and actor in dramatic text and the therapeutic use which can be made of this. It is interesting to note that, to my mind, Klein's most vivid discussion of this idea is done by means of analysing a piece of literary, not clinical, material, a short story about a man who projects himself into other people (Klein [1955] 1988a: 145–75). In projective identification the individual enables the other person to feel, emotionally and/or physically, the feelings which he or she cannot tolerate bringing into consciousness. This serves the dual purpose of defending against those feelings and omnipotently controlling the other person. For this there must be some degree of role responsiveness, a tendency in the other person to be able to empathize with the projected feelings (Sandler *et al*. 1973; Holmes 1992: 126). We shall return to see how the relationship between this concept and counter-transference operates and, in the next chapter, consider the contribution this idea can make to dramatherapy.

In order to make the point of the necessity for splitting and projective mechanisms to come into being, I have taken a reductionist approach to a complex set of ideas. It needs to be stressed that projection and introjection are ongoing and intricate processes that form a vital part of the relationship of the child with the primary carer. They are processes which enable the child to build up a strong enough ego and super-ego. It is not simply a question of 'good out, bad in'. Good aspects of the self are also split off in order to find a response in the other and be able to be re-introjected. Not all 'bad' parts are projected out. The result of the gradual process of engaging with projection and introjection in the primary relationship leads to the formation of a healthy sense of self and of a helpful super-ego which helps to manage the infant's destructive impulses but is not disabling. Lack of successful engagement with these mechanisms can lead to imbalance and disabling states of mental functioning of varying degrees of severity.

The theory in the theatre

To see how these early mechanisms are echoed on an individual, family and societal level, I shall look at Edward Bond's play, *Saved*. In this play we have a metaphor for aspects of phantasies of the life and death conflict which Klein writes about. It can be seen both as a stark metaphor of the infant's phantasy experience and as an illustration of what happens when early parenting has gone badly wrong. Written in 1965 it is set in South London. A young man, Len, sexually insecure, forms what is initially a sexual relationship with Pam, who lives with her mother, Mary, and father, Harry, who do not speak.

The play shows us a stark cycle of deprivation. It aroused enormous controversy when first performed at London's Royal Court Theatre before a members-only audience, the play having been censored for public performance. I suggest that one of the reasons for the revulsion, horror and Lord Chamberlain's ban was because it shows us, the audience, who by and large are apparently not the people of the play, a mirror of our own potential depths of sadism and violence, a glimpse of our own repressed deprivation and the consequences which are possible. As such it is a metaphor for social and cultural conditions too. In the play a baby is stoned to death. Why? One critic called it 'mindless violence' yet this seems to me the opposite of what it is. For it is surely in the psyche – the mind – of the young men that the violence is born. If by 'mindless' 'lack of thought' is meant, then in this context the careful dialogue in which the young men discuss what acts of brutality they will commit seems to be ignored. To call it mindless is to dismiss the impact of early infant experience in the formation of the mental topography of ego and super-ego (Freud 1973b). Such criticism also dismisses the play itself, which points up the consequences of deeply inadequate parenting and the grave implications of this for our whole society. Such criticism also dangerously distances the events of the play from its middle-class audience with its patronizing projection onto a scapegoat of a particular social group. Bond wrote in the introduction to the play, referring to the murder:

> The scene is typical of what some people do when they act without restraint, and is not true of just these particular people and this particular occasion. Everyone knows of worse happenings. This sort of fury is what is kept under painful control by other people in the play, and that partly accounts for the corruption in their lives. Clearly the stoning to death of a baby in a London park is a typical English understatement. Compared to the 'strategic' bombing of German towns it is a negligible atrocity, compared to the cultural and emotional deprivation of most of our children its consequences are insignificant.
>
> (Bond 1965: 6)

As dramatherapists we may work with any of the characters in the play in real life in family centres, in day units, in hospitals or prison. Yet it is important to remember that it would be all too easy to think of deprivation as outside ourselves, in other words as therapists we can project our deprivation into our clients. This would be to ignore precisely what Bond is telling us and to ignore what I have called the actualization of the paranoid-schizoid position which serves to remind us of the dangers of projecting our own repressed terror and sadism onto others. Within the scope of this chapter it is not possible to explore the play in great detail, but we can look at some of the essential elements which bear out aspects of Melanie Klein's theory and which can help us not to ignore this play which, as Sir Laurence Olivier said at the time, we should have the courage to look at. How much more so now when, as I write, the James Bulger case in Britain and others in its wake in other European countries, force themselves on our unwilling ears, and also as we commemorate the fiftieth anniversary of the liberation of Auschwitz.

In the play mothers are inadequate and fathers absent either physically or emotionally. There are two examples of mothering in the play. One is Pam, the mother of the baby, the other is Pam's mother, Mary. Mary's mothering of Pam was clearly inadequate for Pam has internalized little good-enoughness herself. We see Mary as a woman who lacks appreciation, who dishes up the food, lives with her husband to whom she never speaks and takes Anadins for headaches. The dull pain of the lives of the characters and their deprivation is symbolized by the baby who cries perpetually throughout the evening and is left abandoned in its misery. All that the baby can introject at this time is the 'bad breast'. Nothing else exists. Just before its death Pam

41

has drugged it (we never learn whether it is a boy or a girl) with aspirin, thus underlining the pain of the baby which must be shut out so that it cannot remind the mother of her own neglected child within.

The dramatic event leading up to the baby's death is that the mother leaves the child in the pram in her fury at the refusal of the man she claims is the father to visit her and resume his role of lover. I read this as the syndrome of neglect being repeated as the young men set on the infant. It is as though this image of abandonment evokes the most primitive fury which is acted out. It is the attempt to ward off the internal persecutors which torture them by reminding them of their own neglect. The fury is directed outwards and they become the external persecutors as a way of protecting themselves from the threat of annihilation. Yet it is also metaphorically an action not only of destruction but also of self-destruction because the infant they murder is the very image of their own early experience of deprivation. In order to cope with the overwhelming feelings the baby brings up in them they kill it. And, by projection, they kill off part of themselves in doing so.

Metaphorically Bond creates an image of a deprived section of society, 'sinking deeper into a form of poverty we do not yet recognize – poverty of culture' as another critic wrote. If it was so easy for a middle-class audience successfully to displace the horror onto another section of society why then was the play so unbearable? Perhaps because it reminded everyone, regardless of class, of those deeply unacceptable parts of ourselves – our own vulnerability and consequent terror of annihilation and our own sadism, both of which are inherent in that early paranoid-schizoid position. This then in turn becomes projected onto the play and its author with a violence of its own. That such terrors exist is clear in any group which examines its own process; early phantasy life is evoked and it is common for group members to feel themselves to be murderers or to fear being murdered, to feel guilt and anxiety and loss when a member leaves. Sometimes such groups are ridiculed as indeed therapy itself can be shunned, in an attempt to avoid recognizing that early infant experience exists in all adults. However successfully we may have worked through the infant stages and formed a strong ego and super-ego, the early struggle between life and death and its attendant defence mechanisms of projection and splitting are easily resurrected in times of stress where danger can be deflected out by means of projection of the 'badness' which threatens, originating from the death fear (Klein [1946] 1988b: 6).

In dramatherapy not only are these powerful mechanisms to be echoed in the work as essential parts of the methods of enactment but they also enable the therapist to be aware of the needs of the individual or group.

The depressive position

Klein proposes that the paranoid-schizoid position is succeeded by one in which the characteristics are those of love, guilt and reparation. She calls this the depressive position, which the infant experiences around the middle of the first year of life. The mechanisms of the earlier position – projection and introjection – do not suddenly disappear but the new characteristics emerge as the months of the infant's life proceed. So far the infant's main relationship has been with the breasts and is therefore a 'part-object' relationship. During the depressive position the baby comes to realize that the good and the bad breast are indeed one and the same thing and are part of that central 'other', the mother or other primary carer. Klein calls this the depressive position because the infant has to accept that this object which it has split is in fact not two but one. Inherent in this recognition are attendant fears that because of its feelings of hate and its sadistic attacks, the child has damaged the mother. The depressive position occurs around the time of weaning, which is therefore a time of loss when the baby experiences the loss of the breast and all that means in terms of 'love, goodness and security' (Klein [1940] 1988a: 345). These are felt by the infant to have been lost through its own greed and destructive phantasies. It is here that reparation must be activated. Guilt feelings therefore come into operation to be succeeded by loving feelings towards the mother. If these loving feelings are returned the infant's optimism is increased; gradually it is able to introject a good-enough ego from a good-enough mother. There will be less need to project badness outwards as the positive process is continually being reinforced. As both good and bad feelings begin to be tolerated towards the same object the defence mechanisms of denial and idealization can be employed less. It is worth quoting Klein herself here for she sums up the position which contains many complex elements thus:

> The ego comes to a realisation of its love for a good object, a whole object and in addition a real object, together with an overwhelming feeling of guilt towards it. Full identification with the object based on the libidinal attachment, first to the breast, then to the whole person, goes hand in hand with anxiety for it (of its disintegration), with guilt and remorse, with a sense of responsibility for preserving it intact against persecutors and the id, and with sadness relating to expectations of the impending loss of it. These emotions, whether conscious or unconscious, are in my view among the essential and fundamental elements of the feelings we call love.
>
> (Klein [1935] 1988a: 270)

As the reparative efforts of the infant are rewarded a benign super-ego is developed. If this process is not successfully engaged upon the individual will continue to fragment, or split off those aspects of the self which are intolerable. These can then be projected onto another. This process of projecting the negative feelings outwards can then be experienced by the individual as external persecution rebounding upon the self. The processes of splitting, projection and introjection do not disappear in the depressive position but they

43

are mitigated by the activities of the super-ego and the experience of mourning.

Saved?

So is there any redeeming feature in *Saved* which mirrors the positive working through of the depressive position which for Klein is crucial to mental health? Bond himself called the play optimistic and says of the ending:

> The play ends in a silent social stalemate but if the spectator thinks that this is pessimistic that is because he has not learned to clutch at straws. Clutching at straws is the only realistic thing to do. The alternative, apart from the self-indulgence of pessimism, is a fatuous optimism based on superficiality of both feeling and observation.
>
> (Bond 1965: 6)

We must look to Len for the straw at which we can clutch for a sense of hope. Len was Pam's lover at the beginning of the play. When she rejects him in favour of his friend Fred he stays on in the house, a kind of good presence. When she clearly cannot manage the baby he attempts both to look after her and to show concern, however ineffectual, for the infant's welfare. The sexual element of his relationship with Pam's mother, Mary, is of an Oedipal nature, as Bond himself points out in his notes on the play. After Len helps Mary to stop the flow of the ladder in her stocking, Harry, Mary's husband, comes in. He pretends not to notice but later in one of the usual rows with his wife he refers to the 'filth' of the older woman and the young man in a compromising position. In his fury he attempts to go for his wife but collides with a chair. The chair leg comes off. In the struggle between the young man and the old the Oedipal symbol is obvious. The killing off of Harry's sexuality is symbolized by the phallic chair leg which comes off during the row about Len's position in the household as Harry's rival in the sexual affections of 'mother' Mary. At the very end of the play Len is mending the chair. Here is the reparation which involves both 'parents'. Len's mending of the chair symbolizes the need to make reparation to both parents, to keep the good objects intact. The chair still wobbles a bit, but it is mended. Against all the odds there is some 'goodness' in Len. One of the important things which he does in the play is to acknowledge that he could have intervened in the killing of the baby. He saw it but did nothing and admits that he should have done.

> LEN: I didn't know what to do. I should a stopped yer.
> FRED: Too late now.
> LEN: I juss saw.

In a way Len is perhaps acknowledging his own implication in the murder by projection; that Fred has acted out his murderousness for him. His acknowledgement is a withdrawal of projection, an acknowledgement of his own

44

murderousness. The fact that he can do this is an important ingredient in his representing hope, albeit in the nature of this particular play this is hope at its lowest common denominator, hope of the 'clutching at straws' variety. For in acknowledging his own projected 'badness' he can move into a more integrated state. He 'mends' the chair. This is an act of reparation, after a fight with Harry in which Harry has brandished a knife at Len in rivalry. In mending the chair there is submission to the Oedipal reality of accepting Mary and Harry's relationship of which he is not a part. He represents the possibility of guilt, reparation and love. And therefore of growth.

The depressive position and the dramatherapy group

In working on a play in dramatherapy the depressive position can be seen as integration starts to occur. It is possible for both the individual and the group to come to an acknowledgement of the different roles they play, that what is projected out into the role is introjected also and is part of the personality. It is not uncommon to work with a text onto which a group can project its own unwanted feelings such as hate and fear, loss and vulnerability – they will say that the text is awful, horrible, depressing, the parts are the last things they want to play – yet through the process of working on it together, paying attention to their individual and group process as they go, the group members both draw closer together and allow the play to work for them as it enables them safely to acknowledge those things of darkness. Here the group has reached its depressive position where it must settle with the reality of good and bad together. The group can be a 'good-enough' mother, as can the play and the therapist. There may be regressive moments at this stage. This is clearly evident in groups where there is to be a performance; the members, having realized that the group, the therapist and the play are good enough, and realizing also that the work must come to an end, can resort to those splitting mechanisms of the earlier paranoid-schizoid position. The anxieties about performing and acknowledging the integration publicly are converted into projection and the agreed task of performance is used as a scapegoat for all things bad, the therapist is experienced as punitive and the group retreat into a state of part-object splitting. If the performance heralds the end of the life of a particular group, the imminent loss of the group, the therapist and the play itself is one of the reasons for the regression.

The group may also split itself in an attempt to manage the anxiety which all members are experiencing. Some people will project out the internal persecutors, attacking the task – and probably the dramatherapist – who is 'making them' do it. Others may then rush to defend, thus taking refuge in the defence-mechanisms of denial and idealization. If the group is in a healthy state of being strong enough to work through its depressive anxieties, members begin to own their ambivalent feelings, get in touch with feelings aroused by ending, begin to mourn the imminent loss of the good-enough group, task, therapist and fellow group members. Helpful guilt activates the need to make reparation and the performing of the task becomes possible. It is an act of love.

In an account of the process towards performance by psychiatric patients, Emunah and Read Johnson (1983) describe the variety of regressive behaviours exhibited as performance draws close. Similar behaviours can frequently be seen in the theatre experience also where the depression of a cast in the period leading up to the first night is manifest in a not-good-enoughness feeling, poor dress rehearsals, squabbles and rows, threats of walking out, etc. In *Our Country's Good* we see this as the company prepares to perform (Act II, Scene 11). The depressive position is one which has mourning inherent in it. The regression is therefore partly a cry which reflects a wish not to move forward, be weaned, grow towards independence and therefore experience inevitable loss. One of the losses will be the opportunity to play the roles again once the play is over. There can be a fear that what the roles have 'stood in for' will disappear, that there has been no integration, that all that will remain is an empty shell. But mourning can give way to creativity, and ending precede a new beginning.

We have seen that the potential chaos of terror, neglect and abandonment, the potential violence, sickness and pain are not a million miles away. This is what Bond is saying. He is also saying that there is a kind of resolution, even at the depths, which is possible. In a therapy group we cannot afford to forget that potential and that possibility as well as the possibility for creativity and celebration we found at the end of *Our Country's Good*. One of the ways in which group members are enabled to look at their own most painful experiences, work with what they have repressed and, it is to be hoped, find the possibility of both ease and change can be understood more fully in the light of the next concept I discuss.

CONTAINER, CONTAINMENT AND HOLDING

Related to the concepts of projection and projective identification is that of the container, a notion first developed by Wilfred Bion (1963). The idea of a container is very concrete. It makes me think of Greek amphorae containing wine, oil or water, or Henry Moore sculptures with their huge hollow forms containing the essence of man, woman and child. It can be useful to bear one's own container image in mind, for when we think of the phenomenon of projective identification there is a very concrete aspect to it, for the feelings are actually felt by the person into whom they have been projected. The therapist can therefore be a container for such feelings. In analytic practice the therapist can gradually hand back to the client those feelings which have been split off by means of projective identification. In this process the therapist actually feels the feelings the client is repressing. The handing back can be done through oral interpretation which can help the client to start to understand

46

and own the feelings as belonging to him or herself and, like Prospero, to acknowledge the things of darkness, the things they have been 'in the dark' about. The therapist can be said to be holding the feelings for the client. Because these feelings are as yet intolerable for the client, just as they were for the tiny infant, the therapist must find ways to hand them back in a form which is tolerable and does not provoke unmanageable anxiety. The careful work which continually has to be done by the therapist in order to enable the client to hear truly what has hitherto been too painful to bring into consciousness has been well explored by Casement (1985; 1990). Because of the fear of 'the return of the repressed' (Malan 1979), the therapist may be required to hold the feelings for the client for some considerable time as it is only gradually that more and more can be allowed in.

Ogden (1992) gives a very clear account of the effects of projective identification on therapists and draws attention to the disabling effects that this can have on the therapist's functioning. As I write I recall a group session working on a text, after which I felt that I could hardly conceive of continuing. Supervision helped me to locate my feelings as a massive group exercise in projective identification in which the issues raised by the play were so threatening to the group that the only way they could cope was to give me the feelings to hold. Having realized that and understood what they were requiring of me at an unconscious level, I was able to work with the group with a greater awareness of how to work with the text, so that it became accessible to the members in ways which they not only could handle but also benefit from. Part of the work I had to do on myself was to understand the shadows this play also raised for me. This points up the role-responsiveness which is a condition for projective identification to take place (Sandler 1987). I was then able to 'hold' the group in the sense in which Winnicott used this term:

> it was only when the infant or patient was being held . . . that the truly spontaneous gesture, the revelation of the self to the self, could arise and be felt by the infant or patient to be safe.
> (Davis and Wallbridge 1981: 36)

Winnicott's sense of holding was that of providing a safe environment where the infant – and by analogy the patient – could feel that the parent – or therapist – would be there for the person without putting his or her own feelings and concerns in the way.

> Over and over again a mother deals with her own moods, anxieties, and excitements in her own private life, reserving for her baby what belongs to the baby.
> (Winnicott 1947 quoted in Davis and Wallbridge 1981)

We can see how the therapist's receiving of projected unwanted feelings and being able to think about them and help the client own and manage them can help to maintain the containing environment. A good teacher, a good

47

manager, a good theatre director may well use this approach either instinctively or as a result of training, to help the students, the staff or the cast find their own way to foster an effective and creative working environment.

In the next chapter we shall see examples of the practical application of the concept of containment in dramatherapy work with texts. Here we need to note that the text itself can provide a container for difficult feelings and unexplored parts of the self. I remember someone once jokingly asking me if dramatherapy worked on a prescription basis so that if a person was experiencing great difficulty with murderousness he would be prescribed so many lines of Lady Macbeth. At the time we both laughed but in fact the reality is not so far away. The character can hold for us those parts of ourselves which we have yet to meet in consciousness. By projecting them *into* the character they can find a home, be kept safe for us; the character becomes the container, like a Henry Moore figure. Here Kernberg's point that part of the mechanism of projective identification depends on the individual needing to retain empathy with the projected feelings is highly relevant, for in playing the role the container, which is the character in the text, enables the individual to stay in touch, at an unconscious level, with the projected feelings. In projective identification there must always be a relationship in order for the feelings to be received, to be identified with. This is one of the ways in which projective identification is different from projection. In projection we project *onto* the object and therefore no relationship need be involved (though of course it might be).

Working with a dramatic text the character provides the container for the projected feelings. I believe that this is nearer to the concept of projective identification than projection because of the feature of projecting *into* rather than simply *onto*. Two people are necessary for projective identification, so the work with the character cannot be called projective identification for there is no 'real' person to receive the projections, no one who will be controlled by the feelings, no one who will either act them out or extricate themselves, think about what is happening and return the feelings in a more manageable form to the actor. What happens, rather, is that the individual allows another part of the self to hold, or contain, those projected parts and enable them to have life in the role. It is as though part of the self acts as the receiver of the projected parts and feels them. The character is 'standing in' for another object relationship, either a part of the self or significant person in the individual's object relations. In Pirandello's *Six Characters in Search of an Author* this mechanism is beautifully symbolized. The characters are created by the writer and are therefore part of the writer's objects. They roam the theatres looking for actors to embody them, to give them life. They and their story are alive just as the split-off parts of ourselves are alive and await a home in which they can be felt and lived. They are part of Winnicott's safe environment, which indeed can be very concrete, as I shall shortly discuss. So what we have is the actor projecting part of himself, by means of a character, into the part of himself which can act that character, so that it can be both contained and acted out, held and expressed.

In *A Midsummer Night's Dream* Bottom, 'translated' into an ass, talks and experiences himself as no different from his usual self. He does not know that he has been acting the ass. He does not recognize the ass in himself. Rather he recognizes Pyramus, the lover and hero whom he performs in the mechanicals' play. This role in his fantasy is nearer to his accepted and acceptable image of himself. That of the ass is more deeply unconscious. The play on words between ass and Bottom, his name, serves to underline that he is out of touch with his essential identity. If Bottom were in a dramatherapy group the playing of the role of Ass could be something that he would gradually be able to do willingly, as opposed to it being forced upon him; playing the role supported by sympathetic group audience witnessing, and by the holding provided by the therapist, the text and the setting. But at what cost to us!

TRANSFERENCE AND COUNTER-TRANSFERENCE

So far we have looked at a single actor taking on a single role. We have considered mainly the relationship of self and self; that is the relationship between actor-self and character-self. We have begun to look at the mechanisms of projection, introjection and projective identification as they operate for an individual in enactment. In this section the focus is on the relationship between actor and therapist and actor and others in the group within the framework of two key psychodynamic concepts.

Transference

The concepts of transference and counter-transference are essential to the practice of psychoanalysis and some humanistic therapies. The term transference is used as a clinical term to describe the transferring of feelings and responses from the past into the present within the therapeutic relationship.

In essence we do this often in our daily life, treating another person in ways prompted by the ways in which they remind us at an unconscious level of someone of great significance to us in the past, such as a parent or sibling. Sometimes the unmanageable difficulties of such transference experiences bring someone into therapy. These earlier aspects of object-relating are usually transferred onto the person of the therapist but can also be onto other members of a therapy group. Yalom (1975: 21) draws attention to Sullivan's term 'parataxic distortions' for those transference responses which occur in everyday encounters which result in 'the distortion of interpersonal reality in response to intrapersonal needs'. A fascinating account of the unpicking of the transference relationship of a social worker to his boss, which is then traced to his relationship with his father, forms the exemplar in Holmes' (1992) exploration of psychodrama and object-relations theory. Differing

49

uses are made of this phenomenon, which has been acknowledged to be part and parcel of the therapeutic relationship. These range from ignoring it to interpreting everything that happens in the therapeutic relationship as a repetition of an earlier significant relationship, with many positions in between (Sandler *et al.* 1973; Rowan 1983). In psychoanalytic psychotherapy attention paid to the transference forms the very cornerstone of the work. Enabling the client to form a transferential relationship with the therapist sets a climate for the unresolved aspects of the primary relationships to be given a life which can be explored and understood through the process of the therapy as it is lived and enacted. The past is re-lived and re-enacted through the mechanism of transference.

The therapist may stand for more than one person in the client's earlier life and the transference need not be only gender related. For example it is perfectly possible for a therapist of either gender to represent a male or female client's mother at one stage in the therapy and father at another. Analytic psychotherapy is usually regarded as completed when the transference is worked through or 'dissolved'. Two of the major tools of transference are projection and projective identification, where aspects of past situations and relationships are projected onto or into the person of the therapist and the therapeutic setting. Projective identification is a frequent means by which the therapist begins to understand the intricacies of the client's inner world, as we shall see when we come to look at counter-transference. In dramatherapy the therapist may or may not pay attention to the transference according to training, theoretical bias and personal style. However, it is my belief that transference is always present and is an extremely useful diagnostic and therapeutic tool.

What is of interest to us here is that whereas in analytic psychotherapy the therapist normally takes a consistent role seated in a chair as the one who listens with 'free-floating attention' (though there may be sub-roles and different stylistic stances within this) the dramatherapist has many overt sub-roles. The therapist is at times initiator, at times the listener engaged in free-floating attention, at times a director, at times another actor, at times a side-coach, at times a skills teacher, at times the boundary keeper for the task, etc., etc. Whilst playing any of those sub-roles, the client's transference phenomena may be in evidence. The dramatherapist has continually to judge what is the most helpful response to the group or the individual client at any given moment in the therapy process, while retaining an awareness of the ways in which there may be a consistent transference towards him/herself despite the changes in sub-role. It may also be the case that the nature of the transference response changes so that, for example, the client may respond to the dramatherapist-as-director in a very different way from the way she or he responds to the dramatherapist-as-listening-facilitator, even in the same session. At its most simple this could be because one parent is being evoked by the therapist in one role and the other in the other. The dramatherapist may choose to make interpretations of the transference but is more likely to find dramatic means by which the client may explore the original object relationship which is being manifest in the transference.

Repeating and rehearsing: working with the transference

Since then, at an uncertain hour,
That agony returns
And till my ghastly tale is told
My heart within me burns.
(Coleridge, *The Rime of the Ancient Mariner*)

Both psychoanalytic psychotherapy and dramatherapy share the element of repetition. In the former the client will turn the psychotherapist into his or her 'significant other' again and again and again. As the original relationship is worked through in the transference and as the client gradually comes to an understanding of this process, change becomes possible. The element of repetition is crucial. In dramatherapy the repetition is through the taking on of roles and working with others in the group who are also in role. The transference is 'translated' into role-play. In dramatherapy transference speaks, we could say, a different language. The actor is therefore provided with two containers for the transference object – the character he or she plays opposite and the actor who plays that role. This of course has bearing on the role of the therapist who, because of the nature of dramatherapy, frequently shifts the focus of the transference onto the enactment and its components. This is important in a form of therapy where the therapist plays such different sub-roles as facilitator, director, etc. Much will here depend on the therapist's style as well as on professional judgement. (For a proposal of some of the differences between dramatic transference in relation to analytic transference see Eliaz 1992.)

In repeating we are also rehearsing. The original meaning of rehearse is linked to that of 'going over again'. The word rehearse is derived from the verb 'to harrow', which therefore implies going over old ground, exactly what one is doing in the process of therapy. I find it helpful to keep the two concepts of rehearse and repeat together, for repetition on its own might simply be a defence against change, a refusal to move forward. If we think of repeating in the way an actor repeats in order to become acquainted with and learn a new role, repeating becomes 'rehearsal' as preparation. An actor in rehearsal is repeating the lines, the moves and the ways of relating the character to the other characters, while at the same time changing and refining those elements to gain the most truthful performance.

In therapy the notions of rehearsal and repetition can help us to view two important components of therapeutic change. First, old ground can be reworked with the intent that gradually the original object-relationship(s) will be de-cathected, that its psychical charge will be dissolved. Second, the

51

process of this simultaneously acts as preparation for the object(s) to be related to in a new way. While the client is going over old ground, he or she is also quietly preparing the soil to nurture new growth. Through the transference mechanism the client can continually repeat and continually rehearse.

Transference and dramatic text

When working with dramatic text something becomes available to the therapist which is not present in quite the same way in other forms of dramatherapy. The therapist can help the client to make use of the text to focus on the relationship which underlies the transference. This is obviously working in a completely different way from individual analytic psychotherapy where the transference relationship is encouraged to develop over several months or years and the transference object is consistently the therapist. However, within the dramatherapy group the object of particular transferences may be anyone in the group as well as the therapist. What the dramatherapist is doing is observing and deducing what relationship(s) the client is re-enacting and then assessing what dramatic interventions might be most useful. For example, a group member who sees her father as a Lear-like figure may explore her relationship with him by taking on the roles of Lear's three daughters. The transference might have been originally manifested by her response to the therapist or a fellow group member. In exploring the words which Shakespeare gives to both Lear and the daughters, she is being able to repeat symbolically her relationship with her father. The same woman, in analytic psychotherapy, might at times behave to her therapist who was carrying the father transference, as Cordelia one day and at another stage of the therapy as Goneril or Regan.

On an occasion working with *As You Like It*, the group's projection onto me was of a strict withholding and distant father who somehow banished their fun, just as the 'bad' Duke banishes his niece Rosalind in the play. Having heard out their feelings I invited them into the enactment space to speak what they felt to whatever character in the play 'my' behaviour evoked. If they wished they then took the role of this character, finding a line or an approximation of a line of the text to speak. This is not to say that that particular transference was magically dissolved but that some taking back of what had been projected onto me freed up the group and they found they could challenge me. The rest of that session was one in which there was much release through creative improvisation with the text. Some time afterwards one participant reflected:

> You know there was some aggro expressed after the first couple of sessions, when some people complained that you seemed overdistanced from events. I accused you of doing it on purpose later on, as soon as I felt safe enough to do so. Whatever may have been happening on vari-

ous personal levels, I remain convinced that the play only began to come alive at this point – i.e. when we became aware of our own new life as a group, capable of feeling and thinking together.

Here the necessity of the dramatherapist taking on the negative group transference and simultaneously returning it to the text enables the group to move with the play. To both hold the transference and let it go – another paradox. It is also important for the therapist to be in touch with the character in the play who, because of the particular stage of the engagement with the text, is the one he or she is being cast in by the unconscious of the group.

Counter-transference

Because transference must involve an 'other' for there must be an object onto whom the original object is transferred, it is obvious that there may be a transference relationship going the other way as well. This phenonemon was seen by Freud as an impediment to psychoanalytic treatment. Whilst he came to view transference as one of the most important disoveries that the method of psychoanalysis had unearthed, he never came to a similar conclusion about its counterpart counter-transference. At first, therefore, the therapist's transference to the client, or *counter*-transference, was thought to be a hindrance to the process of psychoanalysis. Gradually it became clear that this was in fact far from the case. Heimann (1950), whom Sandler cites as being the first to make explicit the positive value of counter-transference, makes a statement which is particularly relevant for the dramatherapist to consider:

> the basic assumption is that the analyst's unconscious understands that of his patient. This rapport on a deep level comes to the surface in the form of feelings which the analyst notices in response to his patient, in his counter-transference.
>
> (Heimann 1950 quoted in Sandler *et al.* 1973)

The interventions of the dramatherapist are largely taken from the realm of metaphor and symbolic action. These phenomena being the fruits of the unconscious, they facilitate a meeting with the client's unconscious. The dramatherapist is constantly allowing his or her associations and intuition to inform the therapy session and to help make the decision as to what structure to create for the work (see Chapter 3 for discussion of the term 'structure'). This is one of the ways that the dramatherapist's unconscious manifests its understanding of the client or the group. It is also by this means that the decision is made as to which sub-role is most important at any one time in the session or stage in the therapy. However, the therapist has to develop the ability to check out or monitor whether or not the intervention is more related to his or her own needs being met than those of the client. The unconscious produces the association or the idea for dramatic intervention and the therapist quickly does a 'rain-check'. If the therapist is acting on the counter-transference then the choice of intervention will be inappropriate. The therapist's job is to understand the impact of his or her own counter-transference reactions and study their meaning to help the client. Some of this can be done on the spot; other aspects of the process are achieved through reflective processing later through written recording, supervision, the dramatherapist's own use of the tools of the trade or a combination of these. In my view it is crucial that the dramatherapist has extensively explored his or her own inner world through in-depth personal therapy in order to be aware of the possible sources and nature of counter-transference reactions.

Kinds of counter-transference

Different aspects of counter-transference have been identified by several writers (e.g. Little 1951; Racker 1968), but it is generally acknowledged that counter-transference falls into two main categories. The first is where the client becomes a transference object for the therapist because the client reminds the therapist either of a significant other in the therapist's life or of a repressed part of his or her own self. The second is where, by means of projective identification, the client gets the therapist to experience the split-off parts of either the client's affect or self.

The first is relatively straightforward; I start to feel a particular feeling, or find myself reacting in a particular way to client X. I examine this feeling and realize I am responding like I did to my father or, in relation to group Y, I realize that my response is linked to unresolved feelings in relation to my mother – maybe I treat the group as I would like to have treated her, etc. Through my own monitoring I, as a dramatherapist, can locate the inappropriate responses where the individual or group 'stands in for' my own significant objects. What is more, through my own therapy or analysis I am more likely to see it coming. This aspect of counter-transference is, in other words, the therapist's transference to the client.

The second main category is related to the concept of projective identification. Although several writers view this as a mechanism related to psychotic states, it is widely acknowledged to be activated in the therapeutic environment and is increasingly seen as a very useful means of understanding aspects of the client which otherwise remain inaccessible to the therapist. In this form of counter-transference the client projects into the therapist so that the therapist feels feelings or finds him/herself drawn to behave in a particular way that would not normally be warranted by the situation. Here a form of counter-transference is being enacted in which the therapist is feeling *for* the client, or wanting to behave like the client might want to behave. The other possibility is that the client is provoking in the therapist the reaction of a significant other in the client's life. So if, for example, I feel protective towards a group, I need to ask myself, 'Do I feel protective because I have issues about protecting/being protected/not having protected or been protected, etc. *or* do I feel protective because they want me to behave like someone who protected, didn't protect them, etc.?'

The mechanisms of projection and introjection are important in understanding counter-transference. Both the subject and its manifestation in practice I find fascinating. Here I can do no more than whet the appetite of the reader unfamiliar with the concept (though doubtless not of the lived experience) and remind the practitioner of its importance in dramatherapy. For in any intervention we make, any sub-role we decide to take, I believe we must consider how to use the counter-transference experience for the benefit of the client, acting on our *understanding of it* rather than acting *on it*. This is particularly important to remember for the dramatherapist who works in role where the spontaneity of being in role may cause a blurring of boundaries between therapist's material and client's material. This phenomenon also raises some interesting issues for drama in the educational context where the technique of teacher-in-role is frequently used. Its relevance to the theatre will be evident in the example which follows.

In practice

When working with dramatic text a very interesting situation occurs which operates on two layers between two people – the people themselves and the characters from the text which they play or represent in some other way. I shall therefore close with an example which illustrates some of the issues relating to projective mechanisms and transferential aspects of object-relating as they can be activated in drama work. The context is that of theatre production.

I was directing an all-female production of Shakespeare's *The Tempest*. I had cast as Caliban a woman whom in audition showed considerable versatility and the ability to play a 'bad guy' with power and conviction. As rehearsals wore on she seemed less and less capable of getting the venom with which Caliban speaks to Prospero. I would discuss, create opportunites for improvisation, demonstrate, use every directorial device I knew and the more I did this the more she retreated and the worse our relationship became. I never got the Caliban I wanted and she grudgingly performed the only one she could do. All the time I felt she performed the only one she *would* do rather than *could*; now I think differently. I now think that deeply unconscious mechanisms were at work and that the play tapped into some of those early inter- and intra-object relations. As actor Jill was playing a role in the play, as director I was not – apparently. However, we were doing *The Tempest*, and Prospero is master. In the early part of the rehearsal period, when I perceived Jill was having difficulties, I felt I was being reasonable and understanding, not critical but enabling. Gradually I began to lose patience when I felt that my plan, my vision of the play, my production, was going to be spoilt, as I perceived it, by her performance. And I began to get angry and critical, cruel in my lack of understanding of how hard this part was for her to play. She became my scapegoat. None of this I realized at the time. Now the lines stare out at me from the page and I wonder why I was so blinded then. Except that I know that that is exactly how projective identification works; when we are locked into such deeply unconscious mechanisms we cannot become conscious of them without effort and tools to help us, and sometimes not even then.

> CALIBAN: This island's mine, by Sycorax my mother,
>   Which thou tak'st from me. When thou cam'st first,
>   Thou strok'st me, and made much of me; . . .
>   . . . . and here you sty me
>   In this hard rock, whiles you do keep from me
>   The rest o' th' island.

> PROSPERO: Thou most lying slave,
>   Whom stripes may move, not kindness! I have used thee,
>   Filth as thou art, with human care; and lodged thee
>   In mine own cell, till thou didst seek to violate
>   The honour of my child.
>   (*The Tempest* Act I, Scene 2: 347)

Whilst there may be several explanations to our interaction one stands out clearly; that when it became clear to me that 'my child', that is my 'baby', my play, was being spoilt or 'violated' then I behaved in a punishing manner. But more deeply than that the question is also in the air, was I projecting onto the actor the need to have someone express the Caliban in me and was enraged that she would not perform this task for me? At the end of the play Prospero says of Caliban,

>   This thing of darkness I
>   Acknowledge mine.
>   (*The Tempest* Act V, Scene 1: 275)

The Caliban in all of us is hard to acknowledge, the shadow, the parts we would rather not know about, the sadistic, greedy, abusive, violent parts, the parts that as infants we project outwards. And as adults too. I cannot speak for Jill but can only 'acknowledge mine'. If I had been able to analyse why I needed her to play the nastiness of Caliban maybe I could have helped her to do it because then I would not have been projecting my Caliban into her, giving her an intolerable burden. If this had been the case then I could also have been freed up to acknowledge the kind of Caliban which she was actually playing – the wounded, weak and vulnerable Caliban. As director I could then have allowed my vision of the play to have been enriched. But maybe that was also a part of myself I did not want to acknowledge at that time and therefore must get rid of it, project it out and punish it.

What is happening here in terms of the psychodynamics of working with dramatic text is that two individual adults, Jill and Marina, are in role together as actor and director respectively. Within them two individual infants, little-Jill and little-Marina, are activated from the moment of encounter. Marina invites Jill to take the part of Caliban and Jill agrees. Marina thinks she is operating as a director and Jill as an actor and on a conscious level they are. However, in both of them the infants in them and the unique life lived by each up until that point, their conscious and unconscious experience are all sending out signals to one another. These signals are caught by the transmitter which is the dramatic text they are both working on, Shakespeare's *The Tempest*. Now activated, these signals clamour to find expression and the transmitter obliges. Jill's unconscious finds roots in Caliban and Marina's in Prospero, the 'director' of the island. In the play Caliban represents or 'stands in for' aspects of Prospero which Prospero would rather not know about (until he comes to an understanding of this at the end of the play); in other words Prospero projects onto Caliban the unwanted self-threatening aspects of himself. Marina as Prospero therefore projects onto Jill as Caliban those unwanted self-threatening aspects of herself and Jill finds it increasingly difficult to play the role. Because both Marina and Jill are not conscious of the *intra*psychic forces being activated they are also not conscious of the dynamics of their *intra*personal relationship. They therefore *pretend* that they are two adults (which of course they are but in their object-relations are not) and blame each other for the difficulties in their *interpersonal* relationship. They remain angry and disappointed with one another.

At the time of this event I was new to dramatherapy and 'but green in judgement'; I didn't let the dramatherapist and the director in me talk to each other. If I could have integrated them I might have understood more about what was going on. Clearly there were transferential aspects to the relationship being lived out through projective mechanisms. The theatre is not an area where 'supervision' is practised as it is in clinical work but I know I would have benefited then from looking psychodynamically at what was happening between Jill and me – and indeed exploring what our struggle might have been 'acting out' projectively for the whole cast.

In all of us there is a Caliban and a Prospero, an oppressed and an oppressor. In order to do some of the most difficult work in therapy we do well to hold on to that awareness, uncomfortable though it might be. To truly educate children and to provide a mirror of the human condition in the theatre, we do well to stay in touch with that awareness in which the most painful and 'unacceptable' aspects of inner feeling and life experience can be named and understood. We can then more easily remember that anger is often the result of hurt and remain compassionate towards both ourselves and those we work with.

CONCLUSION

And so we come full circle, back to Susan in the drama class with whom we began this journey. Through the potential space of the drama class Susan was able to act out her fears of life and death, her pain, her fury and her need. She did this by means of the mechanisms of projection and introjection contained both by the sub-system of the school setting and within the dramatic enactment. Through these means and those of a transferential relationship with the teacher and the support of her peers she was able to engage with aspects of the paranoid-schizoid and depressive positions. Daily in dramatherapy groups, in theatre casts and in drama classes these processes are being visited again and again and again. For the therapist, the teacher and the theatre director the road is always an unknown landscape. For me the concepts touched on in this chapter are some of the signposts which help me to find my way around the country that I am in and help me to complete the walk when I get lost. How I do that will be the focus of Chapter 3.

3

THEORY INTO PRACTICE
Means and methods

INTRODUCTION

In order for the dramatherapy and psychodynamic processes discussed in Chapters 1 and 2 to be harnessed for healing, growth and change, the potential space must be created and maintained. Within this the context of dramatic text work itself can become another potential space. Certain conditions must prevail in order for that potential space to exist. They are not different from those I would use in any dramatherapy group in essence and the principles offer much to those working in education and in theatre, as we shall see in Chapters 4–10. I realize I may be covering very obvious ground for some of my colleagues but I hope they may move on to areas which may be less familiar later in the chapter.

What follows explains my methods of working as a dramatherapist to create the means whereby people may move through a text, continually trying out new ways of relating to it. My aim is for them to find their way via the text towards development and change. Over the years I have become convinced that the concepts of containment and holding are crucial to the effectiveness of the work. In Winnicott's words,

> so there may come into being the potential space in which, *because of trust*, the child may creatively play.
>
> (Winnicott 1971: 129, my italics)

In order for trust to be built up in the dramatherapy group, the therapist needs to foster the experience of both holding and containment in the group setting and within the dramatherapy structure used. This is, in my way of working, crucial in enabling the group members to move deeply into their own process safely. Then I can trust that they and the text will meet and do the work of therapeutic enhancement together. Text, therapist and the group provide both containment and holding for the work to be engaged on, deepened and concluded. Aspects of the self can be projected and gradually re-introjected.

In addition to this, I design structures. My role is to invite the participants to engage in dramatic structures within a holding environment for the discovery of their own processes which they are ready to explore at this moment

59

in their lives. The journey is not for me to determine – rather I provide the means of transport.

The importance of containment as an enabling factor in the effectivenss of the work is pinpointed here by a participant in a workshop on Ibsen's *Ghosts*, who said to me several years later:

> I remember the introduction as being extremely powerful. We entered at quite a deep level very quickly which I haven't often experienced. I don't know what that was to do with, whether it was the structure you provided and the containment you provided with that structure which enabled us to get so involved. The structure was set out and contained. As a participant I didn't invent the structure, I just entered it. The text is like a structure I entered into as well.

In providing this environment I attend to five main areas. These are a high priority in the way I think, plan and execute the work.

1 Contracts and boundaries
2 Design of the dramatherapy context
3 Function of the group and the therapist
4 Structure and management of dramatherapy methods
5 Text as container
6 Planning and management of dramatic structures

CONTRACTS AND BOUNDARIES

Three essential contracts need to be made (and there may be others according to the particular circumstances of the work). The first is between the therapist and the organization in which the group is to run. Time spent on clarifying the aim of the dramatherapy group within the context of the primary task (Rice 1965; Coleman and Bexton 1975) of the organization is crucial, but in large organizations undergoing stress and change this is by no means easy. At least grappling with the issue will help the therapist to become aware of some of the difficulties which might arise; any negotiations with the organization or institution before the group is to be run is time well spent. (For many relevant essays see Obholzer and Zagier-Roberts 1994.) A well-made contract between the institution or organization and the group ultimately in itself provides support and value for both therapist and clients.

The second contract is that which is made between the group members and the therapist; and the third is made between the group members themselves. The aim of a contract is to safeguard the rights of those making it, clarifying their purpose in being together and thus preparing the ground for the work to bear fruit. A contract carefully made should be empowering for all concerned. Contracts should not be entered into lightly; we have the lesson of Dr

Faustus to remind us of that! The external making of the contract can also be empowering in terms of releasing the clients into making a contract together. It is about valuing themselves and one another and therefore being valued. The contract is the first act of containment that the therapist provides the client. It is the first act in a relationship which says, in effect, 'I respect you and will do what I can in your interests according to our agreement as to why we are both here.' In such conditions there is a chance that the client may be enabled to internalize the therapist's modelling of value. Each group member may then be able to make a contract with him or herself. This helps the participants to stay with the work of the therapy.

The contract with the group will agree the aim and purpose of the therapy and the method of the work. I have known dramatherapists, particularly in training or newly practising, to be tempted to call the dramatherapy group a drama group out of fear of alienating or frightening off either prospective clients or the organization. In these circumstances therapists need to analyse their own counter-transference reactions and try to understand the meaning inherent in their relationship to the dynamics of the clients and institution through careful processing and discussion in supervision. It is helpful to remind oneself at such times of the role of dramatherapist and that what is on offer is dramatherapy. (It is, of course, another matter if the dramatherapist is genuinely offering a drama group which might be more appropriate than a dramatherapy group in a particular setting and context; in this case the contract will reflect this.)

Lest the making of contracts feels a little mechanistic let us look at the emotional and psychological truth of its importance as feelingly suggested by this passage from *Mary Barnes* by David Edgar (1987).

MARY: Duggie.
DOUGLAS: It's O.K.
MARY: I've come –
DOUGLAS: Don't worry –
MARY: Come to have a breakdown. (*Pause. Quickly Mary pulls out the sheet in the typewriter, puts in another sheet and types*) Dear – Matron – Thank – you – for – the – interview – but – I'm – otherwise – engaged – Yours – (*She takes out the paper, signs it*) Mary Barnes. (*Pause. Mary reaches to her hair and pulls out the pins. Her hair falls down*) I'm cold.

(Edgar 1987: 101)

Here Mary is being given permission by the therapeutic community to which she has just arrived to do what she needs to do – to regress and slowly, painfully, build her life up anew. In writing the letter to the hospital cancelling her interview she is making her contract with herself. Douglas, the therapist, acts as witness to her process and provides her with the holding necessary for her to make this pact to explore her inner world and reject the outer one. This is symbolized by the letter to the Matron rejecting the job interview and therefore rejecting her struggle to hold on in the outside world. Through the playwright's device of having Mary write a letter declining the opportunity of a contract with the external world, he underlines the powerful contract she is making with herself and with the institution which is to provide her with the containment necessary for her to 'go down', as she puts it, to embark on a journey into the darkest recesses of her chaos.

The establishing of the contract is a vital part of creating a holding environment. As part of the contract practical boundaries will be established. They are crucial in psychodynamic therapy but can deepen the work done in both educational and theatre settings. This is because a firm basis is set which helps to diminish anxiety and thus provide for risk-taking within a safe environment. Holmes (1992) discusses the relationship between anxiety and spontaneity, pointing out that Moreno, the founder of psychodrama, 'believed that it is a loss of spontaneity which results in increasing anxiety'. I agree with Holmes' response to this that it is, rather, the presence of anxiety which is the cause of loss of spontaneity. In an active creative therapeutic medium such as either psychodrama or dramatherapy, the loss of spontaneity, or the difficulty in establishing its presence, is an important inhibiting factor. Attention paid to boundaries can sometimes be experienced as inhibiting, perceived as barriers, especially by adolescent groups who will test out the boundaries to the utmost, or an adult group which is in an adolescent developmental phase. But their very testing out is to help them feel a sense of security, of knowing where omnipotence ends and how to discover what is possible through discovering what is not possible. Once boundaries are established, feelings are clearer and can be fully experienced and explored because one is acting in 'relation to'. Faced with consistent boundaries growth and development of 'me' as opposed to 'not-me' become possible, as I discussed in Chapter 2. Also spontaneity becomes more possible because the boundaries enhance the feeling of safety through the containment they offer.

So what kinds of boundaries are needed? An approach that I find helpful is to think in two categories, that of negotiable boundaries and that of those that are non-negotiable. Non-negotiable boundaries are those which I set as a therapist, ones which I feel enable me to work and offer my services to the clients with the possibility of successful work taking place. As a dramatherapist I need certain conditions and certain containment myself; knowing where I stand in relation to my own work is an important part of what I have to offer my clients. Therefore for me to be clear what I can offer or not offer helps the clients be clear as to whether or not this is a group for them. Usually my non-negotiable boundaries will be about consistency regarding the dates and time and venue of sessions and, if it is a closed group where new members are not admitted after an agreed time, a commitment to attendance. Where confidentiality is concerned I shall also need to protect my right to share information with people in particular roles relevant to the client's well-being when that well-being is, in my professional judgement, at stake. Examples of such roles might include the school headteacher, the day-centre manager, the consultant psychiatrist. Confidentiality is not secrecy, a therapist is not a priest bound by the confessional, and, in my experience, exploring the issue of confidentiality with group members has always been a rewarding exercise for both them and me. Setting my own boundaries about it helps the group members to discuss their own issues and explore what needs they have for confidentiality with one another. This latter then forms part of the negotiable boundaries, and helps to develop the culture of the group.

Being clear about the primary task of the dramatherapy group – its purpose, why it exists – also falls into my category of boundaries. For if I know the boundary of the work, in other words what the group is there to do and what it is not there to do, then I can help the group to be anchored in that defined environment. From where the ship is, we can explore the surrounding waters, not sail off into other seas and founder on rocks because the group has gone adrift. When the winds are blowing and the waters are high the group can pressurize the therapist to weigh anchor and sail off ill prepared into uncharted seas instead of staying with the depths that are there to be explored from the safety of that containing environment.

The boundaries we agree together are extremely important in providing the holding necessary for the work to proceed. When they are not adhered to then they are addressed and both the therapist and the group members have a reference point in common. For example a group member arriving at a group bearing a bun or a drink, where the agreement has been that no food or drink should be brought into the session, can be seen to be signalling something to the group members and the therapist. Thinking about what this means for the individual and the group will be the task of the therapist and maybe of the group itself. The therapist might wonder not only why the boundaries are being tested but also why it is that the group member in question might be the one doing this. Only the fact that the boundary is there in the first place can throw this piece of behaviour up and help further speculation as to the meaning for the individual and the group on the significance of food or drink in this context and at this particular session. This is a simple example of the function of boundaries in the group setting. Boundaries encourage the exploration of inner and outer, self and other. When broken or tested they provide clues to these issues which can be helpful in the therapist's understanding of the client.

DESIGN OF THE DRAMATHERAPY CONTEXT

The choice of play is like any form of therapeutic intervention. In an ongoing group it is selected in relation to the particular group and what is happening to that group in its current life. In the situation of a workshop being advertised as exploring a particular play, then the participants themselves could be said to be selecting their own therapeutic intervention in their lives by choosing to work on what that particular play offers.

Once the play has been selected, then in order to decide on the overall structure for the work, I think about various, apparently very simple, relationships between the text and the group setting and aims. Sensitivity to the aims and length of the group are important in designing the structure of the work and in modifying it in progress. Two examples will serve to illustrate this matching of the external constraints to the structural boundaries of the play. One is that of the five-day workshop using a Shakespeare play, such as is often run on a week's course or summer school. The other, a four-week group contracting to work with *Waiting for Godot*, will be looked at in greater detail later in this chapter (pp. 73–81). Both these short-term examples serve to highlight the way in which the issues of holding and containment are addressed through the structure of the work. The principle can be applied to any work, short or long term.

Five-day workshop example

Working with a five-act play focusing on an act a day is a way of paralleling the play's basic structure with the structure of the group event. It is in itself a form of containment. It means that the wholeness of the play is available to the participant who cannot get stuck with one part of the play or one character. An example is *The Tempest* and the character of Caliban. One might call him 'id' personified. Stuck in Act II with Caliban might mean an unbalanced focus on the chaos that Caliban represents, which within the context of a one-week event is not helpful and might even be damaging. I always find that groups want to linger with Caliban; his pull is as attractive as Satan in Milton's *Paradise Lost*, the fascination of our own shadow selves given body and form. As we move through the play the encounter with Caliban can be developed, can be balanced by the other characters, by the other aspects of the self, and therefore contained. Encountering Caliban and finding he can be integrated through the lines of the protagonist, Prospero, in Act V, 'this thing of darkness I acknowledge mine', can enable the integration of aspects of the shadow self which the individual has hitherto found difficult. At the very least a moment of recognition is possible. This is possible if work on the play moves as the play itself does. The work is therefore grounded in a structure which takes account of the external world from which the group members have come and to which they must return very shortly. It helps them to engage meaningfully, to move through the text and to be aware of movement towards the ending. The groundedness is always there. This does not mean that the work is superficial, rather the opposite, as the safety of the parallel containment allows the participants to take risks and work spontaneously, allowing the drama to work at an unconscious level. Moving the group through the 'act-a-day' design also takes care of the danger of one individual carrying the projections of the group. In this way all the members can encounter all the roles and engage fully with the way the metaphoric values of the play are developed. If we stay with Caliban as an example, it could be convenient for the group if one member remained with Caliban throughout the work, for the 'thing of darkness' can, in their phantasy, be acknowledged to be belonging only to that person. For the experience to be meaningful in that the play is allowed to work on each person, the whole play must become accessible to them in a way which means they can safely leave the island of the summer school or course on the last day of the event.

If I had five weeks on a Shakespeare play I would still use that basic structure, translating it to an act a week, as this allows for the participants as individuals and as a group to move through Shakespeare's structure, thus engaging with the integrity of the logic of the text. For I find that this logic works its way into us as we work on through the acts. I am now used to walking into the group at the start of the Act III session and finding the lostness, the confusion, the stuck feelings of the group which exactly mirror the events of *The Tempest* in Act III (though it will be manifest in a way totally individual to each particular group). It is not only that the group is working on the play, but also that the play is working on the group.

The overall design of the work is extremely important in order for the group members to allow themselves the freedom to surrender to the text and discover what it holds for them.

FUNCTION OF THE GROUP AND THE THERAPIST

The group has a containing function in itself. Members may act as containers for the projections of others which can be acknowledged and understood within the boundaried context of the group's life. The playing out and handing back of projected material is made possible by the work with the text through the means of enactment and the use of the audience function, as we saw in Chapter 1.

The group also provides a holding function, particularly as it becomes cohesive. Group members begin to support one another, sharing feelings and thoughts, struggling with difficulties and conflicts and generally valuing the potential space of the therapy group. In doing so they validate one another and the dramatherapy work and thus create a 'good-enough' environment. This plays a vital part in creating Winnicott's conditions for creativity and growth.

The therapist's part in this is to help to promote this 'good-enough' group by being a 'good-enough' dramatherapist. In addition to good boundary management this will include being able to contain both positive and negative projections, helping the group members to begin to own their own split-off or projected material as the group's life is lived. The management of the dramatherapy methods and of dramatherapist sub-roles are important ways in which the therapist addresses projections and transference phenomena.

Above all being consistent and staying with the process of the group, not losing sight of the overall task, is what gives the group members a sense of being 'held' by the therapist. The ways I find useful in helping me to maintain this position will I hope be evident in the section on 'planning and management of dramatic structures' later in the chapter (pp. 72–81), and indeed in the succeeding chapters.

STRUCTURING AND MANAGEMENT OF THE DRAMATHERAPY METHODS

The issue of boundaries explored in my first category applies equally to the management of the dramatherapy structures. Important in itself, it also reinforces the overall issue of boundaries as being part of the culture of the work. This is another aspect of holding because there is consistency of approach. This is illustrated by the experience of the participant I quoted on p. 60 and is in accordance with the holding function of parental primary care outlined in Chapter 2.

The dramatherapy methods themselves will be those of role and enactment as explored in Chapter 1. It is almost impossible to think of working with dramatic text without the concept of role. In order to portray a character a role must be embodied. Playing within the context of a dramatic text in dramatherapy many roles may need to be taken. Management of this process of taking on a role, occupying it and taking leave of it is of paramount importance and must be seen in relation to the boundary provided by the enactment space.

En-roling and de-roling

In dramatherapy it is in the area of en-roling and de-roling that the therapist must be alert to possible boundary confusion. I have found that the more clearly someone engages with the process of taking on the role, the greater the focus once in role and the deeper the work which becomes possible. The person feels safer that the boundaries are engaged with, so the fear of merger and becoming lost is minimized. The defence mechanisms, which can lead to superficial work, which the individual might automatically employ as a safeguard against such confusion, are rendered unnecessary. The knowledge that the role can safely be entered into and safely left enables the participant to be fully in role, allowing the role to work for him or her. When I have worked with dramatherapy students in training, spending time on exploring the transition space between being out of role and being in role, they have frequently been amazed at the powerful experiences of emotion and of perceptions of fantasy and reality which the transition allows them. My belief is that these powerful experiences are being experienced even when one moves quickly into or out of role, but they are being experienced at an unconscious level. If they are too threatening to the personality then they are defended against and therefore cannot be harnessed for working in depth. The work with the students makes conscious what I believe happens unconsciously and is either at best defended against and therefore rendered useless for insight or at worst leads to internal chaos. So often when working as a trainer in management and organizational contexts I have been greeted with participants who say anxiously, 'Are we going to have to do role-play? I hate role-play.' Experience has taught me that the reason they hate it is usually because they have not been properly prepared for it and have experienced fear, embarrassment or ensuing inner confusion by being exposed to a method which is not understood by the trainer.

Enactment space

The creation and maintenance of an enactment space is crucial to role boundary management. I therefore create or invite the group to create a clearly defined enactment space in one part of the room, which is entered into and exited from. The management of this boundary helps the group members to be aware of the 'not-me' aspect of the role and strengthens the ego to enter safely into the 'me' aspects, that is to allow themselves to suspend their disbelief and enter fully into the role with the parts of themselves which do not, or might not, otherwise find expression. The containment is provided by the structure of the world of the theatre form. Working with a group of only two it is possible for both group members to enter into role and have the experience deepened by the audience-as-witness function provided by the therapist, who remains outside the enactment space. If for any reason the therapist feels that it is appropriate to enter the enactment space, for example to 'double', then the cushions or chairs outside the enactment space symbolically hold the group space which the therapist has just left and to which he or she therapist then returns. Time and time again I have been told that the working space has felt safe enough for risks to be taken and participants have therefore felt able to engage fully with what the role work offers. It is the strengthening of the 'not-me'/'me' boundary that enables this to happen. Role work is risky, which is what the participants on those management courses instinctively know; it is living with the paradox of being and not-being simultaneously.

Three stages of role work

If we go back to Peter Slade's (1954) definition of projected play and personal play we can see the three stages of role involvement quite clearly. In the first stage individuals need to *en-role*, that is to take on the role. In doing so they project into the role, they project aspects of the self onto the role itself in order to make it live. Before actually taking on the role, the person who is about to play it sees the role 'out there', like the toy waiting to be played within Slade's projective sense. The character in the play is there waiting in the script to receive the projections about to be put upon it. The individual needs to be prepared to approach this waiting role. The aim of this is to help participants prepare themselves for the role, to dress themselves in it, so it is a bit like becoming familiar with the colour, texture and design of the clothes one wishes to try on in a shop. This might involve trying out particular characteristics of the character's movement or voice, picking out particular lines and finding different ways of saying them. It might simply be quietly waiting and focusing on the enactment space and preparing to work in it with the sincerity and absorption mentioned in Chapter 1. I try to help participants not to rush into the role, but to wait at the boundary between the rest of the group and the enactment area, to become focused, just as I encourage actors, whether adults or children, to get into the place of the role, the inner space of it, quietly before going on stage. This process slows down the transition; it is a gathering of the forces of the individual to allow maximum presence in role and therefore maximum effectiveness within it. All this is the process of en-roling.

The second stage is the process of *occupying the role*. This is the time of being and not being simultaneously, as Landy (1986) pointed out. Once in role the role must be maintained. Here the therapist can help with possible suggestions of role reversal, reworking particular lines, etc. In terms of providing the containment necessary for the individual to do their own work the therapist must help that person to achieve the appropriate aesthetic distance. This can be obtained only by the clear management of role and enactment space. Creation of distance allows greater safety to allow the unconscious aspects of the personality to emerge and work in the role. The therapist's help in maintaining this distance is manifest in side-coaching, such as, 'Not your real name, remember', or 'Are you talking as yourself or as the character now? If you're not the character at the moment come outside the enactment space', or' 'You've slipped outside the enactment space; make sure you respect the boundary.' Here the therapist is safeguarding and maintaining the enactment space and encouraging the client to do so by modelling. It echoes good parental boundary reinforcement which enables the child to practise autonomy within safe limits. I see it as the management of the potential space in dramatherapy. Here the therapist's sub-role will be that of the side coach, which will include reminding the actor of the boundaries when these become confused.

Finally there is the taking off of the role, the process of *de-roling*, when individuals leave the role behind but take with them aspects of it. At this stage the bearer of the role may be clearly separating out aspects of the role with which he or she identifies. Projections may become clearer and more conscious; the role-bearer is in a position of spectator rather than participant, looking at how it was to be in the role. De-roling may take many forms. To my mind there is nothing worse than asking group members simply to jump about or shake out when there is no relationship between this activity and the role which has just been played. If, for example, the role has been a very static one, and the actor has been deprived of physical movement while playing it, it might be very helpful as a way of de-roling to suggest that some physical movement is done as a way of putting the participant back in touch with other aspects of the self not engaged with in the enactment. If, on the other hand, the role has required a lot of movement, allowing the body to become still and reflective might be a more effective method of de-roling. The aim is to help the participants to contact parts of the self not much used in the role-play, to enable a transition from role to their usual way of being present in themselves.

I remember a client who had extreme difficulty leaving his improvised role because he had chosen the name for his character which was the same as one of his brothers, of whom he had not previously spoken, and contrary to my general instructions to the group to avoid using names of people known to them. I led him gently round the group asking him to de-role other players by telling them who they were no longer playing and calling them by their real names. They had already de-roled themselves, but he needed to de-role them for himself in order to start to regain a sense of the reality of the group members and gain some distance from the drama. He was then able to feel more present in the here-and-now reality of the therapy setting and let it come back into focus. Then he was able to gain enough distance to see the role he had just played more objectively. He was also able to identify for the first time some unacknowledged boundary difficulties with this particular family member. The man could have left the session very confused and the other group members unduly anxious had the de-roling not been attended to. Enough time needs to be left for this.

The practising of taking on a role and taking off a role also has implications for beginnings and endings. To pay attention to them therefore helps to reinforce the most fundamental of boundary experiences which human life contains, that of living and dying. Paying attention to moments of letting go and moments of starting anew reinforces the vocabulary we all need, to learn to come to terms with death both in the experience of mourning and of coping with our own mortality. It is noticeable in groups that individuals who have difficulty with boundaries and also have difficulties in saying goodbye tend to rush into the enactment space and blur being in role and out of role.

69

One woman I recall who epitomized this, arrived in the group exibiting great confusion and difficulty in being authentic in her feelings and relating to others. She found the endings of sessions particulary difficult and silences almost unbearable. Gradually she began to be able to be more authentic in the group as the boundary management of the dramatherapy structures was consistently held for her. The kind of chaos she exhibited showed her own boundaries to be extremely confused. She both projected unmanageable feelings into others and received theirs to a high degree. In the dramatherapy context the sorting out of what is part of oneself and what is part of another is helped by clear management of role-taking.

The enactment space itself has to be de-roled for it can collect the accumulated energies of the group and remain in the unconscious as well as the conscious memory. I have known sub-groups working within the context of the whole group who have not heeded the instruction to de-role the space find considerable confusion arise as a result. One role merges into another and the space is charged with feelings spilling over.

I feel that this issue could be particularly useful to teachers, for however well the drama is structured, an awareness of the potency of projected unconscious material in enactment is helpful in managing the drama work effectively. Keeping a clear boundary between what is enactment and what is not is the difference between a chaotic drama class and one in which the drama can work at a deep level for the children. I remember many years ago I was experimenting with drama in education before much had been written about it and certainly before I knew anything of dramatherapy. I learned several practical lessons about the containment needed without understanding the concepts involved. I simply knew that I needed to find a way to avoid the wrath of the Maths department to whom my drama class would go after my lesson! Here the hurling of paper darts reached epic proportions after the exciting wars of drama were brought to an abrupt conclusion by the school bell. The children were left with their inner worlds engaged by the roles, uncontained and unsupported, acting out their chaos in an inappropriate setting. Neither the enactment space nor the three stages of role management had been attended to, with congruent results.

Setting up the conditions conducive to effective role work also means that the actor–audience dynamic must be catered for in the structure and management of the session. There must be enactment space and there must be audience space. I find it helpful for the audience space to be similarly defined. The sense of the ritual of the theatre is increased and so is the quality of absorption. A clear demarcation between actor space and audience space clarifies the role of audience. It allows the audience members to take on their role as audience, not merely as people blurred in with the action. It enhances the relationship between audience and actor. If there is to be performance I tend to invite the group which is performing to decide on where it wants its audience; this is often an important part of members' understanding of another layer in their relationship to both the text and the audience. There is a creative tension which occurs in a theatre space in a dramatherapy session when the room is clearly demarcated into action and audience areas. Jean Genet, writing to the director of his play, *The Screens*, said that he wanted the house lights and stage lights on at the same time.

> With the collective ass of the audience scrunched down in its seats, its immobility imposed by the acting – that was enough to make a distinction between stage and house, but the lights are necessary for the complicity to be established. A poetic act, not a spectacle, would have taken place.
>
> (Genet 1972: 51–52)

This does not mean blurring of identity but heightening of both separateness and identification which enables

> 'both actor and audience to be caught up in the same illumination, and for there to be no place for them to hide, or even half-hide.
>
> (ibid.: 52)

Thus the space is created in which things can happen. I like to think of dramatherapy as a poetic act in the way Genet speaks of the theatre, where no one individual is a detached audience to another, observing the spectacle, but is involved in their own role of audience both to bear witness and to touch and be touched by the action; the poetic act is that of creating new meaning through metaphor. This is especially evident in text work since a text is primarily a piece for the theatre and therefore needs to have the theatre dynamic reflected in the setting of the dramatherapy group.

The therapist's awareness of nurturing the delicate but powerful relationship between audience and actor role at all times in the session reinforces the containment while enabling the dramatherapy group to be a 'potential space' and the play a transitional object.

TEXT AS CONTAINER

I find that Shakespeare's 'wooden O' (which we met at the beginning of Chapter 2) describes the containing aspect of working with text very well. A play has its own structure and form; it is complete in itself. It is, therefore, to my mind a very containing way of working because it can hold an infinite number of projections, be an infinite number of mirrors, and yet be finite at the same time. Ultimately it ends. Prospero, in *The Tempest*, goes back to the mainland just as the group does at the end of every session and, more finally, when the group's life is over. Yet within the circle, the 'O', many things are possible. 'Things new, or old as the circling year', as the chorus in *Oedipus Rex* addresses Apollo. 'Healer of Delos', they call him. A play can provide healing precisely because it provides a place to which people can bring the unconscious text of their lives and, by meeting the form and structure of the play, find new ways to shape their experience. I hope the reader will find ways of seeing the text as container in the chapters which follow on individual plays.

PLANNING AND MANAGEMENT OF DRAMATIC STRUCTURES

So far I have stressed the necessity for providing and maintaining an environment where the group members' inner worlds and external life experience can meet the world of a play in a way which provides an opportunity for creative and reflective exploration. I work through dramatic structures which, if I get them right, operate at the point of aesthetic distance. By dramatherapy structures I mean moulding dramatic techniques into a form in relation to individual and group process. This form is designed to enable the individual and/or group to engage in unconscious processes through symbolic dramatic means. Here thought and affect are engaged, conscious and unconscious are free to range together within the possibilities provided by the limits which the structure gives. This may seem a paradox. However, over the years I have learned that these limitations act as containing mechanisms and holding structures which enable exploration at depth.

There is a difference between technique and structure. Techniques, drama games or exercises may all be used in dramatherapy but they remain empty shells if they are not moulded into a structure. For example, a sculpt in which group members form themselves into a shape with their bodies to express a particular idea, concept, feeling or relationship could be called a drama technique. However, when and at which point in the process it is introduced, the way in which it is worked with, entered into and exited from, harness a complex process which I think is better served by the term 'structure'. Structure implies building; the feeling of the word when used as either noun or verb has the richness of both these grammatical functions hovering in the air around it. The word implies something solid, yet something which is built up stage by stage, separate parts being in relation to one another and forming a whole. It is a word which for me echoes the experience of dramatherapy itself which depends so much on understanding and utilizing the many different kinds of bricks of which the dramatic art-form is made. An individual structure therefore may contain many elements echoing and complementing one another. I sometimes call this the *layered effect*.

To achieve this layering the dramatherapist needs to think in terms of levels of meaning and process in order to devise aesthetic structures which support, underline and echo one another. (I use the word aesthetic because these may not always be exclusively dramatic structures. They may involve an aspect of movement, art or music. The aesthetic values of these media support the dramatic engagement with metaphor.) The greater the congruence between these layers or levels in terms of their truthfulness to the text and to the aims and process of the work, the more they will support the group members' discovery of the ways in which the text is *their play*. By this I mean that every play will be the play of the particular group working on it. It will delve out the themes that are in the group, just as every theatre performance is different every night according to the audience present on that occasion; the nuances of the shared meaning created between audience and actor can change.

In order to discover what might be facilitative structures I have constantly to keep in mind both the aims and the processes of the work. There will be many examples suggested and referred to in this book. Here I want to spell out the thinking and planning process by following one example through, sketching in the early work and dwelling in detail on the final session.

Four-week group example

The example is that of *Waiting for Godot* worked on by a group consisting of two men with myself as dramatherapist, over four sessions. What options are open to me in providing a parallel experience such as I did with *The Tempest*? I could think of four main characters and four sessions but this would work only as a paralleling of the mathematics and not fulfil the purpose of finding parallels to provide containment for effective exploration. Being left with any of those four characters at the final session would leave the participant in an unbalanced relationship to both the play and his own inner world which has engaged with it. It also leaves out the character of the boy who brings messages from Godot. The question is how, in four sessions, to make the text of the play available dramatherapeutically which, for me, means by definition in a contained way?

In the case of the Shakespeare play the decision for the context design was arrived at in advance. In the work with *Waiting for Godot* it evolved during the work. Perhaps I could have decided on two acts – two sessions per act; I think this might well have provided the appropriate containment structure but might not have helped me to fulfil the different aims for the group. In this instance I wanted to find out what were the themes and issues the two men might bring to the work from their own unconscious so that they might move quickly into a deep relationship with the play and their own inner worlds. I therefore wanted them to have access to the whole play from the beginning. In this way a therapeutic effect might be achieved even in this short time. The brief was also a training brief so they needed to experience my methods; I needed to offer them a range of techniques to consider and I needed to engage them critically and consciously as well as unconsciously. There were therefore several 'external' considerations to hold in my mind and the task was to find both an overall structure in which enough risks could safely be taken, and enough containment found to hold deep work in a short-term context. The structure devised was therefore as follows.

Structure for Waiting for Godot

The first decision I made was to decide on allowing myself to develop the overall structure as I went along. This contrasts with the structure I designed for *The Tempest*, for example. In this instance I decided on the first session structure only, with the intention of facilitating an exploration which would lead me to discover the appropriate structures for the remaining sessions.

After the first two sessions the two men had allowed themselves to work together at a high level of trust, opening up important issues for themselves, to each other and me. In a longer-term group this work could have been pursued more slowly but in two sessions to go there was a need both to extend it and not to leave it hanging, but at the same time begin to close it off and take leave. Here is where the deepening function of a containing structure was vital to discover. I decided to work using the text as this container, while introducing different ways of working on it.

In Sessions 1 and 2 the two members of the group had explored connections between their own lives and aspects of their inner world. They had done this by means of a variety of improvisations, mimes and sculpts related to the play's content and form, the characters and the language. I also introduced the use of a defined personal space from which they took the role of actor in their own lives and spoke from there at different stages in the sessions. This was like a concrete potential space in which they could gather together the work in each session. In both these first two sessions the work had a kind of collage quality; words were taken from both acts of the play and John and Jack began to identify with particular characters. In Session 2 there had been a lot of exploring and sharing by talking and the atmosphere had been very thoughtful. In Session 3 I felt that it was important to design a structure for engaging with the whole text of Act I. John and Jack made life-size 'puppets' of each character from balloons and different kinds of papers, placed them in a large enactment area and 'doubled' from each of these as they read/moved the act. Both the process of making the puppets and the puppets themselves made a very powerful impact on them and took them to further depths in terms of their responses to Beckett's characters.

Session 4: an example of preparation

Preparing for the fourth and last session, the overall session structure with its component sub-structures arose from my internal monologue which went something like this.

They're very involved still and we need to close off tonight, yet there's still more work to be done. Act II will be the real container, in its entirety. We agreed to work on the whole act and I mustn't be tempted not to do that. But we need time for reflection and making conscious connections. There's the teaching aspect too, the contract which says I'll illustrate my methods, so although I could stay with last week's structure they won't learn another way of doing it if I simply do that. There's been a lot of questions raised. Is this text just about raising uncomfortable issues – I feel uncomfortable with that if it's true – no, what's going on for me is that I'm holding their discomfort for the moment until after the work is over. I'm being asked to carry that and still have faith. Of course! That's why I've been asked to carry the materials around this week and bring them back for the final session; I haven't felt too easy about doing that and yet I couldn't leave them in the building as they might get damaged or thrown out. It wasn't right to dismantle them last time. It would have been too abrupt. That lack of continuity isn't in the play, rather the opposite – last week and this week are definitely intimately connected and I knew that when I said I'd look after the materials. I must keep the faith just as Vladimir and Estragon do, the way they wait and return day after day. This is where I'm experiencing the play, offstage. Jack and John need me to do that otherwise how can it work for them? I need to know their suffering through the play too, I can't be in tune otherwise, won't find the right structures in the sessions. I suppose I'm like Vladimir and Estragon as well, tramps carrying around the debris of creativity – all those pieces of paper and burst balloons which made wonderful puppets last week, like the tramps' memories. 'Keeping faith', that's what was happening when Jack said to John, in the de-roling at the end of Session 2, 'I hope you'll be here next week.' And John replied, 'I'll be here next week.' I was so moved by that, both for them and for us and the work we're doing, and for the fact that the play was working on them – it's what Estragon and Vladimir do, keep faith with each other and with Godot. Yes, I need to be sensitive to how deeply these two men have worked together in such a short space of time and facilitate their leavetaking of the work together.

I've just noticed what I wrote after Session 2: 'the moments of silence *were* the waiting and in that waiting perhaps the leaves are growing – maybe in the last session do something about building a tree and having leaves on it which represent things for them'. I'd forgotten I'd thought that but it feels even more right now. There is hope in the play and there is hope in dramatherapy; I need to keep that connection to find the right form for tonight's session, since the work's not only about the play but about dramatherapy. Inside them there will be a gathering of the work so far; the sculpts, the images, the puppet characters of last week and the whole text of Act I. There'll be the statements they made in Session 1 about what the play meant to them and there'll be the powerful theme of Session 2 – they welcomed the chance to work on this but also found it disturbing. There'll probably be anxiety about whether they'll be left feeling rather uncontained with it all. And we're in another room to-night. I need to be aware about my own fury about being messed about re the room – but in a way it's like the tramps in the play being moved on, and Pozzo and Lucky on their interminable journey. I need to be aware of these echoes, yet still find a session in which this particular journey stops. The work continues inside them but the play and what it has evoked in these four sessions needs to be let go of.

I keep thinking about the tree; the fact that there are four or five leaves on it in Act II and none in Act I. If there's been any growth in the sessions the leaves would be an appropriate symbol for this. There needs to be a balance bringing things into consciousness and enabling the unconscious to work through the metaphors in the play and in the dramatherapy structures. There needs to be a fine balance in the dis-tancing used – too much will mean that things already engaged with won't get tapped tonight and they'll go away with material which be-longs in the work repressed; too little distance will mean they'll prob-ably go deeper instead of being able to close off. They need to work together but they need to start to separate out too, and from me as well. And I need to hand back what I'm carrying for them, I need to close off too.

What I am doing by this process is sifting through the various layers which re-sults in formulating a session structure which fulfils the different, but related, aims for that session. In order to find the most appropriate structures for these aims to be achieved I need to think of those which will be most contain-ing. That way many of the aims are catered for anyway. The structure eventu-ally arrived at is set out below. The rationale relates to the aims and I set it out here to illustrate the final journey of the thought process.

In reality many of the ideas for the practical structures are arrived at intui-tively – what is clearly thought through is the rationale. The structures are tested out against them in my mind as part of the planning. This is of para-mount importance in sifting through the many ideas which come to me as I design the session. I must select from my ideas those which fulfil as many of the aims as possible. The different strands inherent in any one activity must reinforce and strengthen the webbing of the whole. In the course of planning, many of the individual ideas are jettisoned if they do not match the aims. The more rigorous the design of the house the more effective a building it is and the more freely one can move around in it.

During the actual session things may well change, indeed they should change if I am in touch with what's happening in the group. So how do I choose what and how to alter of such a well-planned structure? My rule for myself is simple; any deviation must be chosen in relation to the pre-session thinking coupled with an awareness of the here-and-now events and process of the session. There will be some examples of this in later chapters.

Having clarified for myself the aims, the next stage is to have a dialogue between my creative imagination and the part of me which is skilled and practised in questioning and analysing thoughts, feelings and processes. I should stress that these parts are continually working throughout the session itself and will often change or modify the design for the session. They will serve me all the better in this if I am clear about what I am aiming at beforehand. That way whatever is brought into the session by the group is greeted by a facilitator who has attempted to be in a state of balance between 'knowing' and 'not knowing'. New ideas, shifts of emphasis, re-creating or altering of the order of the structures in the session may be slotted into place more accurately if the basic aims and rationale for the existing session design have been fully internalized.

Designing 'on the hoof' is a rigorous business, just as any therapeutic work is. It is a skill which every dramatherapist develops whether working with text or not for in dramatherapy, as well as attending to the projections which abound in the group and processing transference and counter-transference dynamics, the therapist has to translate these into practical activity. Working with a text I try to design structures which will enable the individual and group to move through their own processes in which these dynamics can be worked with through a projective and introjective relationship with the text.

Here, however, I am deliberately taking an example of some of my most highly structured work which did not alter much in practice in order to illustrate the structuring process. This session is an ending session of a very short-term piece of work. I am often very prescriptive in an ending session working with text, whereas in a dramatherapy session not working with text my style will tend to be far more fluid, the more so the longer the group has been running, finding a form in the here-and-now to acknowledge the struggles between awareness of ending and the wish to avoid the painful feelings which this may produce. This particuar session of *Waiting for Godot* is designed very tightly; the shorter the term of the work the more tightly I tend to structure the ending session. I find this helps to promote maximum depth of work at the same time as ensuring that the participants are not left in an uncontained way with unfinished business and nowhere to go with it.

Final session: Waiting for Godot

From my internal monologue, described above, the aims emerged as follows.

A To move into the final phase of the work, whatever this might be for each person.
B To engage with Act II of the play, making sure the whole act, not extracts, is encountered.

C To work within the context of the five characters, helping the participants to find the aspects of those characters which they need in order to complete their journey in this work.

D To continue to mine the play, by means of close attention to Act II.

E To introduce new methods and techniques in accordance with the training aspect of the contract.

F To strengthen ego-functioning prior to leaving the work, each other and me.

G To avoid regressive work which cannot be completed in the session.

H To hand back what has unconsciously been given to me to hold, in a manageable form.

I To close down the four sessions' work.

J To ensure feedback and processing time and facilitate evaluative comment.

Now the session can be planned. (Italicized sections illustrate the way the planned activity stays in touch with the aims.)

Practical organization before the session

1 Put out on a side table all the materials used so far in the sessions.
To create an awareness of the previous work and underline by implication that this is the last session. Smooth access to using the materials when the time comes. Give them a sense of being 'held' by the room being set up since we are in a different room tonight.

2 Place the materials for tonight's session on another table.
We still have tonight; it's a separate piece of work; the principle of boundaries enabling more containment and therefore more depth, hence keeping them apart from the artefacts of previous sessions. Also modelling for teaching purposes.

The session

1 Check out feelings, mood, etc. of Jack and John then select appropriate warm-up activity.
To be selected with particular sensitivity to this being the last session.

2 J and J to decide on the area for the enactment space for the session and mark it out in whatever way they choose.
Consistency with previous session and style of work – containment, especially because we are in a different room.

3 Build a tree from the objects in the environment and the materials provided.

Ego-strengthening function of the tree as symbol.

Engaging in a final task together, while still fostering the bond to enable tonight's work to begin to move towards separation – projective play rather than personal play therefore.

To provide an actual structure to hold the leaves (see 5 below), linking the characters and words to the symbolic function of the tree and strengthening the process of internalizing the words projected onto the characters.

4 Each person to make five leaves, one for each character. Write the name of the character on one side and on the other a word you want to give that character tonight.

To allow feelings which have been brought to the session to find a symbolic container. They can then be modified or strengthened and further understood through the reading of the text later in the session. Trusting the inner logic of the psyche which is engaged in this work to usefully use these stepping stones.

5 Ceremony of hanging the leaves on the tree.

Using a ritual of stepping into the enactment area to hang each leaf will reinforce the boundary of inside and outside the enactment, especially important as the enactment space will not exist after tonight.

To give a sense of dignity and importance to the hanging of the leaves echoes the value Beckett gives to seemingly unimportant events and objects in the play.

Giving weight and time to the hanging of the leaves underlines the relationship between the ego-strengthening tree and the messages the group members are giving themselves through the projective symbols.

6 Each person to choose five objects, one to represent each character, from the large selection of small objects, then set out a large sheet of paper under the tree in the enactment space and take up positions opposite one another. Task is for participants to read text of Act II choosing to speak whichever line they wish (and in chorus if they both want to speak certain lines). As they speak they move the 'characters' on the paper 'stage'.

The projective technique of using the objects enables the unconscious internal processes already engaged in previous sessions to move forward by means of the shapes and forms made on the stage. The reading of the play should be the container for this process if the boundaries are adhered to.

7 Come out of the enactment space when finished reading the text, time to talk about the experience and make any connections they are ready and wish to make.

The work has been intensely focused so far; now create a space for sharing and reflection, making connections and beginning to move into the winding down section of the session.

79

8 De-role the objects used in this session.

Closing off the session. Leaving the tree in the enactment space to gather to it the artefacts of the previous session (see 9 below) links the whole four weeks, allows the opportunity to put the 'jigsaw' pieces together both consciously and unconsciously. They are all visual and tactile symbols which are endowed with meaning.

9 Put all the materials which have been used in previous sessions with the tree in the enactment space. View them all from outside, commenting, making statements, connections, thinking about leaving the work.

Bringing back into consciousness the whole four sessions, working towards closing down, gathering up, taking away. It also gives me a chance to see where they are, to input if I feel it is necessary.

10 De-role the materials, deciding what they want to take away, if anything, and what to put in the bin. Leave the tree till last.

Engaging with the materials used throughout the work – the various statements held on the paper, the various paper and balloon images of Act I's characters – helps to leave, to distance and to integrate. Also talking together whilst doing it is helpful in consolidating the work done together, celebrating the relationship which made the work possible. The tree has been an important symbol, much is gathered into it, and leaving it till last is particularly containing and reinforcing.

11 Viewing the empty enactment space, speaking to it, saying what it has held for them. Then entering it for the last time and making a statement to the playwright, looking outwards. Then de-roling it by taking away the boundary markers.

Enlarging the ripples of saying goodbye to the work. Related to teaching aims it reinforces the importance of the concept of a clearly defined enactment space. Roots the dramatherapy firmly in the play by 'speaking to the playwright' as the last symbolic act of the work. Faces the external world as they prepare to leave. Acts as bridge between this and the group experience.

12 In circle where we started, sharing thoughts, feelings. Moving slowly into reflection on the whole project, then to feedback and evaluation.

Time to let go of the work and relationships, voicing feelings to me about the work; the opportunity to create some distance prior to leaving. Saying goodbye, to me and I to them as well as to each other.

Very little was changed in this particular session. I suggested a warm up which was designed to enable the two participants to be separate and yet together through movement first, to feed into the theme and aims of the session right from the beginning. Then I added a short sculpting exercise to connect with the previous sessions, the text and each other.

I had had some reservations about reading the act and using objects simultaneously; I was concerned that the activities, instead of complementing each other and deepening the experience for the participants, which was my intention, might instead cause a split in concentration. In the end I decided to stay with it because of the training brief where as many different ways of working as possible could be introduced. I knew there would be time for Jack and John to discuss this if it hadn't worked for them. In the event it did and they commented positively on it. This is an example of how staying with the primary task of the work and the contract helps to keep one on course and survive one's own inevitable doubts. This is crucial when one is designing or re-designing the structure as one goes along in the session. The process which I have spelt out here has to be engaged with while the session is in progress. Decisions have to be made and implemented quickly, and feeling, intuition and reason harnessed harmoniously. Without the therapist having internalized the primary task, it is hard to utilize the possibilities of layering, where activities echo and support one another at conscious and unconscious levels, providing a richly textured experience for those working therapeutically on the play.

CONCLUSION

Imitation is natural to man from childhood, . . . he is the most imitative creature in the world, and learns at first by imitation. And it is also natural for all to delight in works of imitation. The truth of this second point is shown by experience *though the objects themselves may be painful to see we delight to view the most realistic representations of them in art* . . . the reason of the delight . . . is that one is at the same time learning – *gathering the meaning of things*.
(Aristotle, *The Poetics*, in Bywater 1920: 24, my italics)

In succeeding chapters we shall continue to explore particular works of drama to discover how, by engaging with the pain through dramatherapy – a means which we could say involves delight in its deepest sense – we may engage with what must surely be at the heart of therapy, the gathering of the meaning of things.

4

BEGINNING

Roots by Arnold Wesker

I'm tellin' you the world's bin growing for two thousand years and we hevn't noticed it. I'm telling you that we don't know what we are or where we come from. I'm telling you something's cut us off from the beginning. I'm telling you we've got no roots.

(Beatie, *Roots* Act III)

'I'm beginning, on my own two feet I'm beginning' are the final words of the protagonist, Beatie Bryant, in Wesker's play, *Roots*. How often in our lives do we think we are beginning afresh when we are not; when we are simply moving on from school or moving house, leaving a job or changing partners. 'Simply' may seem a grossly inaccurate description, for it might feel complicated at the time and might be an important rite of passage, but if in fact we are taking our old patterns with us, beginning again is not really what is happening. Real change is hard, demanding work for it means engaging with what has been in a new way. Then we can free ourselves of aspects of the past which bind rather than liberate us.

I have chosen to explore *Roots* because it puts into sharp focus these themes of change, transition and beginning in the context of family relationships, the context where we all 'begin' and within which our issues of separation must be seen. It shows the protagonist, Beatie, in that place of hard, demanding work within a context where the background is that of denial of the need to change and an ostrich-like response to social and environmental changes. I have also chosen it partly because it is a play in which the unconscious dynamics of mothers and daughters can be explored by our attention to metaphor. This is an important theme in our society where many more women are in therapy than men and women dramatherapists in Britain greatly outnumber men.

THE PLAY

The play is direct and accessible and, although set in a particular place and time, I have found it to be a text which members of a group relate to easily and is as relevant in essence now as it was when I first worked with it at the beginning of the 1960s. In fact it has, at the time of writing, enjoyed recent revivals on both the National Theatre stage and television. But first, for those unfamiliar with the play, a résumé of its events and themes.

Résumé of the play

The play is in three acts and set in the Britain of the 1950s. The protagonist, Beatie Bryant, is a young woman of 22 now living in London. The action of the play takes place in rural Norfolk where Beatie grew up. She revisits her family, first of all her married sister Jenny and her husband Jimmy, who is a garage mechanic. Through their conversation Beatie's London world of talk, ideas and politics is sharply contrasted with rural life. Beatie uncomfortably straddles both worlds. She loves Ronnie, a left-wing Jewish intellectual, but admits to Jenny that she often does not understand what he is talking about. Beatie then stays at her parents' cottage. Ronnie is expected to join her in about a week's time to meet the family and Beatie is anxious that family squabbles are patched up and that the family do not let her down. The depressed aspect of both family and rural life are revealed in Act II in family tensions and in the fact that Beatie's father has been given the sack, as new styles of farming management impinge on the old estates. The day Ronnie is expected finally comes and the family arrive in their best clothes to partake of Mrs Bryant's wonderful spread. As they prepare for Ronnie's arrival a letter comes from him to say that he realizes the relationship with Beatie is a mistake, their lives are too different. As Beatie faces the shock and pain of this and finds herself alone amongst her family she realizes she has stopped quoting Ronnie and finds her own voice at last.

In Chapter 1 I referred to Wilshire's (1982) notion of 'standing in'. In discussing *Roots* I am going to take this idea to help us explore the relevance of this play to our own lives and to the way we might work with this play in practice. Each character in the play stands in for those aspects of another to which the latter has no access, only potential. For us, outside the play, the central character, Beatie, stands in for all those who strive to find themselves, and for all daughters who struggle to separate from their mothers and for all who try to find, in T. S. Eliot's words, 'the still point of the turning world', a constant reference point to which to return and from which to draw nourishment.

So who is Beatie in this play and which other characters or aspects of characters does she 'stand in' for? Such an exploration could undoubtedly be more extensive than this chapter will allow, but in sharing just something of my dramatherapist's way of reading the themes of women's familial relationships, the family and society, I invite the reader to make other journeys through the play, making connections with different aspects of personal and professional experience.

Mothers, daughters, sisters

It is in the first scene that we find the relationship between Beatie and her sister, Jenny, delineated. Before exploring this let us look first at the context which Wesker gives us in that opening scene. He presents us with the contrast between Beatie and the life she has left behind now that she lives in London with the Jewish left-wing intellectual, Ronnie. Jenny and her husband Jimmy, a mechanic, live in a remote cottage surrounded by sandpits, without mains water, gas or electricity. The scene gives us important information about the society in which the family live, the family itself, and introduces some of the themes of the play.

We find ourselves in a social context of Rock 'n' Roll, strikes, and the advent of television, a Britain where the nearness of the war still gives a *modus vivendi* for men like Jimmy, for whom the Territorial Army stands in opposition to the threat of nuclear arms.

Jimmy, on entering, complains of physical pain which Mrs Bryant has apparently diagnosed as indigestion. He also tells us that the local doctor is dying of cancer. Already the themes of sickness and health, metaphors in this play for social and psychological issues, are being introduced. Beatie embodies the aspects of change and no change; she has learned different ways while she has been away and she tries to influence her sister and brother-in-law. This she does by jumping up and making speeches which are a reproduction of Ronnie's ideas. She uses his words. At the same time she shows them that she is still part of her background by explaining that she would put a comic behind the *Manchester Guardian* while pretending to read Ronnie's approved paper. Jimmy becomes angry as Ronnie's words about culture and class and the need to communicate pour from Beatie's lips and her attempts to talk about more personal matters like 'love in the afternoon' as recommended by Ronnie draw sarcasm from Jimmy and a reversal to the topics of food, local accidents, weather and the allotment. Eventually Beatie's inability to stay with these safe subjects draws an angry response from her brother-in-law:

> don't you come pushing ideas across at us – we're all right as we are. You can come when you like an' welcome but don't bring no discussion of politics in the house wi' you 'cos that'll only cause trouble.
>
> (*Roots*: 94)

When Jimmy has gone leaving Beatie and Jenny together, we see both the closeness and the distance which typifies their relationship. We learn that Jenny has a child but the identity of the father is a secret she is not prepared to share with anyone, including Beatie. Jimmy has married her. Beatie asks:

> Are you in love with Jimmy?
> JENNY: Love? I don't believe in any of that squit – we just got married and that's that.
>
> (ibid.: 97)

Beatie herself has chased Ronnie:

> I chased him for three months with compliments and presents until I
> finally give myself to him. He never said he love me nor I didn't care
> but once he had taken me he seemed to think he was responsible for me
> and I told him no different.

(ibid.: 95)

Beatie's and Jenny's experience with men may in fact be not so different, in
spite of differences in outcomes of their lives, in relation to the opposite sex.
Jenny became pregnant – how do we know that she did not pursue the
father of her child just as Beatie pursued Ronnie? Clearly the difference is in
the actions of the two men, where Ronnie appears to have some sense of responsibility towards the 19-year-old country girl he slept with. And with his
greater sophistication and his sense of responsibility – and, it still being the
1950s, we might suppose that it is Ronnie who took care of the contracep-
tion arrangements. So in some ways Jenny and Beatie could be interchange-
able – the point is that they are not; that Beatie is in a sense 'standing in' for
Jenny, for her potential, for the Jenny who might have moved away, but who
did not; who might have found a different kind of man from the one who
fathered her child.

We learn more about why the two girls have gone along these different
paths through the reminiscences they share in Act I.

> JENNY: And I know someone else who always wanted more'n she could
> get.
> BEATIE: (*sulkily*) It's not the same thing.
> JENNY: Oh yes it is.
> BEATIE: 'Tent.
> JENNY: You liked anything you could lay your hands on and Mother
> used to give in to you because you were the youngest. Me and Susan
> and Frankie never got anything 'cos of you – 'cept a clout round the
> ear.

(ibid.: 99)

Beatie's view of the situation is, not surprisingly, different. But from Jenny's
angle Beatie is the one who is different, who has been given opportunities; the
dialogue continually draws parallels between the two contrasting life styles
where Beatie now seems out of touch with Jenny's reality; a reality which is
presented as the lack of possibilities.

> BEATIE: Are you going to live in this house all your life?
> JENNY: You gonna buy us another?
> BEATIE: Stuck out here in the wilds with only ole Stan Mann and his
> missus as a neighbour and sand pits all around. Every time it rain look
> you're stranded.

85

JENNY: Jimmy don't earn enough for much more'n we got.

(ibid.: 99)

And again:

BEATIE: I'll buy you some coat hangers.
JENNY: You get me a couple of coats to hang on 'em first please.

(ibid.: 100)

Symbolically Wesker makes us aware of the isolation and lack of spiritual growth which comes with the economic trap in which Jenny lives. 'Every time it rain look you're stranded.' While the crops may thrive and receive nourishment for real growth, Jenny can eat only to comfort herself and deny her own potential for individuation.

JENNY: Well, there's nothin' wrong in being fat. (*Placing bread on a large oval plate to put away*)
BEATIE: You ent got no choice gal.

(ibid.: 98)

Jenny continues to play the role assigned to women by virtue of her gender (Chodorow 1989) and to compensate for lack of opportunity to have a different life from her mother, by eating. She too is a provider and carer. Beatie's reference to choice is a hard truth.

But lest we fall into the trap of thinking that Beatie's position at this stage of the play is any different, we need to listen to what she says about babies and about her own relationship with her body.

BEATIE: Once we're married and I got babies I won't need to be interested in half the things I got to be interested in now.
JENNY: No you won't will you! Don't need no education for babies.
BEATIE: Nope. Babies is babies – you just have 'em.

(ibid.: 96)

And then:

JENNY: You hungry again?
BEATIE: I'm always hungry again. Ronnie say I eat more'n I need. 'If you get fat woman I'll leave you – without even a discussion.'

(ibid.: 97)

If we look at this relationship in terms of who stands in for whom, it is as though Beatie returns home to look at her other self again in the form of Jenny. Whilst Beatie stands in for Jenny in terms of potential, Jenny also stands in for Beatie as a reminder of her heritage as a gendered woman in a gendered society whose role is to have babies and not to think. However enlightened Ronnie may be, he is still a male who holds views which do nothing for the possibility of real change in Beatie. It is as though in this opening scene we are shown the whole woman, together; by looking at how each character stands in for the other we are given, as it were, two parts of the same woman who appears woven into life before our eyes as they weave the experience of all women's heritage into life before us on the stage. This then paves the way for our introduction to the mother of both girls in Act II.

This next act takes us into the parental home where Mrs Bryant is talking to Stan Mann, Jenny's elderly neighbour. The Bryant home is a tied cottage on the main road between two villages and Mrs Bryant's days seem regulated by the hourly bus which passes outside the house.

Mrs Bryant, 50, bemoans her lost youth and Stan his lost sexuality as they note the passing of the seasons. With Beatie's arrival Mrs Bryant's life is revealed as monotonous for she says to Beatie, 'You do bring a little life with you anyway' (ibid.: 116).

When Beatie expresses surprise at her mother revealing how she feels, Mrs Bryant retorts, 'The world don't want no feelings, gal' (ibid.: 116). Perhaps Mrs Bryant would rather not have her own feelings for, as we see in the speech from Act III quoted below, we learn of the painful feelings to which she never gives vent.

As mother, Mrs Bryant has both an actual and a symbolic function in the play in relation to both Beatie and the wider themes which Beatie represents. Beatie is what her mother could never be, does what her mother could never do. In treating her youngest daughter most favourably Mrs Bryant is giving herself what she has never had; in a sense therefore Beatie stands in for her mother. But to stand in for anyone else's potential is a position which brings with it envy and anger. These emotions as experienced by mothers in relation to daughters have been well presented elsewhere (Ernst and Maguire 1987). Here let's simply listen to Mrs Bryant in Act III.

> When you tell me I was stubborn what you mean is he [Ronnie] told you you was stubborn – eh? When you tell me I don't understand you mean you don't understand isn't it. When you tell me I don't make no effort you mean you don't make no effort. Well, what you blaming me for, blaming me all the time! I haven't bin responsible for you since you left home – you bin on your own. She think I like it she do! Thinks I like being cooped up in this house all day. Well I'm telling you my gal – I don't! There! And if I had the chance to be away working somewhere the lot on yous could go to hell – the lot on yous.
>
> (*Roots*: 145)

We could say that Beatie is the lived-out potential of her mother, having left home and worked in London. So 'standing in' has brought its own rewards in terms of a new kind of freedom. Seemingly, for her separation is only superficial as we shall see. Beatie has berated her mother on this visit home. She accuses her of not thinking, of not being alive. In fact the standing in works two ways, for Mrs Bryant stands in for Beatie's shadow side. As the shadow is that part of ourselves which is hidden from us in the unconscious Beatie is unaware of these aspects of herself. She therefore projects them onto her mother. It is Mrs Bryant herself who can perform the therapeutic function of bringing that truth into consciousness as she, in effect, makes Beatie aware of what she is doing. In this speech she forcefully pinpoints the projective function she performs for her daughter. 'When you told me I don't . . . you mean you don't . . .', etc. The speech quoted goes some way to redressing the balance so that Mrs Bryant is freed from some of Beatie's projections and Beatie must literally stand on her own two feet, shadow and all; her mother can no longer do it for her. When Beatie says despairingly, 'I can't mother, you're right – the apple don't fall far from the tree, do it?' (ibid.: 145), she arrives at an understanding of who she is in relation to her mother. At this point the projections have to be withdrawn. By acknowledging the inarticulateness she has projected onto her mother she is in fact able to find her own way to communicate. It is then, I think, that she does actually 'begin' to begin. She continues

> You're right, I'm like you, stubborn, empty, wi' no tools for livin'. I got no roots in nothing. I come from a family of farm labourers yet I ent got no roots – just like the town people – just a mass o' nothin'.
>
> (ibid.)

She begins to find her voice, for it is only at this point that she can be apart from her mother. The separation is painful, for Mrs Bryant must harshly reject Beatie before this can happen and yet, paradoxically, she does this through recognition of their symbiotic closeness: 'The apple don't fall far from the tree do it?' (Mrs Bryant, ibid.).

Beatie, the fruit of her womb, is like her mother, incapable of falling from her and from what she, Mrs Bryant, represents or stands in for – the whole rural society in which she has grown up, in which she has her roots. It is Mrs Bryant who finds the language which Beatie needs in order to move away into beginning the journey of discovering who she really is. While she was a symbiotic representation of her mother, including her mother's hidden wishes to move away, she was capable only of mimicking growing away just as she mimics Ronnie. She quotes Ronnie's words throughout the whole of Acts I and II, she cannot find her own words or her own language. Yet significantly it is through her mother's metaphor that she can begin to do so. She recognizes her mother's being in touch with herself in the provision of a metaphor so apt because it is literally rooted in the rural culture of which she is totally a part.

If we look more closely at the metaphor we can see how this happens. 'The apple' – the association with breasts, with femaleness, and with Eve, symbolically our first mother – combines sexuality and motherhood and women's carrying of guilt and the fall from grace, the role given to their gender in a patriarchal society. All these are conjoined in this image given from mother to daughter. In Chapter 2 we saw how the struggle for separation and autonomy was manifest in the infant's struggles with her earliest object relations. Here we see how the metaphor of the apple and the tree in relation to mother and daughter is so potent for it highlights that very struggle. And it is precisely because it is a metaphor that it can be of such use in the play. By being able to use a metaphor Mrs Bryant at that moment engages in a creative act. In engaging in a creative act she is finding her own voice. And it is precisely because it is also the voice of her backgound – her 'roots' – that it lends weight and authority. The fact that the words may be borrowed does not diminish that authority, but rather enhances it, for these words are the words of generations of country dwellers who have found their particular relationship between the action and the word, between meaning and expression. It is the very erosion of that culture that Beatie feels so passionately about in her final speech (ibid.: 148), which we shall return to later. By the use of this proverb-like metaphor Mrs Bryant here stands in for those generations of ancestors and it is this that gives her her authority. And it is precisely because she can speak with authority that her words can have such an effect on Beatie (see also Wilshire 1982: ch. 5).

Mrs Bryant is at this point part of a whole line of mothers and daughters and at the same time totally herself. This gives her an additional authority within the mother–daughter dyad and it is this authority which can release Beatie. She speaks of her own self as a subject – 'If I were away working the whole lot on yous could go to hell.' This is not Mrs Bryant the feeder, the perpetual giver and caretaker. She is not at this point only the object of another's needs but is in touch with a different self which Beatie has 'stood in' for, the self which has the possibility of a different life. When her mother is able to release herself, even for a moment, into that part of herself (albeit in relation to loss rather than potential) Beatie can then begin to find her own individual self. When her mother begins to talk and use her authentic voice then Beatie is freed to find hers. When her mother is, even if only for a moment, a subject as opposed to an object, then her daughter can begin to find herself as a subject too (Chodorow 1978; 1989).

Painful though this is, Beatie has to recognize that in order to be truly separate we must first understand how truly close we are. To be in touch with the object and know that it is separate from ourselves is to begin to separate. We must mourn the leaving of that symbiotic state, to begin the journey towards individuation.

It is at the moment of greatest pain that Beatie cries out:

Look at you, all of you. You can't say anything. You can't even help your own flesh and blood. It's your problem as well isn't it. I'm part of your family aren't I? Well help me then! Give me some words of comfort! Talk to me – for God's sake somebody talk to me. (*She cries at last*)
(*Roots*: 144)

It is indeed their own problem. What she is going through is the struggle of working towards separation, of being able to find her own voice and her own language.

Here we have seen Beatie stand in for some important aspects of women's experience. The dramatic presentation of these relationships between Beatie, Jenny and Mrs Bryant authorizes the experience of all women who find themselves imprisoned by their gender and by their background. Beatie therefore 'stands in' for them. In the next section I shall explore one of the ways in which Beatie stands in for her own family and how this relates to the theme of beginnings and change.

Families

We have seen Beatie in the play as someone who is able to begin to change and who does this through facing the reality of herself. She faces her pretence, she allows herself to feel pain, to be alone, to experience her separateness from the family. In doing these things she finds her voice. In contrast we see her family who do none of these things. Beatie stands in for that part of them which is denied. She therefore stands opposed to their inability to face the reality of painful feelings and events. She stands in for that part of them which could reject avoidance and denial as a means of survival and which could lead to a greater sense of reality and the finding of their own potential. The most powerful way in which Wesker presents this is through the metaphor of food.

All four scenes begin with references and actions to do with food. The message given is the need for the child within these adults to be given something which comforts, a panacea against the pain and difficulties of living. The play is also full of characters complaining of indigestion which indicates that the customary way of dealing with life is not working. Beatie is presented as being the same as them in her relationship with food at the beginning of the play but significantly different at the end. She stands in for the alternative which they turn their backs on. Let us look at this in more detail.

The first scene opens with Jenny's little girl calling out for a sweet from the bedroom. She is given one instantly, the comforter, the panacea, and she is told to go to sleep by her mother, 'I don't wan' you grumpy wi' me in the mornin'.' Being grumpy is not allowed. Why the child might be grumpy no one wants to know – give her a sweet. In other words deny the feelings.

When Jimmy comes in the first thing we learn is that he is in considerable physical pain. Even though this has been thought by Mrs Bryant to be indigestion, the cure seems to be to pile on more food.

JIMMY: There's a pain in my guts and one a'tween my shoulder blades. I can hardly stand up.

JENNY: Sit you down then an' I'll git you your supper on the table.

(ibid.: 86)

Later in the conversation when Beatie attempts to talk with her sister and brother-in-law about 'love in the afternoon' Jenny replies with 'Shut you up gal and get on wi' your ice-cream' (ibid.: 91) and offers Jimmy some more which he accepts. Food is there to ward off any awkward topics; it protects and consoles. Wesker gives his reader some information in the stage directions following this scene:

> *Throughout the play there is no sign of intense living from any of the characters – Beatie's outbursts are the exception.*

(ibid.: 92)

Perhaps food takes the place of intense living and is a panacea for a life in which both social conditions and mores make intense living difficult, impossible or indeed undesirable.

The next scene opens with Mrs Bryant calling the cat in order to feed it. She is annoyed by its non-appearance. This is the first we see of Mrs Bryant. Her role as the feeder is our first glimpse of her, a role we see her in again and again. Beatie as the daughter echoes this role for, as her mother prepares the dinner, she begins to bake a cake for Jenny. (Later Mrs Bryant's support of Beatie using her parents' electricity to do this is the cause of a row between Mr and Mrs Bryant – conducted by a refusal to speak to each other.) It is as if the three women are united in the context of giving and receiving food. As we saw, it is Mrs Bryant who is able to give Beatie the image of the apple. In contrast to this Mr Bryant does not want Beatie baking in his house – perhaps he does not want the real food which Beatie can provide him with, the food of feelings and words.

As they prepare food together, Beatie fills her mother's ears with Ronnie's quotes. Mrs Bryant's way of dealing with her discomfort is to say, 'Well I'm sure I don't know what he's on about. Turn to your baking gal look and get you done, Father'll be home for his lunch in an hour' (ibid.: 116).

Food can always provide a way of dealing with difficult feelings or avoiding a challenge. Almost immediately we see this even more clearly:

MRS BRYANT: Thank God you come home sometimes gal – you do bring
  a little life with you anyway.
BEATIE: Mother, I ent never heard you express a feeling like that.
MRS BRYANT: (*She is embarrassed*) The world don't want no feelings gal.
  (*Footsteps*) Is that your father home already.

(ibid.)

Mr Bryant comes in and immediately the conversation is about his guts' ache. The fact that he is ill leads ultimately to his being laid off work. It is as if the

91

perpetual denial of feelings, the inability to communicate which is always dealt with by the panacea of food, is shown to be not enough. The guts react. Feelings cannot be stuffed down inside without a reaction.

There are many other examples of the use of food in the play. Suffice to say here that the family members are locked into a system of displacement of feelings onto food which is in fact a kind of poison slowly making them ill, even depriving the 'head' of the family of his ability to work. When this method of displacement is patently not working they have no other remedy except the poison itself. In this sense food is like a destructive drug upon which they depend.

We find that Beatie's response is different from the others'. She has some sense of what is happening: 'You all eat too much. The Londoners think we live a healthy life but they don't know we stuff ourselves silly till our guts ache.'

Here is an example of Beatie's potential for being really different from her family. She has some notion of the unwellbeing of her family. 'Stuff ourselves silly' has a ring to it of 'insensible', even 'mad'. At some level she knows the big lie of the rural idyll – and she is not quoting Ronnie when she says this. Her position is most clearly defined at the end of the play which culminates with these stage directions:

> The murmur of the family sitting down to eat grows as Beatie's last cry is heard. Whatever she will do they will continue to live as before. As Beatie stands alone, articulate at last.

> (ibid.: 148)

In the play Wesker presents us with a family who turns to food whenever there are difficulties. Food is a way of dealing with seemingly insoluble problems. Beatie does not need this for she has taken hold of real feeling, real pain, stared it in the face, experienced the lonely journey which marks the beginning of real change.

In this way Beatie holds the healthy part of them, the possibility that one need not stuff oneself silly but convert food into energy, into words, into creativity. In doing so one takes responsibility for oneself and one's actions in the world. Instead of lying down under social exploitation Beatie shows in her powerful final speech that protest is possible. But the play's message is that it shows that there is a price to pay. The price is that of embracing the real, which includes pain, as opposed to displacing reality onto panaceas. Real food is the creative energy of Beatie's final outburst. The fact that she met Ronnie, the catalyst, in the catering department of a hotel, underscores the symbolic significance of food in charting Beatie's progress which triumphantly concludes with her final lines: 'I'm beginning, on my own two feet I'm beginning' (ibid.: 148).

Wesker leaves us in no doubt that true nourishment is feeling and being in touch with one's own reality. This results in the ability to express oneself in words, to conceptualize and communicate. But this is in itself only a beginning. For true communication is surely a two-way process; Beatie's family need to be able to hear and respond for effective change to happen. Perhaps social change can come only if the panacea, in this case food, can be given up for real food as exemplified by Beatie. Metaphorically the 'mighty head of the Bryant clan' needs to allow Beatie to bake her cakes of words and feelings in his house before old roots can grow new shoots, moving on with the seasons of change in the human heart.

Society

The play itself stands in for the society for which Wesker was writing. Forty years on I think it still does in many essential ways and therefore we can see how it stands in for us too, the members of our own society. It is a reminder of choice between action and passivity.

This aspect is encapsulated by the contrast between Beatie and her sister Susie. Susie is talked about but never appears in person, though she has been invited to the final tea party.

> BEATIE: Shall I tell you what Susie said when I went and saw her? She say she don't care if that ole atom bomb drop and she die – that's what she say. And you know why she say it? I'll tell you why, because if she had to care she'd have do something about it and she find that too much effort. Yes, she do. She can't be bothered – she's too bored with it all. That's what we all are – we're all too bored.
>
> MRS BRYANT: Blust woman – bored you say, bored? You say Susie's bored with a radio and television an' that. I go t'hell if she's bored.
>
> (ibid.: 146)

How many times have we heard the word bored used to mask uncomfortable feelings or depression? It is certainly a word I have often heard used by children and adolescents either to deny or to covertly signal feelings such as need, fear, anger and grief. Perhaps Susie too is bored because the problems of living in a world in which annihilation is possible are too overwhelming, too frightening. It is a world over whose destiny she has no control. But the play as a whole posits that we can have control if we are prepared to take responsibility for our own feelings and actions and relationships. Susan's way of dealing with her life is to cut her mother out when her own social pretensions are rumbled.

> JENNY: Susan brought something off the club from Pearl and Pearl give it to Mother and Mother sent it to Susan through the fishmonger what live next door to her in the council houses. And of course Susan were riled because she don't want her neighbours to know that she bought anything off the club. So they don't speak.
>
> (ibid.: 98)

We are told that Susan and her husband took the television to bed with them with a dish of chocolate biscuits when they first had it:

PEARL: But now they don't bother – they say they've had it a year now and all the old programmes they saw in the beginning they're seeing again.

(ibid.: 138)

Again food, again an attempt at the panacea. And here we find another panacea, this time in the marvels of the still new technology – then the disillusionment.

Beatie stands in for the creative part of ourselves which can try to sort out fantasy from reality, Susan for the depressed part which drives us further and further along the road of 'quiet desperation'. Wesker offers us a choice between the two and in doing so makes this family stand in for the choice facing the wider system of which they are a part. His ultimate tool is that of the metaphor which holds the whole play – Roots. In the context of this metaphor I want to point up aspects of what Beatie's struggle within her family stands in for in us, the audience.

Wesker is writing at the end of the 1950s, one of the famously named 'angry young men' school of new writers. It is post-war Britain, a time of enormous social change which is reflected in the references to the wider society to which the characters belong. The media and the image makers are at work. Material benefits are beginning to tempt as Britain begins to recover from wartime shortages and the earlier Depression. Workers' rights and the existence of unions, the possibility of productive as opposed to crippling strikes make the working class a target for abuse by the commercial world. As Beatie so passionately says in her final speech, 'The whole stinkin' commercial world insults us an we don't care a damn' (ibid.: 148).

The old world has gone and in this play Wesker uses the metaphor of rural life to stand in for the idea of growth which is healthily connected with its past. In the country it should be possible to find a continuous cycle of birth, growth, death and regeneration but in the rural idyll he presents to us the old world has gone or is rapidly going. The idyll is represented by a glimpse of the world to which Ronnie belongs and its attitude to the country when Beatie explains that Ronnie's London-born sister and brother-in-law live quite near because 'he make furniture by hand' to which Pearl asks 'Can't he do that in London?' The idea of the idyllic rural retreat in which those not born to it may pursue crafts and 'alternative living' which was to become so much part of the 1960s and 1970s is hinted at and indeed foreseen here. The reality is quite different. Old Stan Mann, aptly named like a latter-day Everyman, dies in Act II and the local doctor is dying of cancer. Mr Bryant gets laid off from his eighteen-year job as he becomes no longer economically viable in the new management of the estate. He throws the union magazine in the bin; it is not part of his world. So the family eat and the men get indigestion. What role is there for them now in a changing world where the old feudal laws remain only in the use of the word 'Sir' to the boss who is giving you the push. The feeling of impotence is so clear in Mr Bryant's description of the new estate managers, 'Sharp as a pig's scream they are – you can't do nothing' (ibid.:120).

The image is a brilliant evocation of the fear which lies not far from the surface. Fear of the loss of identity. Fear of the rapidly changing world. Fear of the potential for destruction afforded by the existence of nuclear armaments. In the midst of this Beatie struggles to find an integrity of self.

> I come from a family o' farm labourers yet I ent got no roots. .. . Roots! the things you come from, the things that feed you, the things that make you proud of yourself.
>
> (ibid.: 145)

She has sought the answer in her relationship with Ronnie but it turns out that he is as confused in his way as she is in hers.

> (*Ronnie's letter*) My ideas about handing on a new kind of life are quite useless and romantic if I'm really honest. If I were a healthy human being it might have been all right but most of us intellectuals are pretty sick and neurotic – as you have often observed, and we couldn't build a world even if we were given the reins of government – not yet any rate.
>
> (ibid.: 142)

Between them Beatie and Ronnie and Beatie's family represent the crisis of change. There is confusion as the old order changes. Burying your head in the sand (is it without significance that Jenny and Jimmy live surrounded by sandpits?) is one option. Struggling with ideas, as Ronnie does, is another. But Beatie's is to try to find her own authentic voice, her own creative use of her native language. As Wesker wrote in 1958, four years before the production of *Roots*,

> Having tucked my plays under my arm and stepped out – where do I go? . . . Having set my vision I may not be big enough for it. I shall learn as I go along. It means starting from scratch and breaking our hearts again and again, but at least something would be happening. And England would know that its community was alive and kicking and critical and eager.
>
> (Marowitz, Milne and Hale 1965)

The characters, situations and context of this play stand in for any society at any time of change. A time when beginnings are hard and integrity difficult to maintain. As such it 'stands in' for the process of change. It shows us the difficulties of beginning again.

As I write I think of the decimation of the countryside in the years since

Wesker wrote this play, the attack on the natural environment, the farmers' rape of the landscape and natural habitats for over-production in the context of the politics of greed. Surely Beatie's words were prophetic.

This play, in terms of the wider society, stands for the struggle for the integrity of creative identity, a struggle to be a moral being in the least narrow sense of that word. In that sense it 'stands in' for the spiritual part of a society. Beatie's struggle is a creative act. I believe Wesker was concerned with how a society in a time of change can be in touch with its roots and its creative potential and can use them for really effective change. This, as Beatie says when talking about Susie, means taking responsibility.

The play roots individual change within the context of family, inheritance and society; it challenges us to look at responsibility in terms of the relationship between the individual and society, at what one individual can do to contribute to wider change. This is a theme which I shall come back to in other chapters, for it is of the greatest relevance to the therapeutic process.

Conclusion

In each of us there is a Beatie, a Ronnie, a Mrs Bryant, a Stan Mann and so on. The therapeutic and educational processes of beginning again, growing and changing, healing and revitalizing our lives is mirrored in this play. Beatie is the central character. As such she touches all these characters and they 'stand in' for parts of her. As she acknowledges these, integrates them into herself, she can begin to move on. In Kleinian terms Beatie has projected onto Ronnie the role of 'the good breast', the one who can really feed her, give the kind of nourishment her mother never could. Whereas she has idealized him, her mother is seen as the 'bad breast' withholding healthy nourishment. 'What kind of life did you give me? . . . You didn't open one door for me' (*Roots*: 127).

In Act III she has to move from this schizoid position. She, as it were, enters the state which characterizes Klein's depressive position as outlined in Chapter 2. She has to settle for reality and tolerate ambivalent feelings towards both her mother and Ronnie. By ceasing to idealize Ronnie she can find the Ronnie in herself, but the parts of Ronnie which can really nurture her because they are parts of herself hitherto unrecognized which she projected onto him. She can find the mother in herself and nurture herself and can see those parts of herself that she dislikes, which her mother has carried for her, and in acknowledging them acknowledge and integrate a more balanced self. In doing this she can recognize the objects in her life for what they are – human beings with human imperfections which cannot live her life for her. She has to begin the journey.

In doing this Beatie herself stands in for the processes of growth and change. These processes are not easy, either for the individual, the group, or society, but it is the acknowledgement of the different parts of ourselves which we project outwards, the re-integration of them into our personal, group or social system, which can provide the possibility to say, with Beatie, 'I'm beginning, on my own two feet I'm beginning' (ibid.: 148).

IN PRACTICE

Education, performance, therapy

In the previous section I explored aspects of *Roots* to show how the play offers us ways of thinking about beginnings at an individual, family and societal level. I showed some of the ways in which the characters and events of the play 'stand in for', and through the drama therefore authorize, aspects of our internal and external worlds.

So how does it work in practice? How can the ideas and feelings involved in 'beginnings' find a voice through engagement with *Roots* as performance, as part of an educational curriculum and as a therapeutic mode?

My first experience of *Roots* was as a performer, aged 19. I can still remember the fierceness and passion with which I said those final lines which Wesker gives Beatie at the end of the play. Like her a young woman from Norfolk, although engaged in different struggles from hers, I was nevertheless given words I needed to help me engage with my own struggle; I could articulate some of my feelings through the metaphor of a character in a play, a written text. No doubt at that time I chose to do it only because I was a good mimic and could do the Norfolk accent – the conscious and superficial reason. In fact my real motivation would have been far more complex. It was because the text could hold me that it could also give me a voice with which to explore those unconscious reasons to do with growing up, leaving home, separation and male–female relationships.

It is not surprising therefore that a few years later I directed that play with a group of young people who were also struggling with beginnings. They were 16–18-year-olds living on the outer fringes of London, struggling to move on from the constraints of a class structure and an educational system which was only just emerging from the tyranny of the 11-plus examination. Beatie was played by someone whom I shall call Joanna. A so-called 11-plus failure, she was a highly imaginative and creative young woman who, at the time of our work on the play, was beginning to realize that she had a great deal more ability than most of her teachers had ever either realized or given her credit for. She was also aware of her family background in which there was no expectation that she should go to college, train for anything, let alone have a career. So, not surprisingly, she played her role with a conviction which held the audience and moved them to tears. Because the play was for her a mirror of her own struggle to find her voice, she played the role with an authenticity which enabled her to stand in for parts of themselves too; feeling for Beatie they were able to feel for themselves.

In this production we worked through improvisation constantly, forging the links between real-life experience and the life of the play. The result was astonishing – these young people had never acted before. I believed simply that they could do it – not by technique but by what Dorothy Heathcote calls 'living through' (Wagner 1976). Technique could be taught – and was – but the heart of the experience must first be found so that technique can be grafted on. Of all the plays I directed at that time that was the one which I remember with the greatest affection and excitement. It was also the most successful piece of theatre.

I think now that because I had engaged with its themes myself, had played that character at a time when it was the right part for me to play, it had worked its therapeutic process on me. David Read Johnson (Jennings 1992) speaks of the therapist's wide range of roles. Now, nourished by my earlier experience, I was able to work as director in such as way as to allow the play's therapeutic possibilities access to the young performers for whom this play was also the right play at the right time. My own engagement as a performer had released me; it had taught me its language and had given me sufficient distance not to work out my issues through my actors. I believe that if I had not been through that process I could not have directed Joanna in the way that I did. At this stage I knew nothing of dramatherapy but now I firmly believe that our way of working on that play was, though not contracted or defined as dramatherapy, certainly 'dramatherapeutic'.

Now, with many years' experience as teacher and dramatherapist, I know more about structuring the processes, enabling people to move more deeply into the text and into their own lives as reflected by it. At that time it was the text that held the function of the therapist; the text itself was the therapist, its voice was constant and containing and its structure boundaried yet affording as many possibilities of interpretation as the members of the cast allowed it. They could take up the playwright's words and allow their own engagement with them to reverberate. Through improvisation the group was able to reflect on the reality of the play's world for them. On all three levels of individual growth, of family relationships and social context in which they lived, the play 'stood in' for their experience and therefore helped give it voice, externalize it and authorize it. Through improvisation they re-created the fathers who did not communicate or understand, mothers who were trapped by their class, gender and environment, sibling envy, affection and distance, and their own feelings of conflict, loss and the struggle to 'begin' as adults. In rehearsal they debated the issues of social change, disarmament, strikes. (It was at that time that the first teachers' strikes in England took place.) Creative dramatic work led to creative intellectual activity. For 17-year-olds this process was a cathartic experience (Scheff 1979; Landy 1986). Each tried others' roles so that no one was locked into only one role. Their personal role repertoire was therefore extended by this process. Just as Beatie contains in her internal world the roles of the other members of the play, these young performers could try out those roles that seemed distanced from them by age, background or gender but which were part of them too. They were, in fact, exploring the concept of standing in by allowing all the roles in the play to speak for them, to help them find their own voices for their own life experience and inner realities. This led to their performing with an authority which amazed the audience. I was not surprised; the authority came from the authenticity of the inner experience being congruent with the outer representation.

The confidence that had been gained through the work was put to the test and won hands down one night in performance when the tilley-lamp used in Act I nearly caught fire. The actors dealt with real-life danger simultaneously improvising script and action – and all this in the Norfolk accent. Audience members were impressed with how such a tricky bit of stage business had been done – they had no idea it was a real-life emergency!

Both the process of the rehearsal period and the performance were, I would say, therapeutic. The performance validated the process and the process validated the lives of the performers who had allowed the play to stand in for them and their experience. The part played by improvisation as a rehearsal method was crucial to the success of the performance. In the final stages, pruning and trimming improvisation rigorously make the marriage between the truth of personal experience and the truth of the playwright's text. This enabled the form to be retained, together with the truth of the 'as if' of theatre when improvisation had to be resorted to in the near-fire incident within the actual performance.

As a dramatherapist I have found the play equally rewarding to work with. Wanda, a woman of 28, found that working with the play evoked intense feelings in relation to her sister and she was able to work on the three-way relationship between mother, self and sister. After positioning herself as Beatie in a sculpt in relation to Jenny (sister) and Mrs Bryant (mother), she broke down and wept with a feeling understanding of the real-life roles she played. The cathartic moment enabled her to try out other positions and roles of the triangle and work towards a greater understanding of her own needs. She was in danger of moving too quickly through the roles and thus avoiding the insight she could gain through the moment of 'seeing feelingly' (*King Lear*; Witkin 1974) I invited her to slow down and speak lines from the play of her own choosing in each role and position. After trying the three out again, this time with the lines as well as the positions, she returned to Beatie. 'What do you want to say as Beatie?' I asked her. 'No, you can't help me mother, I know you can't,' she replied. At this point she broke down and wept with the acknowledgement of the reality of her relationship with her mother. She was able to begin to mourn at the moment of understanding her longed for fantasy and her reality. Eventually she could focus on the relationship with her sister and elected to leave the work by choosing Beatie's final words, 'I'm beginning, on my own two feet I'm beginning', more aware now of the work she needed to do to be able to be truly in that position. She was beginning to begin.

In another group a male member, Jim, elected to play the role of Mr Bryant in a short group sculpt of the final scene of the play. For many years he had felt constrained by his unsatisfactory relationship with his father, though this had not openly come into the group until this session. Jim played Mr Bryant looking fixedly out of the window, unconnected to the rest of his family, apart and alone. Jim had also been apart in the group, unable to integrate himself fully into its life, remaining detached or cynical in relation to the three women and the four other men in the group. After playing Mr Bryant he quietly observed, 'I never realized how lonely my father was; he spent his time "looking out of the window" and none of us could ever reach him and I've always blamed him for being a useless role-model to me as a man.' He paused. 'I simply never realized how lonely he was.'

It is in such a way that a text can become a turning point, a moment of transition. Jim was not using Beatie's words, 'I'm beginning, on my own two feet I'm beginning', but this in effect is what he was doing in his own way in this group. One of the things the play is about is the struggle which beginning involves. The choice to begin or to stay where one is. It was because that very choice is inherent in the play and because the text stands in for our own struggle that Jim was able to find in it a moment of his own possibility.

The potential space discussed in Chapter 2 was allowed by this sculpt of the final scene. Winnicott's notion of potential space is that something is possible, something can happen, there is potential for development through creative playing. *Roots* is itself a text about issues of growth and change. It is therefore, in a sense, a 'potential text'.

In dramatherapy the participants can explore this potential space afforded by the text because the actors can take all or selected roles; they are not limited to one. The Beatie who speaks these lines at the end is in every member of the group. Just as in my discussion of the play I showed that characters stand in for one another in the text, so they are all in us and stand in for parts of ourselves. In the dramatherapy group the members may focus on the character that most engages them in terms of their life-processes at that moment. But because all the characters are within us, the ways in which each character lives his or her life is available to us.

So how can this, 'having the characters within', help Jim to arrive at that moment of understanding about his father which helped him to shift his own stance, not only in relation to his father but also to the group? I have discussed the concept of aesthetic distance in Chapter 1. At the moment of aesthetic distance we are 'in balance' to use Landy's (1986) words. At the moment of being Mr Bryant, Jim was 'in balance' in his relationship with his father and therefore the trap in which years of projection had held him was weakened and movement within these constraints became possible. Jim projected out the image of a cold withdrawn father which he had originally introjected. He could not see that his own behaviour was felt by the group to be cold, withdrawn and unconnected. Once he was able to experience aesthetic distance through the drama, his father became available to him symbolically and he was able to be present both as himself and, through the role, his father, experiencing and in that moment exploring the introjected and projected aspects of this relationship. Consequently he was able to begin to withdraw the projections, to own them as part of himself, and to find another aspect of his father which he could gradually understand within himself, feel and give voice to. The group fed back to him how authentic he sounded now and the hostility which had been mounting towards him visibly and audibly changed. That was another moment of beginning for the group, a new shift had taken place. Others were able to acknowledge their own feelings of loneliness and what they had projected onto Jim they could begin to own. They could thus release him from some of the behaviours he had been acting unconsciously on behalf of the group.

Beatie is inauthentic when she keeps quoting Ronnie – at the moment she recognizes her own loneliness she can weep, feel the reality of her situation and begin to change it. Because Beatie's situation is the central pivot around which the play turns, then her experience permeates the play. The individual beginnings of the dramatherapy group do not need to be her beginnings; they can be arrived at through engagement with the other characters while the whole text still holds the central themes. Unlike Joanna, playing the role of Beatie in performance, the participant in the group need not mirror Beatie's situation so closely. In Jim's case his beginning was linked with finding a new element in the intrapsychic dynamic between him and his internalized father. Working on *Roots* we know that beginnings are central to the play. There is therefore the potential that 'beginningness' inherent in this text can feed any character in any situation and therefore any member of the group working on the play. Jim is one such example. At some level he was ready to look at his relationship with his father differently and unconsciously chose to do so. The structure of the play itself could contain and allow this need and readiness to emerge. He chose to let the role give him access to an area he was now ready to address.

A dramatherapist prepares

This chapter is about 'beginnings'. Let us look therefore at one way in which a dramatherapist might start to prepare for using a text. Everyone prepares in a way unique to themselves, especially in the early stages. This is an example of my own approach. It echoes the example in Chapter 3.

This play has a title which is a metaphor. This determines the form the first part of my preparation will take; it will be free association around the metaphor. While doing this I shall put my conscious knowledge of the play on one side, ready to refer to it when, and only when, my associations lead me there. This method will take me to the heart of the play and allow me to be in touch with several layers at once, such is the function of both free association and of metaphor. It is only after this that I shall think in more specific terms about the actual group I am to work with and shape a structure which will be both containing enough and free enough to enable group members to make the exploration through the play which is right for them at that moment in their lives in relation to the aims for that particular piece of work. Today my internal monologue starts off like this:

> *Roots* – interesting how I get a picture of things growing rather than 'roots' immediately – perhaps the play's more about growing – but why's it called 'Roots' then? 'The things you come from – the things that make you proud of yourself' . . . So that's where the text is taking me. . . . I'm starting to get an image of a tree's connection with the ground now, attached yet itself. It's quite a physical image – ah yes, movement, getting the group's bodies to connect with the feelings of being rooted, grounded and growing might come in somewhere. Ah, I hadn't thought of 'rooted to the spot' – that's more about being stuck. Fear perhaps? My stuff? Don't think so but I'll need to explore that a bit more. Oh yes, of course – Susie. 'Susie's afraid that ole atom bomb'll drop and she'll die', . . . maybe the group'll need to explore what rooted to the spot means to them; I've made a connection, I wonder what theirs will be. If I structure this in at the beginning it'll give me a sense of where the group is at, their own connectedness, readiness to move towards communicating with each other or not, after all that's one of the main themes. I'll hold that in my mind. It's beginning to feel like a good opening because already the essence of the play can be held within it – the tension between being stuck and being able to grow; it's being true to the whole play and will help to get the group right in there from the beginning. Interesting how I seem to be planning the beginning before really sorting out the central structure – I don't usually do that – maybe it's to do with how important beginnings are in this play. Since they are so important I'll need to come back to this again before deciding on the opening exercise. . . .

A group member has the last word

We were working on *Roots* making group photographs. I had taken the role of Beatie and had chosen to stand in front of the other characters, looking forward and up, my foot unconsciously positioned on the brink of taking a step. Holding that position for a sustained period was a powerful experience and the questions put by the group helped me to focus on its significance. I felt a real sense of liberation:

> Shackles loosened
> There's sky above
> And light

102

The family were still there but behind me, not my focus. I had not discounted them but was concentrating on stepping forward, moving on. When another group formed their photograph I noticed that Beatie was positioned on a step ladder looking down on the tangled web of her family in front of her. Out of idle curiosity really, I decided to respond to the invitation to observe this Beatie's perspective. I didn't expect to feel anything so I was quite shocked when I took up the position on the ladder. It felt truly dreadful. I was above the family but they were my focus and, although I was physically above them, my whole being felt dragged down. My energy drained away and I could see no way through them or past. From that perspective there was no way I could move on. It powerfully demonstrated a fact I had in some sense known for some time – how we see things makes all the difference. It is something I now know to the very root of my being and that is due in no small part to the experience I've just recounted. And because I know it deeply it informs more of my life.

5

PAST INTO PRESENT – THE WIDER CONTEXT
Cloud Nine by Caryl Churchill

As we leave Beatie setting out on her journey we can speculate on what she would have woken up to had she, like Rip Van Winkle, slept for the next twenty years or gone back in time a hundred years. Would she, I wonder, have found a place in Caryl Churchill's *Cloud Nine* (1980) play?

THE PLAY

The dramatic structure of our next play invites us to reflect that time is relative to the social and cultural experience of the mores it supports. Act I and Act II are separated by a hundred years, though in the life of the characters this is experienced as only twenty-five years. The point is starkly made by this device that things change slowly and the play itself raises the question of how superficial or fundamental is any change that is made in the inter-related areas of race, class, sexuality and gender of British society.

Résumé of the play

The play is written in two acts. The first act takes place in Africa during the Victorian period. Clive, a British colonial administrator, is married to Betty. They have two children, Edward aged 9 and Victoria aged 2. Ellen, the governess, Betty's mother Maud on an extended visit, and Joshua, the black servant, complete the household. An old friend, Harry Bageley, arrives as does Mrs Saunders, a young widow who seeks refuge because of local disturbances. Beneath the respectable façade of the characters, emotional and sexual passions inform their actions. The hypocrisy is revealed during a Christmas picnic and a game of hide and seek. Clive has sex with Mrs Saunders, Betty declares her love for Harry, Edward wants to repeat his sexual experience with Harry of the previous year, Betty declares her love for Ellen, Harry has sex with Joshua and makes advances to Clive. Later there is a local uprising in which Joshua's parents are killed and he apparently disowns them. The act ends with the wedding of Harry and Ellen instigated by Clive, who has been outraged on discovering Harry's homosexuality. The final image before the blackout is of

Joshua raising a gun to Clive seen only by a silent Edward. Act II takes place a hundred years later in south-east London of the 1970s, though this is only twenty-five years in the life of the family who, apart from Clive, reappear to form the centrepiece of the action supported by four new characters, Cathy, Lin, Martin and Gerry. Lin, a working-class lesbian with a child from her marriage, forms a relationship with Victoria, who is married to Martin. Edward is working as a gardener in a public park and living in a gay relationship with Gerry. Betty has left Clive and, at the age of 65, begins to try to find who she is. The act shows the characters struggling with the inheritance of the past in the political and sexual mores of the present. Various permutations of relationships are explored by the characters and the act ends with Betty of Act I and Betty of Act II embracing one another after the brief and only appearance of the disillusioned Clive.

I had encountered *Cloud Nine* some time before I read Jean Baker Miller's *Toward a New Psychology of Women* which was written three years earlier in 1976. I was struck time and time again by how this book by a psychoanalyst was in some essential ways saying exactly what *Cloud Nine* had said to me through the dramatic form. Theory and life form a pleasing unity, for if we look at both acts of *Cloud Nine* we can see how Baker Miller's ways of thinking about the concepts of domination and subordination are exactly borne out.

The play was the result of the collaboration of the actors in telling their life stories, answering questions about their personal sexual experiences and improvising around this material (Howe Kritzer 1991: 112). First let us listen to one of the central tenets of the psychoanalyst and then explore the playwright's presentation of these same concepts.

> Once a group is defined as inferior, the superiors tend to label it as defective or substandard in various ways. These labels accrete rapidly. Thus, blacks are described as less intelligent than whites, women are supposed to be ruled by emotion and so on.... subordinates are described in terms of, and encouraged to develop, personal characteristics that are pleasing to the dominant group.... in general this ... includes qualities more characteristic of children than adults – immaturity, weakness and helplessness. If subordinates adopt these characteristics they are considered well adjusted.... dominant groups usually impede the development of subordinates and block their freedom of expression and action.
>
> (Baker Miller 1976: 6–8)

Whilst Baker Miller's thoughts are subsequently worked out in relation to the position of women, her overall thoughts about dominance and subordination can be extended to the issues of race, class and sexual orientation as we read this play. (For any reader interested in the implications of the relationship between the traditionally male world of psychoanalysis and what women traditionally carry for men, her book is still immensely valuable.)

Act I

Act I takes place in a British colony in Africa in Victorian times. The entire group of characters is gathered round the Union Jack singing a patriotic song which embraces the world under the flag of England. Clive's opening words are ones of ownership, and therefore domination. They echo on an individual and family level those of the song which embraces a wider social and political framework.

> This is my family. Though far from home,
> We serve the Queen wherever we may roam.
> I am a father to the natives here,
> And father to my family so dear.
> (Act I, Scene 1)

Patriarchal society is embodied in him and this sets the scene for the whole play. Within the context of this patriarchal society the dynamics of sex, gender and race will be played out.

The relationship between the patriarchy and the apparent matriarchy of an Empire ruled by a woman is indicated in theatrical terms, for when Clive comes to introduce his daughter, who is named Victoria, the audience see that she is played by a doll. She is therefore identityless and mute. The tension between this and the words,

> She our Queen,
> Victoria reigns supreme . . .
> (ibid.)

which follow immediately after his presentation of his daughter to the audience, emphasizes that the matriarch is a figurehead, an absent 'mute' figure, the evidence of whose existence, the play suggests, is in the attitudes and behaviour of her male subjects who maintain her Empire:

> The forge of war shall weld the chains
> Of brotherhood secure;
> (ibid.)

What are the projections which are put upon the queen, Victoria? Is she a doll created in man's image, a tabula rasa for what is, in effect, a patriarchal society in which 'the forge of war shall weld the chains/Of brotherhood secure'? Women's place is clearly defined in the words Clive uses to introduce his wife, Betty:

> My wife is all I dreamt a wife should be,
> And everything she is she owes to me.
>
> (ibid.)

To underscore the words Churchill again presents us with a theatrical shock, for Betty is played by a man. The male actor introduces the female character with the words:

> I am a man's creation as you see
> And what men want is what I want to be.
>
> (ibid.)

There are several layers of meaning which become accessible to the audience through this device. One is that to men, women are invisible; another that men see the world through their own eyes, with other creatures being made in their own image; a third is that we are presented with the possibility of Clive's repressed homosexuality. It also raises the issue of the status of a wife and the aggressive denial of woman's subjectivity. If everything she has, that is, her very self, she owes to Clive, she is not only an object but also a mere cypher. Even to be sexual is not the role of a wife, for the sexual function is split off from the wife and acted out on another woman, Mrs Saunders, later in the act.

Other women are dismissed,

> No need for any speeches by the rest.
> My daughter, mother-in-law, and governess.
>
> (ibid.)

The split between the apparent reverence of woman as symbolized by Victoria and the reality of woman's place is emphasized by the juxtaposition of the opening lines of the song which immediately follows these words of dismissal:

> O'er countless numbers she, our Queen,
> Victoria reigns supreme.
>
> (ibid.)

What is being emphasized here, therefore, is that women can have authority only if they are figureheads of almost mythological status. Real women for Clive are terrifying. He complains that Mrs Saunders gives him a twenty-four hour erection and goes on to tell her:

If you were shot with poisoned arrows do you know what I'd do? I'd fuck your dead body and poison myself. Caroline you smell amazing. You terrify me. You are dark like this continent. Mysterious. Treacherous.

(Act I, Scene 2)

Later he tells Harry, whom he does not realize is homosexual,

> There is something dark about women, that threatens what is best in us.
> Between men that light burns brightly ... women are irrational, de-
> manding, inconsistent, treacherous and lustful, and they smell different
> to us.
>
> (Act I, Scene 4)

We might ask what Clive is projecting of his own shadow side onto Mrs
Saunders and what women are being asked to carry for men.

The male perception of women is split between woman as mother/
madonna and woman as whore. We see Clive playing his role as martyr to
his Queen and country simultaneously with that of the little boy who wants
both to impress mother and be nurtured by her. This duality is economically
expressed in the following conversation with Betty:

> CLIVE: I have a blister.
> BETTY: Oh my poor dear foot.
> CLIVE: It's nothing.
> BETTY: Oh but it's sore.
> CLIVE: We are not in this country to enjoy ourselves.
>
> (Act I, Scene 1)

Clive's way of dealing with his own unconscious forces is to use women as objects for displacement; for example in order to cope with the little boy in him
he has to turn his wife into a non-coping little girl, displacing his feelings of
immaturity, weakness and helplessness onto her.

> CLIVE: That's a brave girl. So today has been allright? No fainting, no
> hysteria?
>
> (ibid.)

And in order to cope with Mrs Saunders as an independent woman, he has to
project onto her those 'mysterious' aspects of himself which terrify him; she
must be 'irrational, demanding, inconsistent, treacherous and lustful' in order
for him to maintain his picture of himself as possessing the opposites of
those characteristics.

What begins to emerge, therefore, as we look at Clive in relation to women
in the play, is that the mechanisms of displacement and projection are the
means of maintaining the dominant/subordinate matrix. One of the important points which Baker Miller makes in her discussion of domination and
subordination is that subordinates know much about dominants because this
is necessary for survival. They need to 'be able to predict their [the dominants']
reactions of pleasure or displeasure' (Baker Miller 1976: 11) but that this can
be at the expense of knowing themselves because 'subordinates absorb a large
part of the untruths created by the dominants' (ibid.). The way in which the
subordinates, the women, are denied access to empowering aspects of them-

selves can be seen through Churchill's presentation of both Betty and Mrs Saunders in relation to the men.

When Betty voices her attraction to Harry she expresses it as 'like going out into the jungle. It's like going up the river on a raft. It's like going out in the dark' (Act I, Scene 2), to which he replies, 'And you are safety and light and peace and home' (ibid.).

Betty must therefore deny her rights to that part of herself, blame herself and raise Harry's status when she speaks to Clive, having been caught by Joshua in Harry's arms,

> BETTY: I'm sorry, I'm sorry, forgive me. It is not Harry's fault. It is all mine. Harry is noble. He has rejected me. It is my wickedness. I get bored, I get restless, I imagine things. There is something wicked in me Clive.
>
> (Act I, Scene 3)

Her guilt and internalization of her status as a mother/madonna subordinate is reinforced by Clive's response of, 'I have never thought of you having the weakness of your sex, only the good qualities' (ibid.).

Betty must therefore apologize for an important aspect of herself, her desire, and in doing so attribute to herself wickedness and elevate Harry to the position she is supposed to be in – that of purity and nobility – for these are the only two positions available to her. If she gives up the mother/ madonna position she will, by definition, be classified as whore, which is the implied status of Mrs Saunders. She must therefore project onto Harry the mother/ madonna qualities of selflessness, purity, honour, etc., and adopt the whore position, for if she were able to retain the two she might be on the way to becoming a more integrated and whole person who might be able to begin to shed these categories altogether. The threat to the male dominant group would then become a reality, for if that group operates by processes of splitting and denial then the striving of the subordinate group towards achieving integration of identity would threaten to overturn the balance of power.

The recently widowed Mrs Saunders is regarded by Clive as a woman of 'amazing spirit'. However she becomes for Clive nothing more than a vehicle for his ejaculation. She explains that she came to his house for protection from a local attack, choosing him because she thought he 'would take no for an answer' as opposed to the old major, her neighbour, from whom she had to defend herself with a shotgun. But because she says yes to Clive once, he sees no question of her having choice in the matter of a sexual relationship. Because she, as she puts it, 'likes the sensation', this puts her in the category of whore with no rights. There is no question of a relationship between equal partners even in the matter of sex, as we see in a moment in Scene 2. After disappearing under her skirt in spite of her request for him to stop, he emerges triumphantly saying:

CLIVE: I came.
MRS S: I didn't.
CLIVE: I'm all sticky.
MRS S: What about me. Wait.
CLIVE: All right are you? Come on. We musn't be found.
MRS S: Don't go now.
CLIVE: Caroline, you are so voracious. Do let go. Tidy yourself up.

(Act I, Scene 2)

As long as Clive gets his orgasm he can leave the woman aroused and unsatisfied, attributing her discomfort to her own voraciousness. His orgasm and his denying Mrs Saunders hers is a way of his ensuring that he is not totally enveloped by her. It is a way of dealing with his fears that the woman is the dark continent in which he can become swallowed up. There is also an implication here of the skirts representing the mother and the wish of the little boy to retreat into the mother's womb. This 'little boy' and the implied incestuous wish has also to be denied. Again the balance of power is threatened and must be avoided.

The denial of vulnerability in the dominant group and the conversion of this vulnerability into the creating of a subordinate culture mirrors the wider society, the British Empire in all its oppression.

This element is introduced through the role of Joshua, the black servant. Clive introduces him thus:

My boy's a jewel, really has the knack.
You'd hardly notice that the fellow's black.

To which Joshua replies:

My skin is black but oh my soul is white.
I hate my tribe. My master is my light.
I only live for him. As you can see,
What white men want is what I want to be.

(Act I, Scene 1)

Joshua's response reveals the extent of his apparent collusion with the annihilation of his identity. Again Churchill uses a startling dramatic device, which is to have Joshua played by a white man, thus reinforcing both Clive's obliteration of Joshua and his culture and Joshua's response to the oppression by the white man. In the next section of the play we see how Joshua is manipulated into playing whatever role suits the white members of society. In an incident where he is accused of making insolent remarks to Betty, he is used by both Clive and Betty and thus abused by them. He becomes a pawn in the games they play with themselves and each other. Betty can complain about Joshua's sexual innuendoes to her – are these perhaps projections of her own forbidden desires? – and can thus give Clive the excuse to be 'masterful': 'Betty, please, let me handle this' (ibid.).

110

At the end of the incident, Clive winks to Joshua unseen by Betty and Joshua provides the foil for Clive to reassert his maleness; Joshua is used as a device for Clive to assert his image at the expense of his wife's. Joshua is invisible; he is simply a tool for the white man and woman; he is invisible as a person. What is interesting to note here in terms of the dominant/subordinate matrix is that Betty moves into the place of dominance in relation to Joshua; the oppressed becomes the oppressor of another oppressed group for Betty clearly hopes to get Joshua into trouble. However, while supporting his wife in terms of accusing Joshua of insubordination, by winking at Joshua he invites him into a more dominant role as ally in oppressing his wife. Thus in terms of male attitudes to women Joshua and Clive, by virtue of their both belonging to the male sex, can be briefly united against the female in oppressing her.

As in the case of Betty's encounter with Joshua, we see the subordinate group acting as dominants to an even more subordinate one. The governess is a lesbian in love with Betty, but Ellen's feelings of sexual passion are denied by Betty and she is stripped of an essential part of her identity, just as Betty and Mrs Saunders are of theirs. When Ellen announces to Betty that she 'worships' her Betty replies by saying, 'Oh Ellen you're my only friend' (Act I, Scene 2).

Later when Ellen tries to spell out her feelings more clearly, Betty points out to Ellen that she must, in effect, be as oppressed as Betty herself is: 'Women have their duty as soldiers have. You must be a mother if you can' (Act I, Scene 4). And when Ellen says she will rather die than leave her, Betty's response is to flatly deny the other woman's experience: 'No you wouldn't. Ellen, don't be silly. Come, don't cry. You don't feel what you think you do' (ibid.).

The oppression of the characters with homosexual rather than heterosexual identity is part of the chain of dominant/subordinate hierarchy. In order to explore this further, we need to look at the roles of Edward and Harry. In his introduction scene Clive presents Edward, his 9-year-old son, third, after Joshua and before the rest of the women – his daughter, his mother-in-law and the governess – who get lumped together and dismissed, as we have seen. This placing in the pecking order is interesting; we might expect him to be introduced second if he fulfilled the conditions of a Victorian son and heir. However, the reason is immediately apparent for this placing, for Edward is played by a woman and his words indicate his inability to identify with the role of 'manly' male that his father prescribes for him; the implication is that Joshua the servant is 'promoted' over Edward by reason of the servant's 'maleness':

> What father wants I'd dearly like to be.
> I find it rather hard as you can see.
> (Act I, Scene 1)

111

Edward is perpetually having his sister's doll taken away from him; the only time that Clive tolerates its presence is when Edward says he is minding it for his sister, which Clive praises him for, as it is 'manly' to look after his sister. Out of earshot from his father, Edward has said that he does not want to grow up like his father and that he hates him. Yet he has watched the local boys being beaten and comes out with the adult stereotype, 'They got what they deserved', though clearly he has not enjoyed the experience. Edward is seen as being on the receiving end of a whole mixture of adult abusive behaviour, being pushed about by expectations for him to become 'manly', slapped by his father, mother and grandmother when he threatens their stereotypes of gender-appropriate behaviour. He has been seduced by Harry, the explorer, on his last visit, and is supremely happy with his 'Uncle Harry', but the abuse binds him. When Harry says he must leave he resorts to the sustaining myth of the dominant group in response to Edward's cry at the prospect of his going, 'I have my duty to the Empire' (Act I, Scene 4).

Harry's inadvertent revealing of his own homosexuality to Clive is followed by successive speeches in which he expresses shame, talks of himself as diseased, and fulfils all the expectations of how he should behave having revealed himself to be in a subordinate role. He agrees to marry Ellen, who, when asked, consents. In relation to homosexuality, the heterosexuals are the dominant group. This marriage serves to shore up the belief in the dominants' order of things and put homosexuality firmly into the closet by pretending that it does not exist. By marrying, the subordinate group colludes.

But Harry, as a member of a subordinate group, oppresses another subordinate group. His invitation to Joshua to 'go into a barn and fuck' is presented as being an act of equals as he adds, 'That's not an order.' However, one wonders how anything presented by the white guest of the white boss, Clive, can be perceived by the black servant as anything other than a demand. In that sense I see it as one of the direct links between politics – in this play the politics of colonialism – and sex which Caryl Churchill (1983) herself defines as central to the play. This I read as an abuse of Joshua, regardless of whether or not Joshua wants to have sex with Harry, because it stems from the oppression of colonialism. It is also an example of a subordinate group seizing the opportunity to oppress another subordinate group, as we saw in the example of Joshua's treatment of Betty. Another example of subordinate groups dominating one another when the opportunity arises is Joshua's abusive treatment of Edward. He cuts up Victoria's doll and blames Edward for it; it is another moment where a subordinate achieves temporary dominance.

Thus, as we look at the behaviours and relationships in the chain of dominance and subordination, we find Baker Miller is again borne out:

Inevitably, the dominant group is the model for 'normal human relationships'. It then becomes normal to treat others destructively and to derogate them, to obscure the truth of what you are doing, by creating false explanations, and to oppose actions towards equality.

(Baker Miller 1976: 8)

Where better, therefore, to set this play than nineteenth-century colonial Africa? The scenes are riddled with examples of 'false explanations' and the opposition of 'actions towards equality'. The country itself is seen as a place which evokes fear by its unfamiliarity to the white British; its climate, its terrain and its people are not a source of wonder provoking interest, humility or respect, but something which threatens and disturbs and must be dealt with by superimposing alien customs, by subjection and by both oppression and repression. In Act I of *Cloud Nine* we see how the dominant culture must maintain a distance from those parts which, if they were acknowledged, would threaten their dominant role and the norms that are in place in the society, the family and the wider society, in this instance the British Empire. We see subordinate groups behaving in ways set for them by the dominant group, forced into moulds which bring a mixture of denial, pain and confusion. The drama powerfully presents a picture of what women carry for men, black people for white people, homosexuals for heterosexuals, children for adults, in order that their respective dominant roles should not be threatened.

It would seem that fear is an overriding unconscious motivation for the need to oppress. This is exemplified by Clive. In order to defend against the fear of loss of control and identity, even of annihilation, Clive must oppress, control and deny others their full identity. We are back to the early infant mechanisms. We see the frightened infant in Clive projecting onto Africa the bad breast and the powerful mother which deny him and threaten to destroy him. Both Africa and the feared mother come together in the use of the word darker: 'Women can be treacherous and evil. They are darker and more dangerous than men' (Act I, Scene 4). Africa becomes the container for all that he finds out of his control; he can project onto it his own unconscious, the contents of which terrify him:

> . . . there is something dangerous. Implacable. This whole continent is my enemy. I am pitching my whole mind and will and reason and spirit against it to tame it, and I sometimes feel it will break over me and swallow me up.

(Act I, Scene 3)

We see his own sadism projected onto the Africans: 'spoke to three different headmen who would gladly chop off each others' heads and wear them round their waists' (Act I, Scene 1).

It is as though for him it is a tremendous fight of ego and super-ego over the id, of the adult over the child faced with overwhelming anxiety. The more that is denied the more rigorous the maintenance of the controlling

113

structures. This is exemplified in Clive's treatment of Edward and summed up in his words to Betty: 'A boy has no business having feelings' (Act I, Scene 2).

The price for such denial is high, for both dominants and subordinates. When Joshua raises his gun to shoot Clive at the end of Act I, Edward, though seeing it, says nothing. Two subordinates have had enough, yet sadly their revolution must be expressed through the languages that subordinates learn from dominants. Here these are the language of imitation and the language they are coerced into speaking – in this case the language of the gun and the language of silence respectively.

Act II

Through this setting of nineteenth-century British colonialism, Churchill can explore the connections between race, gender, sexuality and the politics of oppression. By setting Act II one hundred years later, but with the characters having moved on only twenty-five years, she shows how the past and present are inexorably linked. By this dramatic technique Churchill underlines one of the essential truths that the play presents, that people are closely linked to the mores, culture and norms of the past and that change is not simply a matter of individual determination. Whilst in Act II things have moved on in many ways, some more fundamental aspects of our ways of being have changed little and lurk not too far from the surface. The act presents the characters struggling to find themselves, caught between these two realities of change and no-change. One of Churchill's tenets, that relationships are based on the denial of feelings and the negation of honesty inherent in a white patriarchal society, is further explored in Act II by presenting the legacy of confusion and exploring the struggles and attempts of finding new ways of relating to ourselves and others.

This is what makes the play so interesting to me as a dramatherapist. We see people working towards change, endeavouring to discover who they really are, what ways of life they really want, what is possible and what is not, both in terms of identity and relationships. We see what they have inherited and what they have had written on them. These issues are what we are engaged with in the therapeutic encounter and as therapists they are alive for us too.

Although I am writing over fifteen years after the play was written, the issues are still alive and well; in many ways in current British society there exists a closer relationship with the Victorian roots presented in Act I than when Churchill was writing. In a curious way, therefore, the play is the opposite of dated: it has become more relevant as time has gone on. One day whilst I was writing this chapter, I walked into the local newsagent. Staring out at me from the shelves was the headline, TEACH THEM TO BE BRITISH, and a front page article which began thus:

Children should be taught to be British – whatever their cultural or

ethnic background, the Government's chief adviser on curriculums de-
clared yesterday. . . . He said schools must ensure that all pupils have
the English language at the centre of their knowledge, understand
the country's history and literary heritage, study Christianity and the
classical world – the basis of European civilization.

(Daily Mail 8 July 1995)

After reading this I went back to my work on this play with an even greater
sense of purpose!

The relationship between time, personal experience and change is the key
to the relationship between Acts I and II of this play. In order to explore this,
my discussion of the second act will focus on individual characters, and on
pair and triadic relationships, drawing out some of the themes that I find.

Cathy and Lin

The act opens with Cathy, a little girl of 4, singing crude songs and her
mother, Lin, telling her to stop. Lin suggests that she do a painting. When
Cathy asks what she should paint, Lin's list, punctuated by Cathy's 'no' to
each suggestion, comprises a house, a princess, pirates and spacemen. Last on
the list and strikingly different from the offered stereotypes is 'a car crash
and blood everywhere'. Immediately we are back with the same mechanisms
of Act I, thinly disguised. Lin appears to project her own aggression onto
Cathy. She announces she hates men and she encourages Cathy's aggression
towards little Tommy. She has expectations of how she wants Cathy to be and
in doing so she parallels Clive and his expectations of Edward. The aggressive
values of the patriarchal society of the Empire is here in a different form;
Cathy is exposed to violent images, she is given guns, and encouraged to use
them in her play as aggressively as possible. There is a shift of a kind in that
the little girl is being given access to guns as opposed to being protected from
them as in Act I, but in reality the child is still oppressed by the adults' expectations and needs of what role they want the child to play to support them
in their norms: 'Don't hit him, Cathy, kill him. Point the gun, kiou, kiou,
kiou. That's the way' (Act II, Scene 1).

Lin has a brother in the British Army, stationed in Belfast, who is killed
during the course of the play. We are reminded simultaneously of the shrink-
ing of the old British Empire and of the continued existence of colonialism.
It is as though Lin feels that the way to fight male dominance is to adopt its
tools and hand them on to her daughter – a simplistic view of the route to
change power relationships. However, she incurs her father's wrath by going
on a Troops Out march with her Irish friend, so it is as though part of her is
against violence while the part of her which encourages Cathy's use of the
gun sees it as the way to liberation. Her confusion seems to reflect the weaken-
ing power of patriarchy and its desperate attempts to hold on.

115

Cathy is played by a man. Churchill's cross-gender casting highlights the issues of expectations of males as aggressors and also challenges us to think about gender stereotyping. Churchill's own reasons for this casting are

> partly as a simple reversal of Edward being played by a woman, partly because the size and presence of a man on stage seemed appropriate to the emotional force of young children, and partly, as with Edward, to show more clearly the issues involved in learning what is considered correct behaviour for a girl.

> (Churchill 1983)

I find that it also reinforces the issue of projection onto children; it is almost as though Lin in some way has to see Cathy as male in order to project onto Cathy the images of aggression and encourage her to live them out. This is emphasized for the audience metaphorically by the technique of cross-casting. When Cathy learns that her soldier uncle 'who gave you the blue teddy' has been killed, her response is to ask if she can have his gun. But Cathy does not want to be clearly in either a male or a female stereotype box, for whilst Lin wants her daughter not to conform to traditional women's roles Cathy herself challenges her mother by wanting 'feminine' clothes and is delighted when Betty calls her pretty. She dresses up in Betty's scarf, earrings and hat. Lin's response is

> I give Cathy guns, my mum didn't give me guns. I dress her in jeans, she wants to wear dresses, maybe she should wear dresses. I don't know, I can't work it out. I don't want to.

> (Act II, Scene 3)

We are presented with a picture of the struggle between old and new. Lin is clearly confused. The positions seem very opposed but there is also a suggestion of the possibility of integration or at least of dialogue between the two positions which is hinted at through the mechanism of cross-gender casting.

Lin's attitude to men portrays a deep ambivalence. On the one hand she says she hates them and yet at the same time she is grateful that her ex-husband let her keep the children. When she tells Vic she is grateful, she implies that because she is a lesbian she should not expect to have them, adding, 'I'm grateful he didn't hit me harder than he did (Act II, Scene 1).

There is confusion about what she feels she has rights to, even what feelings she can have. Here the echoes of Ellen, the lesbian governess in Act I, are clearly heard, for while Lin seems to have no difficulty in being open about her sexuality she certainly reacts from the position of the subordinate group in relation to her being allowed to keep the children and seeming to accept the violence of her husband. Another important aspect which Lin points up in the play is how hard it is to effect change. With Act I echoing in our ears she is, perhaps, very direct and realistic about the process of change: 'I've changed who I sleep with, I can't change everything' (Act II, Scene 3).

Victoria

Victoria is Clive's and Betty's daughter from Act I. Married to Martin, she forms a relationship with Lin, who is working class and lesbian. By the end of the play she lives in a *ménage à trois* with her brother Edward and Lin. Clearly she is attempting to break out of the moulds formed for her by her parents and their class. Her education gives her intellectual insight, so that when Lin says she hates men Victoria replies, 'You have to look at it in a historical perspective in terms of learnt behaviour since the industrial revolution' (Act II, Scene 1).

Yet this is not much help when it comes to her trying to be free. She finds herself tied in a deeper way by the old rules of men's and women's place. As a subordinate the only way she can see her way to be free is if the tables are turned and she changes places with Martin and becomes the dominant; there is no middle ground. Having been offered a job in Manchester and finding herself in a dilemma she says,

> Why the hell can't he just be a wife and come with me? Why does Martin make me tie myself in knots? No wonder we can't just have a simple fuck. No, not Martin, why do I make myself tie myself in knots? Lin, I'm not like that with you.
>
> (Act II, Scene 2)

She sees it as an either/or situation; either Martin is at fault or she is. The clue to her dilemma lies in her words to Lin, 'I'm not like that with you.' Her confusion is rooted in the boxes into which men and women have been put. This box does not apply to her relationship with Lin because here there are no rules drawn; what is implied is that a lesbian relationship is not encompassed by the deeply ingrained power relationship and role expectations of her marriage. After checking out that Lin would love her no matter what, she says,

> And I feel apologetic for not being quite so subordinate as I was. I am more intelligent than him. I am brilliant.
>
> (ibid.)

Yet Vicky as a child was subjected to all the stereotypical oppression of women by a society whose name she bears, so how can she be otherwise? We need to remind ourselves that in Act I she was played by a doll. Victoria exemplifies the woman who carries within her the assumptions of the patriarchal society; to step outside that produces such guilt that she cannot truly know what she wants or define a new way of being for herself within her marriage or in relation to it. We never learn whether Vicky does take the job in Manchester, but the end of the play sees her caring for her little boy after Lin and Martin have ended up squabbling about child care, and offering to get her mother an ice-cream. Her lines which preceded this had an elegiac Chekhovian quality: 'When I go to Manchester everything's going to be different' (Act II, Scene 4).

Martin

Martin comes across as someone desperately trying to catch up with change, trying to find out what the rules are and to learn them. He is as confused as Victoria, though his confusion stems from a different perspective. As an erstwhile dominant, he carries within him the old need to dominate but as the rules have changed he does not recognize it as such. Whereas Clive used protection as a way of keeping his wife in the subordinate role, Martin, with the changed mores of a hundred years later, uses sex.

> I am not like whatever percentage of American men have become impotent as a direct result of women's liberation, which I am totally in favour of, more I sometimes think than you are yourself. Nor am I one of your villains who sticks it in, bangs away and falls asleep. My one aim is to give you pleasure. My one aim is to give you rolling orgasms like I do other women. So why the hell don't you have them?
>
> (Act II, Scene 2)

His argument seems designed to invoke guilt in Victoria, perhaps as a way of appeasing his own guilt, which he does not understand because it is the unacknowledged guilt the dominants owe the subordinates, the guilt of an inheritance which we saw clearly portrayed in Act I. He continues,

> My analysis for what it's worth is that despite my efforts you still feel dominated by me. In fact I feel it's very sad you don't feel able to take that job. It makes me feel very guilty. . . . God knows I do everything I can to make you stand on your own two feet. Just be yourself. You don't seem to realize how insulting it is to me that you can't get yourself together.
>
> (ibid.)

In his frustration he ends up talking very like Clive; it appears to be a reflection on him if his wife does not do what is expected of her. The fact that what is expected of her now, which is to be able to be an independent woman within her marriage, whatever that might mean, which is as oppressive in its own way as the Victorian expectation that she should be precisely the opposite passes him by. Where matters sexual are concerned, Martin shows an attitude remarkably like Clive's – simply the terms are different. Women are still to blame, but whereas Clive blamed Mrs Saunders for his twenty-four hour erection, Martin blames Victoria for the opposite. Referring to her having indicated to Martin, while making love, what would give her sexual pleasure, he says:

> I lost my erection last night not because I'm not prepared to talk, it's just that taking in technical information is a different part of the brain and also I don't like to feel that you do it better to yourself.
>
> (ibid.)

118

Taking independence in sexual matters is therefore portrayed again as a political act. Where Clive was terrified of being taken over by women, Martin is terrifed of being made redundant in relation to them. In both cases the fear is of a loss of identity.

His true stance on feminism, in spite of saying he wants to write a book about it, comes out when he stumbles on Edward, Victoria and Lin drunkenly having an orgy in the park.

After having sex with them he says,

> Well that's all right. If all we're talking about is having a lot of sex there's no problem. I was all for the sixties when liberation meant just fucking.

> (Act II, Scene 3)

Through the character of Martin, Churchill shows the difficulty of the old order changing and the new being unclear. Martin is helpless and angry because the old rules do not apply and nobody seems to know the new ones. We are shown both his vulnerability and his deeply ingrained adherence to the old values which conflict with his wish to understand and change.

Edward

Edward is clearly living as a gay man at the outset of the act. He is closeted and tries to keep up a pretence to himself, living in fear of being 'out'.

When Lin openly asks him if he is gay, in a question which is in fact more like a statement, Edward's response is, 'Don't go round saying things like that. I might lose my job', and again 'I wish you hadn't said that about me, it's not true . . . someone might have heard you' (Act II, Scene 1).

We are reminded of Harry's closeting of his own homosexuality in Act I. As it was Harry who first seduced Edward there is an underscoring through the play's dramatic structure of the handing down of attitudes. Through the characters of Lin and Edward we are invited to consider both how much and how little has changed through the era of lesbian and gay liberation. Edward's attempt to find his own identity independently of his parents' expectations of him is shown by his mother Betty's complete denial of her son's occupation as a gardener:

BETTY: Edward is doing something such fun, he's working in the park
  as a gardener. He does look exactly like a gardener.
EDWARD: I am a gardener.

> (Act II, Scene 1)

Betty cannot allow him to have this and has to turn his gardening into a reason for doing something much more glamorous like preparation for a television programme. This inability to allow Edward to be who he is seems like more of the same; his Victorian childhood was consistent in turning him

119

away from himself to be the 'manly' man his father wanted him to be. The pressure of the dominant over the subordinate is here again; this time it is not his sexuality which is being questioned but his job, his status in the adult economic and social world; again it has to be denied, be turned into something else.

Edward lives with his gay lover, Gerry. Their relationship in practice resembles a stereotype of heterosexual marriage:

EDWARD: I might knit. I like knitting.
GERRY: I don't mind if you knit. I don't want to be married.
EDWARD: I do.
GERRY: Well I'm divorcing you.
EDWARD: I wouldn't want to keep a man who wants his freedom.
GERRY: Do stop playing the injured wife, it's not funny.
EDWARD: I'm not playing. It's true.

(Act II, Scene 2)

Edward is searching for a role as well as for a gender identity. He asks to touch his sister Victoria's breasts, saying he would like to have breasts because they are beautiful. He concludes by saying, 'I'm sick of men . . . I think I'm a Lesbian' (ibid.).

The language joke here emphasizes the lack of a place for individual feelings or gender experience. There is no place for Edward so he is trying to invent one. Being pushed into a category as a child, he now tries to find one which fits the reality of his experience. Eventually he lives with Lin and Victoria and acknowedges that he has sex with them, but when he speaks of it this aspect of the relationship seems less important to him than the fact that he can look after the children while the women go out to work. We learn this in a later conversation he has with Gerry.

GERRY: Who are these women you live with?
EDWARD: It's Vic and Lin. They go out to work and I look after the kids.
GERRY: I thought for a moment you said you were living with women.
EDWARD: We do sleep together, yes.

(Act II, Scene 4)

He says a little later that he wouldn't want to leave the children 'at the moment'. We are left with an Edward who is seeking new ways, rejecting the old categories and labels, trying out living through and letting go of the old available identities. He seems to represent an ongoing search for finding a way to be, in a time when some of the old norms have gone, yet their underlying fundamental principles which categorize gender, economic and domestic roles have remained.

Edward and Victoria

Edward is engaged in the task of finding out who he is. The search for his true self is a brave and difficult one. Churchill shows us that both he and his sister Vic, who are the direct contacts with Act I, engage in the uphill struggle to discover their identity through the most fundamental challenge of all, sexual identity. The incestuous relationship has metaphorical significance as a merger of male and female, an exchange of identity, and therefore in the context of this play and its themes the possibility of a change of roles. By rooting this in the family sibling relationship Churchill also roots the challenge for the review of social institutions and political and economic balance of power firmly in the inheritance of the past.

Gerry

Gerry is presented as a stereotype of a pre-AIDS-era gay man, a popular image of a gay man's life style, without the subtleties and infinite complexity of an individual. As such he provides a foil to Edward's constant search to understand who he is and what he wants from life. He is shown as promiscuous and his account of picking up a man on the suburban train and having oral sex between stops smacks of Clive's urgent heterosexual exploits in Act I with Mrs Saunders. Like Clive, Gerry separates out emotion from sex; he doesn't even want to talk to the man. Having described the sexual encounter explicitly, he concludes,

> I opened the door before the train stopped. I told him I live with somebody, I don't want to know. He was jogging sideways to keep up. He said what's your phone number, you're my ideal physical type, what sign of the zodiac are you? Where do you live? Where are you going now? It's not fair. I saw him at Victoria a couple of months later and I went straight down to the end of the platform and I picked up somebody really great who never said a word, just smiled.
>
> (Act II, Scene 2)

He walks out on Edward because their relationship is too confining. As such he challenges a homosexual mimicry of heterosexual institutions but it is Edward, and not Gerry, who attempts to find out other roles and other ways of being in relation to others. We learn through his conversation with Betty near the end of the play that Gerry wants to return to Edward. We are given no reason for this other than Gerry's own assertion that he is 'very fond' of Edward. Maybe we are being asked to consider if Edward's changing lifestyle enables some shifts in Gerry, for at the end of the play he is suggesting visiting Betty. When she has tried to pick him up before realizing his sexual orientation, he says to her, 'I could still come and see you.' A friendship with this older heterosexual woman is possible. He is, in other words, presented as a more rounded character than at the beginning. There is an interesting moment when Gerry and Harry from Act I pick each other up – again a reminder of continuity of habit and life style; that Gerry has his roots in the past too, however boldly modern his overt description of sexual encounter.

Betty

The optimism of the play, which is embedded above all in the character of Betty, lies in the message that change, though slow and impeded in its progress by social, cultural and psychological dinosaurs, is possible. She has been the most repressed and conditioned and her ability to change is perhaps the least likely of all the characters. It is therefore all the more refreshing to be given the view that if Betty can change then maybe there is hope.

In the early part of Act II she comes out with the kinds of statements which we might expect of her. She is the one who is a constant reminder of Act I not only because of her attitudes but also because of her direct reference to Africa; she says to Lin,

> Children have such imagination, it makes them so exhausting. . . . I had help with my children. One does need help. That was Africa of course so there wasn't a servant problem.

> (Act II, Scene 1)

When she speaks she appears simultaneously as an anachronism and as a representative of many contemporary upper-class English women who still speak in Betty's tones. This draws together the past and the present, making the past alive and well and living in late-twentieth-century England. When she comes out with comments such as,

> What a pretty child just like a little doll – you can't be certain how they'll grow up. I think Victoria's very pretty but she doesn't make the most of herself, do you darling, it's not the fashion I'm told but there are still women who dress out of *Vogue*.

> (ibid.)

The words could well be overheard in Harrods' tearoom. We can hear them being said today and, through the dramatic structure of the play, we hear the overtones of Vic who as little Vicky in Act I was played by a doll. The message from Betty is therefore that little girls should be seen and not heard, be pretty and grow up into women who dress out of *Vogue*. Betty appears unchanged. Yet in the middle of a long rambly speech she slips in the fact that she is leaving Clive. This is a momentous piece of news which, slipped into the speech as it is, could almost go unheard. Then she reflects that there is no job she could do; considering gardening she says, 'Everything I touch shrivels straight up' (ibid.).

122

Although she is talking about plants the words have echoes of the emptiness within of a woman whose life has been only and in all ways that of the subordinate. In this position self-deprecation is inherent and the words seem to come from a deeply painful place within her.

Betty's credibility as a dramatic character lies in the fact that many of her learnt behaviours remain at the end alongside some very important changes of attitude to herself. The message is much like that of Nora in Ibsen's *A Doll's House*; if she can start to look at herself, her relationship with the external world will be begin to be different too. Betty has so much to unlearn. Her racism, for instance, is so ingrained.

> CATHY: I know a girl got her ears pierced and she's three. She's got real gold.
> BETTY: I don't expect she's English, darling . . .
>
> (ibid.)

In leaving Clive she is undoing not just a lifetime with her husband and her subordinate role but all the weight of the British Empire and its overt and covert oppression. Her inability to value women as important is a reflection of the subordinate group's emulation of the dominant's values:

> BETTY: I've never been so short of men's company that I've had to bother with women's.
> LIN: Don't you like women?
> BETTY: They don't have such interesting conversations as men. There has never been a woman composer of genius. They don't have a sense of humour. They spoil things themselves with their emotions. I can't say I do like women very much, no.
> LIN: But you're a woman.
> BETTY: There's nothing says you have to like yourself.
>
> (Act II, Scene 2)

Later in the act we find Betty getting herself a job, in spite of having said how frightened she is. Shortly afterwards comes Betty's speech about her discovery and appreciation of herself as a sexual being. She has talked of her fear of being on her own, 'I'll never be able to manage. If I can't even walk down the street by myself. Everything looks so fierce' (ibid.).

Her discovery of herself as a sexual person apart from being with a man is linked to finding her own body, her own identity and reassuring herself that she does exist.

> I thought if Clive wasn't looking at me there wasn't a person there. And one night in bed in my flat I was so frightened I started touching myself. I thought my hand might go through into space.
>
> (Act II, Scene 4)

Since having been caught masturbating as a child she had never attempted it again until this time of which she is speaking. As she describes both discovering her own sexuality grounded in a solid body that is herself, and bringing herself to orgasm she says,

> I felt angry with Clive and angry with my mother and I went on and on defying them . . . afterwards I thought I'd betrayed Clive. My mother would kill me. But I felt triumphant because I was a separate person from them. And I cried because I didn't want to be.
>
> (ibid.)

This moving account of a 65-year-old woman finding and giving herself permission to be an individual and to be a sexual woman independent of men also shows us the price to be paid for such defiance. To separate from her mother and her husband brings back the old persecutory anxiety of the infant; she fears they will punish and annihilate her. 'My mother would kill me' if she dares to become separate from her. In Betty's claiming her sexuality for herself she feels she betrays her husband, the man who at the beginning of Act I had said of her, 'Everything she has she owes to me' (Act I, Scene 2). But, as Howe Kritzer points out, 'her attainment of greater sexual freedom follows the achievement of economic dependence, supporting Victoria's glib but significant statement that 'you can't separate fucking and economics' (Howe Kritzer 1991: 127). The link between gender, economic and sexual politics is clear as Betty moves firstly into divorce, then into earning her own money, and then into sexual independence. Having gone through these stages she is then in a position to begin to experiment with making relationships. She tries to pick up Gerry; whilst this is a reminder of her attraction to Harry in Act I (for in neither instance does she realize the man is gay) it also shows a Betty who is attempting to make new relationships. When Gerry says, 'I could still come and see you' after Betty realizes her mistake, she replies, 'So you could, yes', as though her mind discovers a brand-new possibility which she finds she can accept. This is very different from the Betty of Act I who idealizes Harry and denigrates herself; it is a more real, more whole Betty who struggles with the difficulties inherent in creating an independent life for herself:

> I was married for so many years it's quite hard to know how to get acquainted. But if there isn't a right way to do things you have to invent one.
>
> (Act II, Scene 4)

It is in Betty that the possibilities of change are exemplified more, I think, than with any other character. Her defiance feels to her like a revolution and to Clive it represents nothing short of that. In the final words of the play Clive appears for the first and only time in Act II. He says,

> You are not that sort of woman Betty. I can't believe you are. I can't feel

the same about you as I did. And Africa is to be communist I suppose. I
used to be proud to be English. There was a high ideal.

(ibid.)

Clive seems to be implying that Betty as mother/madonna has dared to shake
off that role. His juxtaposition of this with his comment about communism
implies that the collapse of the old order of patriarchy is the responsibility of
her – of 'woman'. Betty's progress, and Clive's demise rests, as Baker Miller
said, writing around the same time as Churchill, on authenticity and subordination being totally incompatible (Baker Miller 1976: 103). Betty, by
striving to become more authentic, automatically becomes less subordinate
and vice versa.

A critic speaks

The difficulties facing the individual who desires to break through the defences of the dominant group are presented forcibly both through the character of Betty and by the reappearance of Clive at the end of Act II. What
Betty is up against is tellingly revealed in the following review extract of the
play's first performance at Dartington.

> Julie Covington . . . made the most convincing tired matriarch who, fail-
> ing to pick up a young man in the modern permissive playground of the
> second [half of the show] turns for the first time in her life to erotic self-
> satisfaction. Her account of this was really rather moving.
> (*Drama. The Quarterly Review* 1979)

The reviewer appears not to have listened to Betty's speech, which he patroniz-
ingly describes as 'really rather moving'. He seems to have entirely missed
these words with which she begins:

> I used to think Clive was the one who liked sex. But then I found I
> missed it. I used to touch myself when I was very little, I thought I'd
> invented something wonderful. I used to do it to go to sleep with or
> cheer myself up, and one day it was raining and I was under the kit-
> chen table, and my mother saw me with my hand under my dress rub-
> bing away, and she dragged me out so quickly I hit my head and it bled
> and I was sick, and nothing was said, and I never did it again till this
> year.

Clearly the violent sexual oppression of the little girl has entirely escaped the
reviewer and with it the whole point of Betty having projected her sexuality
onto Clive, never being able to value her own body as 'wonderful'. I leave the
reader to muse upon the implications of the description of Betty as a 'tired
matriarch'. The fact that he has got the order of events in the play wrong –
Betty picks up Gerry *after* this speech – further show the reviewer's lack of

attention to the stages in Betty's development and the relationship between these and the political issues of patriarchy.

He continues,

> Meanwhile Jim Hopper, another fine actor, who played the randy mother on whom the sun never sets in part one, turned into the park attendant, that same Edward, no less . . . now a fully fledged homosexual. Ms Churchill gives an adroit and amusing exposure of what goes on behind the masks of conventional behaviour. Playwrights who readily avail themselves of the freedom to show things that used to be regarded as disgusting and to mention things that used to be regarded as unmentionable are nearly always utterly humourless about it; or else they have a 'black' sense of humour that leaves me white with boredom.

The review by default reveals the need for such plays; I wonder what the writer means by a fully fledged homosexual and am curious as to his projections onto Betty who is both 'randy mother' and 'tired matriarch'. His own racism seems apparent in his cheap joke about black; his blatantly pejorative use of the word 'black' when writing about a play where the white use of power over black is clearly pointed up I find astonishing. His praise of the play is that it is 'genuinely funny', yet earlier he has described it as being 'a little bit like a Farjeon revue'. I am left wondering about this particular male reviewer's envy of the highly original and political female playwright. Does he, like Clive, find women and the dark continent terrifying? I suspect that what cannot be 'mentioned' is that Churchill shows that there are cracks in the door which separates dominants from subordinates. The play must therefore be reduced to the status of a light, quirky piece of comedy, rather than accorded its true description of satire which points to societal ills through the means of wit and comedy and thereby invites change.

Conclusion

The powerful theatricality of Act I with its Victorian costumes, Union Jack flag, rhyming couplets, and high satire remains strongly in the mind and ear and eye well after the play is over. Whilst Act II shows a much greater celebration of open sexual expression, there are attendant confusions as we have seen which are still tied to systems of oppression. The brutality of the references to local African warrings in Act I and the killing of Joshua's parents over whom he is not supposed to grieve is picked up in Act II by Lin's British Army soldier brother and the father's denying of Lin's right to attend the funeral. The paternalistic society's denial of basic human rights and the right to feelings is powerfully presented by these metaphors and we are led to see in the play's ending another image where the right to feeling and being, and the honouring of the possibility of a different relationship between past and present, are possible. This image is the embrace of Betty of Act I and Betty of Act II. It roots

the possibilities of change firmly in the restructuring of dominant/subordi-
nate roles. Betty of Act I is played by a man and Betty of Act II by a woman
(with the added significance of the original production's casting of Betty of
Act I becoming Edward in Act II and vice versa). The final image the audience is given therefore is a reminder of the complexity of the male and female
aspects of human personality and of the possibility of new and different relationships between men and women. With this possibility there is the chance
that the dominant/subordinate paradigm could be transformed and in so
doing the organization and functioning of society be deeply affected towards
a culture of less oppression; one in which respect is given to the importance
of 'relationship' as enabling authenticity, as Baker Miller points out (1976:
103).

The overall impression I am left with is that, at the time Churchill was writing, what emerged from the actors' workshops and the writer's pen was primarily a presentation of the politics of sex and gender. Both race and class
issues seem to lie in the background; they await awakening. Lin and Gerry are
both working class while Victoria, Edward and Betty carry with them their
old upper-middle-class inheritance and Martin is middle class. But class
issues are not overly exploited in the writing of Act II. There is even less attention paid to issues of race, and what Joshua stands for in Act I, as both oppressed black man and servant, has altogether disappeared in Act II. Whilst
the cross-casting of the black servant being played by a white actor in Act I
seemed to support the condemnation of white oppression of black, the exclusion of the possibility of a black actor taking a white role in Act II begs some
uncomfortable questions. Whilst more recently black/white cross-casting has
become more familiar since this play was first produced, and mixed cast
groups are appearing in theatre companies, this is by no means yet the norm.
My own reading of a text, which tuned to the resonances of metaphor, leads
me to the remark that Lin makes to Cathy who has covered her brightly
painted picture in black paint: 'What do you do that for silly? It was nice' (Act
II, Scene 1).

Is Cathy meant to infer from this that black is not 'nice'? Is Churchill here
showing us an example of the heredity of colonialism where unconscious
prejudice lurks in language and assumptions. It is hard to believe that Act II
takes place in the multi-racial London of the late 1970s – or is it? Does the
very omission of race make its own point? I believe it does, but whether or not
this is intentional is not clear. Howe Kritzer sums up the message of Act
II: 'while sexual patterns show themselves somewhat resistant to change, patterns of societal power are yet more resistant, proving the adaptability of the
prevailing power structure in maintaining itself' (1991: 125). Are not actors,
writers and audiences part of that very society and as such must therefore
have their blind spots?

CONTEMPORARY IMPLICATIONS FOR DRAMATHERAPY

As therapists we are not exempt either; these themes are inside us all. Our own prejudices and stereotypes, our own struggles with issues of identity, our own experience as gendered sexual beings, our own race and ethnicity, our own cultural and political history and heritage are present in our interactions with our clients. These issues must be engaged with in our work if our understanding of our own projections and counter-transference is to bear fruit in the therapeutic encounter. If not, might there not be a danger of clients being a subordinate group to the dominant group called professional and therapist?

With these concerns in mind I invited my peers in a regional group of dramatherapists to participate in a workshop led by myself and another member who was interested in text work. Further discussions were held a few weeks after the event with some of the participants. What became clear was how rich *Cloud Nine* is and how much more we could mine its abundance, given time. What follows is a distillation of just some of our discoveries. I focus mainly on the two areas of role and choice and invite some speculation on the theme of dominance and subordination. I shall not make very specific links with the text or speculate on individuals' verbatim comments but rather let them lie between the play and the experience of the reader so that new connections can be made by each person as individual and professional within their own contexts.

My first point clarifies the way in which the theatrical qualities of a dramatic text can move us quickly and deeply into feelings and experiences which can help us to reflect on our practice as dramatherapists. In this instance I am indebted to my colleague, Jenny McMahon, for coming up with a structure for part of the workshop which achieved exactly this. It needs to be noted that the structure which she devised was chosen with peer-training in mind. The group was formed from members of a dramatherapists' group who meet to exchange ideas of theory and practice, raise issues, support and be supported, challenge and be challenged. The structure used was therefore designed with this particular peer-training aim; its purpose was educational not therapeutic.

She asked the workshop members to discuss together which role they would like to play. The chairs for the characters had been set up with appropriate costumes on each. The group was then asked to get into a line in any order and then, in that order, proceed to the chairs, pin on the costume they found on the chair they arrived at and sit down. Without further discussion they were invited to begin reading the play. They were therefore unable to read the role they had originally chosen.

In the discussions a few weeks later the picture which emerged was very illuminating. That particular structure had been experienced as very powerful. The qualities of theatre, in this case especially costume and space used simultaneously with speaking and hearing the text, had undoubtedly caused this effect. What was commented on was the extreme sense of restriction and of having no choice, but of having to cope with the feelings this evoked by swallowing or denying them. The Victorian costumes had been experienced as 'sculpted, containing and restricting'. The wearing of the costumes had enabled participants physically and emotionally to feel the restrictions of those characters in that time and place – the world of the British Empire – but contemporary experience was also strongly evoked. It made one member think, 'how vividly it brought to life how each role prescribed for us by society has its own uniform'.

The use of space and directions to actors created a similar response. In the words of one participant, 'I was Betty, squashed in next to Clive; squashed in affected how you could relate to one another as characters.' She went on to show how this feeling of restriction both reinforced and was reinforced by the costume, 'I felt strait-jacketed, made to fit in physically, made to fit in in the right place, and this was also because of the costume.'

This feeling of restriction, made possible by theatrical means, led the group members in that particular discussion straight into their own everyday experience at work; one dramatherapist said she had been 'accused of dressing like an administrator', at which point the group began to look at the institutionalization of clothes and how challenging dress is interpreted in a paternalistic setting as challenging the institution itself.

The use of the word 'strait-jacket' initiated a thought-provoking discussion on the issues of the status of patients in the mental health service, and of health care professionals. The question of dominant and subordinate groups which the play explores reached out to the work context of the dramatherapists and then into our own work via the workshop experience. Here aspects of the work on Act I linked with work on Act II. Though less focused on strong theatrical technique, which reflects the difference in style between Acts I and II, the drama methods and structures used echoed the themes of the morning's work on Act I.

As part of the afternoon's focus on Act II, I asked the group to go into pairs and label themselves 'A' and 'B'. 'A's were to go into the adjacent room and identify a character they would like to focus on. 'B's stayed in the room and I told them that they would be playing the role of therapist to a character. I then went to the 'A's to ascertain which character they had chosen and then asked the 'therapists' which character they would like to work with. The 'characters' were thus assigned their 'therapists' to whom they went for a twenty-minute interview. In the setting up of this workshop structure no one dissented. I had expected that there might be some resistance; I was aware that a group of therapists playing the role of therapist 'in front of' other therapists (in that the characters were played by their real-life peers) might not be the most welcome way of spending a Friday afternoon away from work. In the feedback session some people mentioned this and seemed as bemused as I was that they meekly complied with something they had not entirely wanted to do.

What I was left wondering was, were our Act II selves unconsciously following through the patterns laid down by our Act I experience? Had I, as the leader of the second part of the workshop, unconsciously echoed the lack of choice which my colleague had – in order to bring home the essence and quality of Act I – quite deliberately given to the actors in the morning session. In Act II of the play there is apparent choice, as I have tried to show in my discussion of the play, but how real this is is another matter, because the strings of the past still have their hold and can manipulate our movement in the present. In this case the strings of Act I held us all in our patterns. Workshop leaders became dominants and group members subordinates. In the case of the therapist/client role-plays, I had given the workshop participants some choice in that the group playing characters could choose their character. The therapists could choose which of the available characters they worked with. Did both groups somehow feel that if they had a little choice they had to put up with the rest, in other words there could be no ground for refusal?

In the discussion session a few weeks later this whole issue was raised. Some people realized that they had convinced themselves that they had had a choice – somehow it felt unbearable not to have had. When the reality of their compliance was really looked at what emerged was 'an acceptance of the agenda you're born with', particularly as women; another said that there was some comfort in being given a role and not having to choose one, which has direct bearing on the play where, as we have seen, the characters of Act II find choice or its possibility very confusing and daunting. One person's words were, when describing being assigned a role, 'There's some comfort in not having to take responsibility for the choice you make', yet alongside that, 'I remember feeling powerless, a feeling of confusion – what might I be made to do?' Here the feelings experienced within the roles reflect the complexity of this issue which the play in its entirety explores.

In the issue of choice the sensation of being silenced was very strong for some people. One person realized that she had never felt fully involved in Act II because she had taken the role of the doll who represents Victoria in Act I. 'The issues of Act II are about sexuality. As the doll I couldn't breathe or speak so how could I become engaged with sexuality?' Although she had been given the opportunity to de-role, on reflection she felt that she had done this insufficiently as the message of the silenced Victoria had proved to be so strong.

Yet another person related how, in the morning workshop, she had felt extremely angry. 'I could feel the hostility rising; I felt, "I could be reading that part because I could do it so much better."' She said she found herself totally incapable of voicing any of these feelings. Of the afternoon session she said that she had again felt she could not refuse. 'I just couldn't say; I bore the unbearable, I just didn't have a choice.' This had left her reflecting on aspects of her own process.

If the workshop leaders were indeed playing the dominants and the members the subordinates then unconsciously we were all reflecting and living out the issues of the play. I found it both an exciting and thought-provoking experience that even with a group of peers used to meeting and working together four or five times a year, these dynamics of heritage and context were so easily tapped. It reinforced my view that dramatic text is a stimulating and effective tool for challenging learning and thinking about our practice.

So what connections did we make as dramatherapists as we thought about our work with clients?

One person said she found the play

> points up the rigidity we carry within us, such as the predetermined roles – 'You've sat in that chair and that's Ellen so you are Ellen.' That feels very familiar in terms of dealing with clients, helping us to understand the defining box of the client.

Another thought was how we could use the experience people had had of being assigned particular chairs; this raises questions about the physical settings in which we work, the furniture, the way it is arranged, who sits where and what is the spatial relationship between client and therapist and what messages are given and received between them, especially in terms of power relationships.

The person who had contacted the sabotaging part of her said, 'As a therapist I believe I give people choices but do I? As a therapist am I seductive and the client thinks, "She's a therapist, she knows what she's doing, I'll do it."' For dramatherapists, whose intervention involves much suggesting of activity and the initiation of 'doing' rather than interpretative comment, this is an important point.

One participant wrote down the following thoughts some while after the workshop; here what she experienced as the limitations of the play served to trigger thoughts about therapeutic practice,

> What strikes me now, reflecting back, is how satire encourages splitting by denouncing by default everything to do with empire/flag/colonization etc. This works as theatre and as a political statement but has interesting issues therapeutically as without some attempt to integrate the complexities and contradictions there can be no moving on. The stereotyping of the characters in one way robs them of their unique personality, hopes and fears and so arguably victimizes them all over again. This came home to me during the role play when as 'therapist' working with an older woman (who had been the betrayed young wife [Betty]) I realized I was expecting that she would speak of her husband and events in a depressed or angry or anxious way. Instead of which there was much

warmth and an acceptance of that was how things were in those days. This highlighted the importance of listening to the client and respecting their perspective.

She adds that the client might be denying 'on a massive scale' and that this would in time have to be explored. This theme was written about by another participant; the play and the practical work on it had clearly stimulated thoughts about the therapist's assumptions and enabled an empathy with the client's position.

The structure of asking us to choose a character we wanted to read and then being told to take on the part of the character whose clothes we were sitting on was for me a freeing one. I had chosen a part with fewer lines and a peripheral place in the family and found myself playing Betty, who fits neither of these categories. This has made me wonder about the freedom for the characters within their clearly defined roles, that paradoxically the removal of choice and control, as paralleled in the workshop, gave Betty more freedom because whatever she did would be contained within this tight social framework. I was struck, however, by the cost of this for Betty in her adoption of a childlike role with Clive and the sibling rivalry with Joshua – Clive as authoritarian father to them both. I also felt the powerlessness of Betty within the constraints of her position. . . . In the second part of the workshop I was asked to take on the role of a character (I can't remember whether I chose it). I took on Edward who had to go and see a therapist in the room next door. I do remember feeling apprehension at the impossibility of this task. I was surprised to find that after hastily reminding myself of some of Edward's lines I was able to take on the role of the adult Edward. In Edward I felt very strongly the legacy of the restraints of his childhood. The adult Edward, as I portrayed him, had developed a rigidity of not allowing himself feelings, of not admitting to needing, and to a series of stock phrases to hide behind. This was reflected in my posture of rigidity with repetitive knee-tapping mannerisms. He re-peated often the importance of the doll in his childhood, but was not really able to get the therapist to hear this; her words were there but he did not feel he was being heard. In my (therapist's) mind at the time was the memory that the play describes what would be termed by British law a sexually abusive relationship between the 9-year-old Edward and the adult Harry Bagley and I wondered if this was in J's mind (she played the therapist), that perhaps she was assuming or had been told that this was why Edward was seeking therapy. For me playing Edward it was striking how Edward did not see this as a problem but spoke of Harry as a friend of his childhood who had provided escapism with his talk of adventures and who was fondly remembered. For me as a therapist this served as a strong reminder of the importance of the clients' view of

132

their own world and naming things at their own pace. I was using the term 'sexual abuse' as a therapist, not as Edward who would probably have multi-layered disclosures to make and personal realisations to come and who may never see the relationship with Harry Bageley as sexually abusive.

As Edward I felt the transferential relationship, with the therapist as father; J and I discussed afterwards how this had emphasized Edward's restraint, fear and rigidity – the childhood continues.

Any of the characters in Act II might appear as real people in a therapy group. In our work on the play, short though it was, we began to glimpse how themes of sexuality and gender, patriarchy and the relationship between a dominant and a subordinate group are all part of the issue of the struggle towards identity which cannot be seen in isolation from its historical context and the societal mores in which both client and therapist participate. This play can help us in moving towards a greater appreciation, at a feeling as well as intellectual level, of the issues involved in that struggle that contextualize the relationship between client and therapist. Some of these issues are perhaps obvious but I think worth restating here; the experience of people from other cultures being treated in Britain by those professionals who may know little or nothing of the cultural mores and history of the clients, the homophobia of many therapy and analytic training organizations, the greater availability of therapy for those who can afford it, the gender imbalance in the professions of psychology and psychiatry – a lot of men at the top and a lot of women at the bottom (Ussher and Nicholson 1992) – the lack of men and predominance of women practitioners in the arts therapies which is still largely a white middle-class profession. The professional and clinical implications of all these situations, and many related issues, *Cloud Nine* can remind us to continually attend to.

6

'THAT WAY MADNESS LIES'
Thursday's Child by Daphne Thomas

> This night will turn us all into fools and madmen.
> *(King Lear)*

In Chapter 4 we found Beatie, emerging from a chrysalis, on her way, perhaps, to becoming a butterfly, going out into the world to find out who she really is. And our exploration of *Cloud Nine* brought us sharply into contact with issues of repression and heredity and ensuing confusion. The play which forms the centrepiece of this chapter challenges us to look at the more frightening aspects of the issues of identity. Another woman in a different trap whom therapists, working with those who suddenly cannot hold it all together any more, will surely recognize. The aim of this chapter is two-fold; the detailed discussion of the play is intended to link with the reader's own experience of working with clients like this protagonist, for she speaks with the clear voice of authenticity; as therapists we must also be aware of our relationship to our own madness – our exploration of it, our denial of it, our fears of it, etc. The second aim will be apparent in the section on practical application which takes us into the area of acting and the process of play production. As we explore a play in which the protagonist splits herself into two characters we ask – what is it like to be an actor, to be two people at once; what are the implications for the mental health and general well-being of the actor; what are some of the implications for the director and the rehearsal process and how can dramatherapy address itself to these issues?

THE PLAY

In Chapter 1 I suggested that dramatic text is a way in which we can develop the language of dramatherapy, a way of developing our own insight. *Thursday's Child* is an example of this for it provides a mirror of madness ; it is part of the language in which clinical 'case work' can be described. Lest any reader be tempted to think that I include it as an example of a text to be worked with with those whose conditions it mirrors, I hope the powerful nature of work-

134

ing with the play which is manifest in the section on working with actors will
be enough of a deterrent.

Résumé of the play

Carol is a single woman of 35. She cares singlehandedly for her elderly mother
who is now bedridden, in their home adjacent to a boutique which they have
owned for many years and which Carol now runs, in a seaside town on the
Yorkshire coast. Carol's half-sister and half-brother are older than her and
have long since left home. Her mother was a widow when Carol was born to
her illegitimately. The identity of her father has never been disclosed. To
others Carol is a supreme coper; a prosperous businesswoman, capable and
independent. But there are deep undercurrents in her life. She is torn between
her love for her mother and her resentment at having been the least favourite
child. She is deeply insecure because of her ignorance of her true identity. Her
longing to lead the life she would really like to lead is crippled by her insecurity
and her urge to care for her mother. As a woman she has been consigned from
birth to a role which gets defined in terms of others. Desperately she wants to
be acknowledged for herself yet doesn't know that self. To find herself amidst
the contradictions of her life Carol has 'far to go' as in the old rhyme from
which the title is taken. Her journey to do so takes her into a fantasy life that
she has constructed around the shop dummy, whom she calls Sylvie. Carol
invests Sylvie with a glamorous and charismatic personality; Carol shares in it
by regularly changing identities with her. In this way she awakens an inner
world of free exploration, images and movement which enable her intermit-
tently to escape her everyday circumstances. However, her illusionary world
is a borderline place between sanity and madness. By being Sylvie, Carol
leads the life she has chosen for herself as well as her everyday life. But
events force a crisis in which she must face the question of which is fantasy
and which is reality and make a last desperate effort to reach and hold her
own identity, or sink in the attempt. When asked out by a man she goes as
Sylvie, believing that Carol stays at home to look after her mother. She returns
and tells 'Carol' that she has pushed the man into the sea, never to be tied by
him and never to lose him. She then discovers that her mother has died in the
night. This finally pushes her over the edge and she exchanges places with
Sylvie, breaking the dummy and then putting it as Carol into her mother's bed.
The play ends with her bound by her 'invalid', changing the name of her shop
and appearing to continue with a 'new start'. (Adapted from the playwright's
synopsis of the play.)

Thursday's Child by Daphne Thomas brings us passionately, lyrically and
frighteningly into the world of madness. It invites the audience to look into
the looking glass of the theatre and be disturbed by the reflection. The play
shows Carol, the efficient businesswoman, the one who copes superbly

looking after both her shop and her mother who is totally disabled by a stroke. In this it shows the face Carol gives to the world, the face of many women in similar situations, apparently independent in the external world and yet utterly dependent within themselves, tied by the need to belong, to be needed, to be loved. Carol knows this and rails against it: 'there must be a cure to this habit of belonging'.

But her intellectual knowledge of her situation cannot save her, neither can her savage humour. The wars raging inside her make her ultimately vulnerable to a breakdown of her personality. And even then she attempts to maintain a mask of normality. As such the play is both the story of one ordinary woman who keeps a shop in a seaside town in England, and at the same time it is a metaphor for the way in which people cope with deep pain, conflict and early damaging experiences by splitting off parts of themselves and finding a way to live with the splits. Whilst in its literal story the play is about breakdown, in its metaphorical sense it is also about the everyday reality of millions; in an earlier draft of the play the actor speaks, in a role called Actor, to the audience:

> We shall find Carol in your darkest places; places guarded by your strongest taboos – the taboos you have imposed upon yourselves. She haunts the most neglected rooms in the remotest corners of your hearts – rooms you seldom enter – where you dare not linger – where you have laid aside, in silence, your greatest sadness.

So what is it that holds Carol from herself and how can we see, in her, the principle of withholding ourselves from ourselves?

Firstly there is her relationship with her mother. Carol has always craved the love she perceived her mother bestowing on her half-brother and sister. Having never had this and yet still wanting it she finds herself bound in an attachment to her mother which she both hates and wants. We learn of the mental cruelty to which her mother subjected her when she was a child, and we see how in the present, as a woman of 35, she still desperately needs to stay close to her mother. The complexities of this relationship and its effects form the substance of the play.

Let us set Carol's experience in the framework of that of many women, as expressed by Orbach:

> Too often a little girl's attempts at separation take place under conditions of opposition from mother and consequent fear. There is no feeling of strength and wholeness to make the world outside seem exciting; instead it is tantalizing and frightening. In some ways it echoes aspects of the painful inner world of the child's reality. Mother is still a focal point; she encourages some attempts at separation – even forces them – and thwarts others. Because the little girl part of the girl's psyche has been split off, it continues to be deprived of nourishment and contact it

136

needs for maturation. The girl both fears and longs to remerge with mother and to be held and cared for, but the inconsistencies in the relationship push her towards separation, with the construction of boundaries between self and the little girl inside. These are in some sense false boundaries; they do not come from an integrated ego structure which can clearly distinguish between self and the outside world, but are internal boundaries separating one part of herself from another part and keeping the little girl inside shut away from the outside world.

At the same time, the daughter's sense of self is fused with her sense of mother, so that in her attempts to separate from mother she may not know who she is. Trying to be her own person, she is nevertheless confused about where she begins and mother ends. In her early development she has taken her mother into her, and now, because she does not have a strong sense of her own separate self, the sense of the mother inside her may outweigh her own independent identity.

(Eichenbaum and Orbach 1983: 53–4)

As we explore Carol and her life we see how uncannily these statements are borne out.

Let us look first at the vivid pictures Thomas presents of the relationship between mother and daughter as it is lived out by them both. As Carol speaks to her mother we learn about why the present relationship is as it is because we are given a clear picture of Carol's childhood experience of her mother. I would stress that the psychotic breakdown the character eventually experiences would indicate that these memories Carol has of her mother reveal that her mother would have behaved in a similar way to her as a tiny infant. The way we see Carol behaving towards her mother shows the internalized mother at work, the 'bad mother' which Carol has introjected. This internalized mother reveals Carol's mother as inconsistent, caring for the infant in a very basic physical way, sadistic in her mixture of giving and withholding, and using her daughter to fulfil her own needs. Carol has clear memories, too, of being humiliated at the hands of her mother.

Carol therefore treats her mother with a mixture of sadism, care and need and the element of humiliation is also present in the day-to-day relationship with the speechless bedridden old woman. These elements are particularly clear in the scene where she taunts her mother with a letter from her half-sister, Janice.

I've got something nice for you this afternoon. Guess what it is? You can't can you? I'm not surprised either. It's so long since you had one of these. And this one has come so quick. Ah, now you know, don't you. Or you think you do. Shall I tell you then? Shall I? . . . (*Starts to draw the letter out of her pocket*) OK, I will . . . (*but stops*) But shall I tell you now or later? Tears? Oh really!

Then she reminds her mother of the guessing games her mother used to play with her which were much more like tricks played on her than games played with her:

> I had to guess which hand. You'd have some sweets in it – or silver – even a note sometimes: but I always guessed wrong, didn't I. Whatever it was was always in the other hand – so I never won it. You all used to think that was terribly funny. I don't remember any tears then. Not from me. Certainly not from me. You're lucky really . . . (*Takes a letter out and waves it in front of her mother*) 'Cos supposing I hid it? Suppose I left you to find it – like you did with my Easter egg, remember? That was a good game wasn't it? But we can't play that now, can we? Not with you in bed, and there wouldn't be time anyway. It takes hours to find things sometimes doesn't it. Even when you're trying very hard, even when you're desperate to find them! Like I used to be.

When her letter makes it clear that the mother cannot go and stay with the selfish and hypocritical Janice, the old woman weeps, to which Carol's reaction is,

> Oh – more tears! So she's hurt you, has she? Well it's your own fault. You should have seen what she was like. . . . Your little girl! Just ask yourself who really was your little girl. Who did your shopping and your washing, and made the beds? Who sang when you were happy and hurt for you when you were sad? Me! That's who . . . Me! And I'm still bloody doing it aren't I? God knows why, but I'm still bloody doing it! I'm all upset – I'm upset because Janice has hurt you. (*Kneeling by the bed*) Oh don't cry Mum – don't. You don't need her. I'm here. You don't need anyone else. And what would I do if you went to live with Janice, eh? I've always had you.

This is the centre of Carol's dilemma. Forced into an early and lonely independence yet craving the love of her mother, she still waits for what she can never have. She is aware of the trap she is in and therefore sees all committed relationships as a trap, where one loves and longs for but is betrayed. Her mother's withholding of her love and esteem for Carol means that Carol has never been able to develop the capacity to love and esteem herself, an essential part of forming a sense of self. As Orbach says, 'in her early development she has taken her mother into her' and cannot achieve her own separate identity. In Carol's case the kind of mother she has taken in is one who humiliated and in an emotional sense abandoned her. This is the 'mother within', which becomes the persona she must live out in place of a developed self. Mollon (1993) points out that both Wilshire and Mahler, coming from the perspectives of phenomenological philosophy, and psychoanalytic developmental research respectively, see the self 'as not given but gradually achieved'. Through Carol's perpetual relating of her childhood experiences we can see the impos-

138

sibility of her ever achieving a sense of self, for there was nothing to redeem her from her situation. Achievement implies a process over time. It is Carol's fate to be stuck. Her life is like a flawed old '78' record played by a needle which sticks right at the beginning, moving round but always coming back to stick at the same crack. It can never release its music.

Another dynamic of her internal world is Carol's envy. This envy permeates her relationship with her mother whom she attacks – safely now that her mother is incapable of replying. In her attacks she shows how she admired her mother and here we see how linked was this admiration with humiliation and how envy finds its place in this constellation. She remembers holding out her arms, 'straight, shoulder high', for her mother to wind her gold and silver crocheting wool; she remembers her mother's hands with her long red nails, 'I was so proud of those nails'; she saw her mother's hands as 'magic hands that conjured shimmering, glamorous clothes . . . magic hands.' But she goes on,

> But I had to watch out for those hands! If I let the yarn drop or tangle, you'd slap out. You were very free with your paws, weren't you mother. Slap and snap – that was you.

We see the image of the little girl adoring the apparently powerful, glamorous mother, and we see too the humiliation of that same little girl by that powerful adult. But at the end of the speech she says something which shows her mother's insecurity as the base for the power she wielded, 'You were powerful: the awful power of the determinedly dependent.' She lists her mother's success in getting everyone's submission, 'The whole world had to be your foil and your handmaid.'

At the end of this speech in which she lists her mother's triumphs, 'the extra cake slipped into the bag; the free bit of extra ham on the quarter', she asks, 'Why? Because you expected it, that's why. You were wonderful mother! You were wonderful! You were the Snow Queen and I adored you.'

These are all reasons for Carol's envy. And because she can never move out of that position of feeling inferior to her mother she too is determinedly dependent. She in turn, therefore, wields the same power over her mother now that the tables are turned. The mother helpless in the bed is a mirror image of the tiny infant Carol, serving to remind us of the very early relationship between mother and daughter where the patterns for the future were set. This time Carol, on the surface, has the power and her mother is the powerless one; however the role reversal is more apparent than real for although her mother is powerless, speechless and at her daughter's mercy, Carol is as chained to her as ever, 'Why do I let you push me around with your panic attacks, your panting, your lip-biting and your scowling?'

Carol's power emanates from an empty shell moulded only from envy and the desire for sadistic revenge. The deep narcissistic blows she received time after time after time have left her with a carapace, filled only with the foul air of envy, non-productive, non-creative and ultimately self-destructive.

139

But parental failure does not only belong to the mother. A highly significant factor in her life is the fact that her father never lived with the family and that Carol does not know who her father is. Mollon (1993) points out the part played in narcissistic disturbance of the lack of a 'sense of lineage' which he describes as concerning,

> the sense of knowing who one is and where one has come from, of being able to locate oneself in a family line – a sense of being part of a line extending in time.
>
> (Mollon 1993: 15)

We know that Carol is deeply curious about her father, she desperately hunts amongst her mother's belongings for a photograph of him, and she dreads that he is someone local who knows who she is:

> I hope it wasn't anyone I know. It's awful to think he might know me – whoever he is – and I don't know him. And he knows I don't know. It makes me feel stupid! . . and small . . . and nothing.

Not only are the experiences associated with father yet another source of humiliation, but they make her feel 'nothing'. This underlines the void which lies at the centre of Carol, the unnourished and therefore dead centre. Mollon goes on to say that the aspect of self which relates to lineage,

> can be disturbed if in the child's imagination the father is not allowed his appropriate place as husband to the wife – a parental couple understood to give rise to the child through intercourse.
>
> (Mollon 1993: 15)

He adds that the child's way of dealing with this can be to create a fantasy that they came into being by their own omnipotent creation. Whilst Carol does not do this, the omnipotence which she displays in her exploits on the breakwater seem to smack of a desire to create herself again and again, to invent herself repeatedly in order to survive.

Another important consequence of Carol's lack of a father is that she is deprived of a caring male acknowledgement of her as a girl-child. Her own experience of her sexuality has been unnurtured. Carol as a sexual being is chaotic, as we shall see. Yet another consequence is that she is unable to move out of the dyadic relationship with her mother and remains in an undifferentiated relation to her, there is no mediating third party which the presence of the father would give (see Mollon 1993: 28).

In terms of her relation to both parents we can see that her overwhelming envy is also partly caused by her mother's relationship with her father from which she is excluded. We learn that her mother has never even used the word 'father' to her.

> He left us, mother. Not just you. Us. You *and* me. You'd have hurt less

140

you know if you'd admitted that. But no; you had to claim all the pain, all the rejection as yours – exclusively yours. You hoarded grief like you hoarded everything. If only you'd seen yourself in me, you might have shared it; eased it a little. You shared nothing with me. Not even his name. You were jealous of me even then. Jealous of my wanting him, missing him, touching the memory of him. So you didn't spare me a syllable of it; just a suggestion; a vibration. I was left with nothing. Just the face of a stranger.

Here we see Carol suffering much like Electra of the *Oresteia*, of whom Klein says that

> the primary motive for Electra's hate is that apparently she had not been loved sufficiently by her mother and her longing to be loved by her had been frustrated. Electra's hate against her mother – although intensified by the murder of Agamemnon – contains also the rivalry of the daughter with the mother, which focuses on her not having the sexual desires gratified by the father.
>
> (Klein [1963] in 1988b: 284)

Carol's words surely bear out Klein's statement. Thomas's choice of words are those which might be used by a lover, 'wanting him, missing him, touching the memory of him'. That last phrase suggests the ambiguity of the relationship, as though almost physically touching and yet not, for the sentence slides away into 'the memory of him', suggesting safer ground. When she accuses her mother of being jealous of her it would seem that she is projecting her own feelings onto her mother; her envy of her mother's relationship with the father is more easily seen by Carol as her mother being jealous of her potential relationship with her father, indeed of her actual relationship to her absent father. In doing so she misses the irony in her own words, 'If only you'd seen yourself in me, you might have shared it.' The fact that it is not all a case of Carol's projection but her mother probably is actually jealous of her, is precisely because she does see herself in Carol. Carol must therefore not succeed where she has failed; Carol is undoubtedly a rival and must be kept down. Maguire (Ernst and Maguire 1987) points out the damage done to girls by mothers who must continually use the child to reflect themselves in their search to boost their own vulnerable identity; such parents will criticize and undermine their own children. It is likely that Carol, being a constant reminder to her mother of her rejection, receives her mother's projections about failure; the mother can continue to court admiration in the world while the daughter acts out that sense of failure and lives the consequences of having only a very fragile ego as a result. She says to her mother, now that she cannot reply,

> Did he tempt you with pleasures and promises; persuade you that leaving your world for his would be as easy as leaving spring for summer? And you believed him, didn't you? But *he* left *you*. You said it. Oh, not

exactly: that wasn't like you: no admissions: no apologies. But you said it – You swallowed his name. You never said the word 'father'. Some days you would snipe at me; spit out your words as if you wanted them to bruise me, pierce me, scar me. Sometimes – a few times – I'd catch you looking at me like a lost soul: as if you wanted something from me: something you knew I couldn't give.

From this experience she learns that men trap women, leave them lumbered and lost, projecting their anger and disappointment onto the child they have been left with. '"Bloody accident" you called me. Or "Miss Pest" or "your little ball and chain", remember?'

The effect of this abandonment by the man on the mother has its consequent effect on the mother's relationship to Carol. It then becomes part of the trap for the child in that the mother displaces feelings which rightly belong to her relationship with the father, 'You did love me – some of the time. Because of him? In spite of him? – I don't know which.'

These aspects of her relationship with her parents – the emotional deprivation, the exclusion, the lack of a father to whom she can be Oedipally connected, the envy and rivalry, and the role she must play as bearer of her mother's unwanted feelings, help us to understand Carol as both child and adult. As a result of having to create herself from nothing, she must be omnipotent. As an adult she has to run the shop superbly, she has to be 'Wonderfully efficient'. She has to be better than others. Maguire (1987: 138) reminds us of Alice Miller's patient whose experience was of 'walking on stilts', having to make supreme efforts to gain admiration. Carol has been given no opportunity to develop a good enough sense of self through love and consistent support of her developing ego and must therefore walk on stilts too. She has a driven quality about her, a manic way of being in the world which is a desperate way of attempting to cope with the inner emptiness. This driven quality and the reasons for it are chillingly created by the playwright in the description of Carol as a child. Her omnipotence is clearly depicted in the picture of a child doing all she knows how in order to attempt to create a sense of self so as to survive. Carol's playground was the beach and the sea and all that that offered. Where other children might have been building sandcastles Carol would force herself to walk out along the breakwater:

But I went on, with the sea hungry for disaster and sucking at my heels. I went on, with the spray rasping my skin and the icy sweat needling my spine, fear like a cheese wire between my ribs.

Although aware of the extreme danger, she would make herself wait before turning back:

And when I got back, I would stand on the beach like a Viking; head up, eyes on the horizon, outfacing it all; knowing sooner or later I must face it again . . . and again. But that never mattered. I had survived. This is what I had to do. To survive. This was my purpose.

Carol emerges as someone who has suffered severe infant deprivation. She is supremely lonely, unnurtured, not loved for herself by her mother, rejected and abandoned by her father, teased and despised by her half-siblings for not knowing her parentage, the butt of their rivalrous attacks on her as the youngest, the supplanter. Her experience leaves her deeply scarred, split between having no sense of who she really is and an apparently successfully functioning life, filled with unconscious envy which has no power but to destroy. These factors combine to create in her a deep distrust of intimate relationships and contributes to her fear of them. The dramatic action in the play centres around the consequences of conflict between her hunger for relationship and her terror of it. She sees men as trapping women, laying them waste and luring them into captivity much as Hades did to Persephone. She also transfers her feelings of betrayal by her mother and her own sense of being trapped by that relationship onto the idea of an intimate relationship with a man. The prospect of such a relationship is then fraught with overwhelming anxiety. Sexual and passionate feelings which might find expression in a relationship with a man must therefore be avoided at all costs as they have been up until the point in her life at which we meet her.

What then does Carol do with all the passion and the fury? When the play opens we quickly realize that she has found her own solution. She splits off the feelings she cannot allow and projects them. Firstly she projects onto the shop dummy, whom she calls Sylvie, the attractive, sexual woman who has never been allowed to develop in herself, desired and desiring. Secondly she projects onto men the cannibalistic sadistic infant in her who needed to possess her parents and was frustrated. She also projects onto all men the power to possess and trap, which she experiences her mother having been subjected to by her father, and which she also feels her mother has done to her. Finally her envy, rather than being acknowledged, is converted into scorn for those around her, those average people, as Miller said, who do not have to 'walk on stilts', and especially for those who marry, like her sister.

Thomas's use of the shop dummy is a brilliant dramatic device and acts as a psychological container for the play's themes. It is the central symbol which holds both the psychological meaning and the dramatic action and creates a dialogue between them. For Carol the dummy is most obviously a friend, a confidante, someone who staves off loneliness, someone with whom she can share her most intimate thoughts and feelings. The dummy provides Carol with a vehicle for projection of parts of herself which she dare not live out. She literally clothes Sylvie with these unexpressed parts of herself, making her an alter ego whom she dresses, undresses and re-dresses according to her mood. She can try these parts on, like the clothes she dresses Sylvie in; she can clothe the dummy in her own shadow and make it live, find a way to relate

143

to it. Her relationship with the outside world, the weather even, is reflected in her clothing of the dummy. Her opening lines are to the dummy and reveal the intensity of Carol and her method of splitting herself between the two identities right from the beginning of the play:

> Well, Sylvie, we must find you something else to wear. It's not a grey day today – Just look at it. Look at that sunshine lying across the water: you could walk all the way to the horizon on that light.

The Carol of the breakwater, staring in triumph at the horizon is here too, so from the outset the child and the adult Carol are present and Sylvie contains both. We shall look more at the relationship between these parts of her life as they come together in the dummy, but first we need to explore a little more what the dummy means for Carol. To free associate around that allows us to encounter echoes which resonate with other parts of the play. (One of the reasons for the play's power is that Thomas's writing has just that property of poetry where metaphors and images conjure up many layers of meaning.)

The dummy has echoes of the comforter, the substitute for the breast, for the mother no longer there, for the feeding which is not happening but where the parent and the infant ally themselves in a pretence that it is. The dummy can also be a transitional object which the baby can control, throw away, cry for its retrieval, use for its own pleasure and experimentation. It is therefore the object which helps the child to separate and have its own autonomy independent of mother. The fact that this dummy is not that sort of dummy matters little in terms of poetic resonance; the word dummy is a powerful one conjuring up these other associations which resonate so aptly with Carol's situation. Thus Thomas succeeds in underlining the issues Carol has about both unmet needs and separation from her mother. It is as though this shop dummy is a 'grown up' substitution for the infant dummy in the mouth and an attempt to have a life separate from her mother, a relationship which she can call her own. This brings us to another resonance of the word – that of 'dumb'. Carol cannot speak her infant pain. She says this clearly to her mother now that her mother too cannot speak:

> Did you think that because I didn't know how to say it that I didn't know it? But it doesn't work like that does it? Just because you can't say it doesn't mean that you don't feel it – and hate it – and fester inside – does it mother? Does it?

The dummy in this sense stands in for Carol, she is the dumb part of her who could never speak her injuries. It is also an image of the mother who could not speak after her stroke; this serves to reinforce the identification of Carol with her mother. We shall return to these aspects of the dummy when looking at the end of the play.

Now we can begin to see how the psychological and dramatic functions of the dummy relate. For it is through the dummy that the dramatic tension is created in relation to the character who is then introduced but never seen by the audience – the man. The man is a vet who visits the town every week. At the same time each week he comes to stand outside the shop and look in through the window which fronts the street.

As she watches the man looking into the shop, supposedly at Sylvie – for this is the only interpretation of his presence she can afford to give – her desire is evident as she imagines what he is feeling; what we see clearly happening is that Carol is splitting off her sexual self. She can relate to it only by projecting it onto the dummy who can then by proxy receive the man's erotic desire:

> He's looking at your ankles, and now his eye is running upwards to the fullness of your calf, feel it? and on over your smooth knees. What's he feeling, Sylvie, when he sees the line of those strong thighs under your skirt. Doesn't he want to touch, to hold the heaviness of your buttocks in his hand, and to trace the curve up into the small of your back and on up to the shoulder, sliding round and down again, squeezing your breasts under the soft silk . . .

In this speech we see some of the diffusion of Carol's sexuality. As she projects her sexual self onto the dummy she can become the lover; the speech is superbly ambiguous for it has a masturbatory quality to it at the same time as suggesting a fantasized lesbian relationship with Sylvie. Simultaneously Carol seems to be identifying with the man, projecting herself into his male sexuality as she watches him through the window. The lack of her own sexual identity and the ability to act on it for herself as both subject and object in relation to the man is very clear in this speech.

As the speech continues she warns Sylvie that she must not get caught, and immediately, by talking to the dummy, her projections of possession and destruction onto all men, are manifest:

> He wants all of you, remember. He'll try to take it all. First he'll say he loves you and bind you with a silk cord. Then he'll build a wall around you with words like 'stay' and 'together'. Try to step outside it and he'll bar the windows with 'ought' and 'must' and set dogs to guard you called 'Mine' and 'Belong'. If you still won't give up to him he'll lock the door with the word 'forever'. At last he'll draw down the blinds of your vista of what might have been and your view of what could be with the awful word 'never'.

Carol's way of dealing with her fear, which has its roots in her own experience of her mother's situation, her own experience of being abandoned by her father, and in her projected experience of her own unfulfilled early needs, is graphically illustrated by this speech. In order fully to appreciate this we need to remember how she views her mother's experience of being lumbered and abandoned. As she talks to Sylvie she speaks like a mother warning her

145

daughter of the evils of men. It is as though she repeats, not what her mother said to her, but her translation of her mother's experience which is coloured by her abandonment by her father.

If we look at the words which end the 'warning' speech to Sylvie we can see the links between her understanding of her mother's experience with its consequent effect on her and her own unmet needs which are projected out onto men. This combination makes for powerful fears of being destroyed by possession. The speech continues,

> Deep in the lair of his possessing he'll stun you with an anaesthetic pleasure and drug you with a mindless desire, and while you rest in his arms his cannibal love will savage you; tearing great bleeding chunks out of the flesh of your hopes and dreams, grinding the bones of your resolve, digesting your identity. In the pain and the blood he leaves behind he'll sow his seed in yours so you'll never be free of the thousand agonies of his harvest.

What we find here is the infant Carol's forbidden wishes for satisfaction. This is complex, for Carol is so deprived by both parents that her revenge centres on both. Again the poetic quality of Thomas's language sustains a complexity of meaning. Her wishes to possess and punish both her mother and father are layered into this speech. She shows the infant cannibalistic desire to devour the mother and to punish the bad breast for frustrating her. She shows too her own desire to possess and be possessed by the father. But both these phantasies return in the form of persecutors typical of the paranoid schizoid position in which Carol, as we see at the end of the play, remains stuck.

In this speech it is as though the infant Carol has both Oedipal (wanting the parent of the opposite sex) and inverted Oedipal (wanting the parent of the same sex) wishes. With such overwhelming greed and desire for revenge she in turn is overwhelmed; in the threat of being obliterated her identity is 'digested'; in other words she is the one to be eaten, a classic example of the return of projected forbidden phantasies and desires in the form of persecutors.

At yet another level the speech reaches into the oppression of women which Carol evokes by her fantasies of sexual intercourse as rape, 'the pain and blood he leaves behind' which completes the picture of carnage and destruction. Echoes of menstrual blood and pain are here too and so is the ultimate enslavement of women; the act of procreation ensures that they will never be free of the thousand agonies of a harvest which, by the very phrase 'his harvest', implies that the 'food' it yields will be reaped by men on the backs of women's suffering.

Central in this speech is Carol's awareness of the threat to identity; to be rendered mindless, to have hopes, dreams, resolve and identity all be brutally savaged. It is poignantly full of dramatic irony when we see the ultimate destruction of Carol at the end of the play.

Linked with this is Carol's third survival technique which is her envious 'sour grapes' way of treating those who have what she has not. Particularly pertinent is her attitude to those who are married. From what we have just seen, Carol has a terror of such commitment, seeing it as a trap and a place where she would become completely destroyed, yet she murderously attacks from a deeply envious place inside her those who do not have these feelings, those who can be, as Alice Miller (1983) says, 'average'. Just after a long speech to her mother in which she berates her for longing for her father instead of allowing her daughter to be enough for her – 'I should have been enough of a belonging for you' – she returns to the shop area where she resumes sewing lace onto a bridesmaid's dress; while she does so she talks to Sylvie:

> Look at this thing. It's hideous. You could have tea and sandwiches for the town in all this! All this skirt! She'll look like a standard lamp on wheels. It's better in these lights though than white. Green's best I think. Like a druid's shroud; to wear for the passing of summer as the year sinks into the grave. There should be light like this in church. Colour to fill the passionless void of white – like wine poured into a cup. Red. Blood red to drench the little carnivorous pageboys and the vampire bridesmaids, to blood them at the kill. Red to drench the bride as she opens the vein of her love to drain away her blood on the altar of her expectations – Red to drench the bridegroom as he comes like a butcher in his Sunday best to the feast. Then yellow. Yellow to blend and wash the rest into one tribe, one pack, one troupe of attendant clowns in their silly hats, their garish clothes, their trinkets. It's a circus Sylvie. It's all a circus. A great big, fat meaningless push and shove and they all want to play.

Here is Carol's vision of marriage as a brutal sacrificial murder; the images of carnage so similar to those of the earlier speech, redolent of her own murderous fantasies and a reminder of her own experience of the mother who has sucked her life-blood from her. Here too is her own scorn and derision of the 'circus'; she is outside it, she who was excluded from her mother and half-siblings is outside this game too. It is not surprising that she feels that green, the traditional colour of envy, is the best.

These then are Carol's means of survival; the dummy, her projections of her rage and pain and envy, rubbishing what she most desires, making herself special and superior to hide her insecurity. During the process of the play we learn all this about her through her conversations with the dummy and with her mother, and the telephone calls to the outside world, the doctor, her half-brother, Roger, the customers, the Bank, etc. Her inner world is revealed particularly through her talks to Sylvie, her childhood through the way she talks to her mother, and her coping efficient business persona through her telephone interactions. These worlds are set out before us, and during the process of the play we see Carol moving between one and the other until they become

147

inextricably linked, not through the process of integration but of substitution. In order to understand the delicate balance which can be maintained and why it is broken we need to look at the part played by the shop in Carol's life.

The shop was her mother's. Carol helped her run it; she tells us of the little intimacies they shared like doing the accounts with a glass of sherry and having to do them again the next day, moments which Carol clearly cherished, moments when she had her mother to herself. Now Carol runs the shop, 'My shop', 'My phone', she says emphatically. In the shop she has control. In the shop she is not the victim of her half-brother and sister, her mother, her feeling of not belonging anywhere as in the past. She has a place. She is competent, untouchable, in charge. The shop is a place of contracts. People require goods, she provides them, they pay her; the boundaries are clear; shops are for buying and selling, the roles of buyer and seller are defined. The shop for Carol is therefore a container, a place where she can be held and where her identity is recognizable in the eyes of the world and where the world can mirror that identity back to her, as we hear through the various phone calls and answerphone messages from customers. But, for Carol, containing boundaries never existed when she was a child. As we see in her recounting of the games, these turned out not to be fair games, with rules, designed to give pleasure, but cruel games which left her not knowing where she stood. At the beginning of the play we hear her responding to her half-brother Roger, 'I'm your sister, Roger, not one of your sodding retrievers.' She has always been taken advantage of, always denied rights, even that of knowing who her father is; she has never had the kind of mirroring that has helped her see herself and know where she begins and ends.

Thus there are limits to how much containment the shop can really provide for someone whose lack of good parental containment was so great. It is also a symbol of her servitude, the handmaiden she had to be to her mother. Yet on the surface the shop is a place where she can make a statement to the outside world that she has overcome, she has made it, she has not been drowned in the attempts of her family to deface her. On the surface she is a strong woman with a strong personality; the shop sells this personality to the outside world. But on the inside Carol is fragile, her ego far from intact. For this fragile Carol the shop is also a place in which she can play out parts of herself. Here therefore is confusion, for it is in the context of the shop itself that her fantasies are played out. There is no clear boundary between fantasy and reality, for the shop is haunted by her unmet needs and becomes her psyche's playground. The shop is all she can truly call her own so it is the place where she can experiment. There is nowhere else, for Carol, bound by her mother now more than ever, has nowhere she can go.

There is a parallel between her childhood playground of the sea which we heard about when she described the breakwater walks, and the shop. We might conclude that play is a serious business for Carol; it is a pitting of herself against the elements, 'outfacing' all obstacles to survival. It is play to ensure survival more akin to the instinctual practice play of animals. The play which Carol the adult affords herself seems infinitely more gentle, a harmless dressing up of the shop dummy as a child might a doll, dreaming of things this imaginary friend might do. But, as *Thursday's Child* proceeds, we realize that in fact her adult playing has the same quality as that of little Carol on her breakwater. In both there are no boundaries other than those she invents for herself. In both there is a sense of danger, of going too far, of pushing the limits. It is as though the limitations provided by her life with her mother, the minute duties involved in caring for her after her stroke, and the pressures of keeping up the efficient businesswoman persona can be maintained only by means of the outlet afforded by the fantasies she lives out through the character of Sylvie; she must be so bounded in her daily life that she must be limitless in her fantasy world.

Both fantasy and reality worlds are based, as we have seen, on shaky foundations; when the tide comes in at full flood Carol is swept away. Thomas explores both parts of Carol with a passion and lyricism which integrate her in our vision just as we see her disintegrating in herself. The playwright makes Carol perfectly understandable so that we, the audience, can accept the logic of her crime and the tragedy and the braveness of her life.

Let us look, then, at what happens to Carol at the denouement of the play.

At the end of the speech about weddings Carol holds the dress she is making up to the mirror, and says 'I'm spending my life dressing dolls!'

Since the time when she is not running the shop or looking after her mother is spent dressing Sylvie, this comment holds particular irony. In terms of the structure of the play it also leads us into the next scene in which Carol is, as the stage direction tells us,'dressing Sylvie for her night out'. The vet, the man who comes regularly to admire Carol through the shop window, has asked her out; almost in passing Carol tells her mother, in the same breath as reassuring her that she won't go.

As she dresses and speaks to Sylvie we see the Carol who yearns for love, romantic and erotic, the Carol who links herself to the universe, who feels within herself the 'life force' which cannot be cabined and confined. As she speaks she becomes the image of freedom; her earlier murderous, vengeful language has dropped away as, in her fantasies, she takes her power. Men are no longer raging and destructive, they are the lesser partner in nature for a season, fulfilling a purpose, and, ultimately, they are in the power of the woman.

Thus she speaks of men, giving 'Sylvie' permission:

Tonight – waxing and waning through the night, you may choose, at your fullness, to take one of them. Call to him, Sylvie, call to him. Sing to him, soothe him, arouse him, touch him. Feel the strength of his arms around you – just for the brief season of the night. How firm his body is, how rooted in the earth beneath you. He is so definite, so certain, so 'here and now'. You are so indefinable, so various, so ever-lasting. Hold him, Sylvie, hold him. He the link and you the chain, that binds night to night, tide to tide, harvest to harvest, age to age. Hold him, and love him, and satisfy him – and leave him.

    We belong to no one, Sylvie. We belong only to the life force that is in us. It is so strong.

Finally, with ultimate irony, she says,

We shall never be lost in the fog of love, however thick it clings. For we choose to belong to no one.

With that she 'quickly takes the clothes off the dummy and puts them on herself'.

    Carol can take up the man's invitation only in the guise of Sylvie. She suspends her identity as Carol and when she returns at dawn she speaks as Sylvie to the dummy which is shrouded in its night-time sheet. She tells her she 'danced from horizon to horizon', recounts the delights of the night, reassuring 'Carol' that she won't leave her. She even uses the term 'love at first sight'. She feels merged with the man:

I was part of him; without having to do anything, I was part of him. And I'd been part of him all my life. I could never let him go again, you see, because he completed me.

Up until now we have seen her talk as a confidante. For the first time the audience is faced with her having changed places with the dummy. This is perhaps why she can talk with such lack of venom, in such a different vein from the earlier Carol; she can freely allow herself to be a woman who falls in love, feels that merger which goes with the state of falling in love and echoes the blissful state of infant and mother in the primary relationship. She describes the walk down to the sea, the smell of sea and night and the dark cliffs looming. Our realization that she has murdered the man slips into our consciousness almost without our registering it, echoing his experience:

I wanted us to feed one another, to grow into each other, to be each other. So you see, there was no choice. I had to do it. It wasn't my fault. I said that. I said it was just meant to be, that's all. No point in struggling or in resenting it. I only did it because I loved him so much. Otherwise I would never had had the strength. . . . I think he understood. He just stared back at me. Didn't blink even. He looked a bit surprised . . . but not angry . . . or scared. And I don't think it was painful. He didn't struggle at all. Maybe he stunned himself when he fell. But his eyes were open when he fell under the water.

Carol has been flooded by the unintegrated, undeveloped sexuality which has been unleashed. The defences have been destroyed that kept her relatively safe. In doing so she can act only on the script she has learned by heart from her life experience; that men must be left before they leave women, before they trap and ensnare them and abandon them. In splitting off her needing and desiring self into Sylvie she has also split herself off from her super-ego which would have protected her from her crime; as Carol she can have murderous thoughts, as Sylvie she can realize them. Her last words in the persona of Sylvie are,

> If the tide moves him, it'll just bring him to us won't it. Whenever the tide comes in, it'll bring him to us.

These moving lines echo the waves, the movement of the tide; their poignancy is partly because we, the audience, know now that the tide has turned irrevocably for Carol. Her words show the delusory state she has finally entered; in the face of murder and death she must cling to a delusion of a kind of continual resurrection, a state where the man will continue to be there for her, and yet safely since he is dead. In the movement of the tide is the tragic irony of her own womanhood having at last been truly awakened by the man who has appreciated her sexuality as her father never did, a sense of the rhythm of woman's sexuality, of the tide which is pulled by the moon and the cycle of menstruation which is indeed the life force. But for Carol it represents death and not birth.

The play now moves to its climax. Carol goes to her mother for advice for Sylvie's plight, 'She'll know what to do'; she is out of touch with the reality of her mother's state just as she is out of touch with her own. But she has an even greater shock. Her mother has died in the night while she was out; the final exchange of personality with Sylvie begins.

> It must have been last night, Sylvie, while you were out. But I never heard her. I didn't. You were out and I was . . . where was I? If you were out I must have been in bed. You were out. I was in bed. It was you that was out.

She, who could never leave her mother, is faced with the fact that her mother has finally left her:

> Gone and left me with the shop . . . and . . . the other thing.

Carol, who took such triumphant pleasure in running the shop, is now lost without her mother; her world is in pieces. After the funeral, back in her mother's bedroom with the now empty bed, Carol sits in a state of shock. Suddenly the phone rings; her reaction shows that she hopes it is the vet. In anger she storms at Sylvie accusing her of wanting to go off with the man and leave her. The two sides of her have been completely dissociated from one another which is evident in her body movements which mirror her disturbed state. She tries to dance with the dummy, but she herself can make only puppet-like movements. She blames the dummy for her mother's death, getting more and more angry and disturbed. Gradually she exchanges identity with the dummy, and in the persona of Sylvie, in a fit of rage at the absent man and absent mother, she breaks the dummy.

Immediately comes remorse; she kneels beside it,

> Carol? Carol, I'm sorry. I'm sorry. (*She carries the dummy to the bed and lays it on it.*) There now, Sylvie's here. I'm not going to leave you. I'm never going to leave you. (*She draws the blinds and puts on the bedside light and covers the dummy with a sheet.*)

Here the symbolism of the dummy as the child who could never speak her injuries adds to the power of this intensely dramatic moment. Placing the dummy, whom she calls Carol, in the bed is the only way that she can look after this injured child and her resulting broken self. But it is a dead Carol, rather an inanimate object, a metaphor for her death.

What has brought on this final flight into psychosis is that the early emotional, psychological and physical abandonment by her parents in their various ways has been re-enacted. She has lost both her lover/father and her mother. The chasm which threatened the infant Carol can no longer be fought against. The choice now is death or a total schizoid split. The Carol of the breakwater chooses survival, at a price. For suicide is an option if the guilt is to be faced. She has murdered her father/lover and, by leaving her mother alone while going out with him, has 'caused' her mother's death (there is a suggestion of her having given her mother a larger than usual dose of sedatives). Her murderous attacks as an infant were in unconscious phantasy – the envious attack on the mother for depriving her of her father, and the murderous rageful attack on the father for his abandonment. This time they are not in phantasy, they are for real; a man lies drowned in the bay and an elderly woman is buried – the playwright uses the technique of the telephone to confirm these events as actual. Up until now Carol has survived by turning her attacks on to herself throughout her life by keeping herself symbiotically attached to the mother, making no claims on a man.

Her finally turning herself into Sylvie is the psychotic response to the re-enactment of the violence inflicted on her when she was too young for words. The dummy being placed in the bed also stands for the mother whose death and its timing have flipped Carol into splitting herself in two. As such it emphasizes the inability of Carol to separate from her mother even after her death; by placing the broken dummy in the bed the point is clearly made that Carol finds a way to identify with her mother, merge with her again, never to be separated.

The very thing she was terrified of yet was deeply psychologically conditioned to want, the very thing she murdered to avoid, has happened. She has finally lost the semblance of identity she had. Yet, as she had described herself to Sylvie just before exchanging clothes with her before going out with the vet, 'I have Viking in my backbone. I have Viking in my finger nails, that scratch and claw and cling to life.'

The end of the play finds her totally in the persona of Sylvie, telephoning the bank to make arrangements for the shop's new persona, Sylvie's Boutique. She asks them to send her the necessary forms because 'I can't get out, you see. I have an invalid to look after.'

Carol has been lost, has more than taken her mother's place, a speechless, mindless inanimate object. In Carol's place is a woman called Sylvie, who has loved and lost, and is trapped in the repetition of mother's abandonment, bound forever to atone for the crime of having dared to separate herself from her mother whose death comes as a judgement on her; bound forever to atone for the ultimate crime of having murdered and lost herself.

IN PRACTICE

We could say that Carol is possessed. She has become possessed by Sylvie and Carol has disappeared. The notion of possession is one which is highly relevant to actors, who we might say become possessed by their characters. Brian Bates, in his book *The Way of the Actor* (1986), explores this idea through interviews with actors and concludes that, 'the traditional actor has a double consciousness; one part is possessed, the other observes and controls.' If not, he argues, a possession takes place where there is a fusion between the emotions of the character and those of the actor. This immediately begs the question of who the character is in relation to the actor. Bates's answer to this is to refer to Rollo May's idea of demonic possession; that in each of us there are demons, 'parts of ourselves that we have not allowed freedom, and that have remained lost, ignored or hidden' (Bates 1986: 79). This links with the view of role work in dramatherapy which I discussed in the first chapter of this book; that we could say that being an actor depends, like being in role, on being and not-being simultaneously; the actor has to draw up from the depths of the psyche aspects of him or herself which might otherwise be buried. Thus they are expressed as the actor allows those parts to take possession while simultaneously being witnessed by the part which observes and controls.

When it comes to a part like that of Carol in *Thursday's Child* the actor is sailing very close to the wind, for the character is that of a woman who loses herself. In this section, therefore, we look at what it means to play such a demanding role and ask what is it that the actor is providing for the audience? A safe place in which to explore life at its most painful and frightening? A place to be safe with what is unsafe? If this is so then there is a heavy burden for the actor and implications for the director who must support the actor and yet deliver to the audience. Two aspects of these questions are shown here by reference to the rehearsal process of *Thursday's Child*. First the actor speaks, describing an incident in rehearsal. Second, I draw on some of my own notes and memories of work in progress in my role as director. The playwright will have the last word.

First the actor:

The day Marina and I first met to begin the process of improvisation and rehearsal for this play, I read some preliminary notes I'd made to her:

'I am nervous – nervous about where you and I might go in this. I have a personal aim for myself within this experience and that is to move beyond a barrier within myself as a performer, a place where I have only touched the edge, where the life of the performer and the role meet within myself. I want to take risks. I know I am getting near that barrier in myself when I get a tightening in my stomach, an anger and resistance to rehearsing and a feeling of hopelessness and apathy. This is when I need your strength as a director to challenge me and help me move beyond this, to change gear and enter the unknown.'

I once heard Peter Brook likening the process of acting to that of meditation, a process in which the actor has to let go, open himself up to nothingness to discover what is there. As an actress I had the capacity of being able to project myself deeply into a role and to embody the character's psyche. It is, however, only on reflection some years later, having trained and practised as a dramatherapist, and more recently since working on this play, that I have become conscious of, and started to identify, the barrier I described that would rise up in me and limit my ability to really let go and enter that unknown place. I believe now that the barrier was fear; fear of entering the unknown and stepping so deeply into role that I might, like Carol in the play, 'become' the role I am playing, as Carol in her 'play' becomes Sylvie, the shop dummy onto which she projects a split off aspect of herself. She loses herself, who she is in the here and now context of her everyday life, to Sylvie, who represents a part of herself which has hitherto been dumb.

It is at this point that she slips over that borderline place where she has teetered on the edges of reality and fantasy, sanity and madness and becomes floridly psychotic. 'She ends up as Sylvie, stripped naked, a dummy, she can put on the clothes, paint the face of Sylvie, but behind that there is nothing' (notes from a rehearsal). Nothing but a fragmented ego/self that is mirrored in the broken dummy at the end of the play, who is now Carol, a symbol of her own internal brokenness and fragmentation.

There are many areas of interest here for me both as a clinician and as a performer which are worthy of exploration, but I want to focus on one particular incident that happened during a rehearsal to illustrate the fear of splitting and loss of self. At the time of the rehearsal the

154

director, choreographer and writer were in the audience space; I was in the area defined as the enactment space, moving between the Carol and Sylvie personas. There was a chair placed centrally downstage which, though still in the enactment area, represented the actor's space, a technique the director had devised whilst exploring the notion of the actor commenting on her process and playing Carol. It is hard to describe accurately and in a way which may be accessible to the reader quite what happened in this moment I am describing, but as I recall, having moved between Carol's two roles several times and then moved into the actor's space and spoken from there I moved back into Carol's shop area and Marina addressed me. I suddenly felt my heart racing as I lost, momentarily, all sense of both who she was talking to – me in role as Carol, Sylvie, the actor or me Jessica – and who I was at this moment. I could feel a sense of my mind splitting as I desperately tried to grasp hold of what reality I was in, beginning to panic, now, that I'd tumbled into a borderline psychotic state and fearing that I wouldn't be able to find my way back. I said 'I don't know who you're talking to, who I am', and as my heart continued to race and my hands to perspire I said, 'I'm frightened, I don't know what's happening'. Somehow Marina's words then spoken managed to meet me in that place; she said, 'I know you're frightened because I feel it too', and I looked up at her. In her eyes I saw the fear, but also an alertness and total concentration on this moment. I wasn't alone, she held my gaze, I looked at Di, the choreographer; the fear was also there. At this moment I experienced both of them as being totally with me and as Marina spoke again and talked about the splitting and madness as belonging to the roles I was playing, I started to re-enter myself. My mind and my body, which I sensed as having dissociated from each another, became one again and I began to breathe more easily.

I have looked at and thought about what in this moment resonated with my own internal process, that is, the borderline aspects of myself, and with a deeper insight than ever before I have recognized this part of my own reality. I believe this was made accessible because I was engaged in the dramatic reality of Carol's life. The role created a vessel in which my own unconscious was activated, made conscious through embodying the role of Carol. Where these two meet something real is born, with attendant risks but with the potential, if carefully managed as this moment was, to create a moment of truth in theatre. I believe the experience, risky as it was, was contained and creative rather than, as it could so easily have been, damaging; instead it was important in my development as a clinician and performer and as well as to me personally. Equally important was its value to the work on the play itself. This was possible because what happened took place within the context of the dramatic metaphor and, very importantly, because it was witnessed and held by those watching, particularly by the director whose job it was to 'hold' me by being with me in that moment. (There are echoes here of the director/therapist roles and the actor/client roles.)

I also gained a much deeper understanding of what it is to be Carol, to embody her, to stand in for Carol, acting as taking on a character or becoming a role. We could question whether acting is about pretending or being, about taking on a character or becoming a role. Carol is doing far more than pretending, she is becoming the role of Sylvie which she has created.

The role in a play provides for the actor the potential 'dummy', an unspoken part of the actor onto which unlived, split off, dormant parts of the self can be projected. If these parts have hitherto been hard to bear, to hold within the self, then there is a potential risk of breakdown and danger if the actor is not carefully held and the processes present in rehearsal understood. We hear more and more about actors who 'disappear', who walk off stage; one reason for this could be that something in the playing of the role, in the very nature of being an actor, becomes no longer containable within the dramatic structure; the containment provided by the theatrical/performance experience is not enough.

Because projection is such an essential part of acting there is undoubtedly the possibility that splitting mechanisms could lead to a sense of, and sometimes an actual, loss of self for the actor. This is especially possible if she or he has a fragile sense of their own identity anyway and might be unconsciously searching for this identity, or aspects of it, through the roles they play.

I think it is also possible and probable that an actor's sense of identity can become eroded and contaminated by the process of continually taking on the identities of the roles she or he is playing and where no formal attention is paid to de-roling. I have pondered much on the roles I have been cast in and their resonance for me personally, by directors who seemingly knew very little about me; was it simply that the director saw a 'good likeness' or did the role and I also unconsciously find each other?

In this small vignette I have touched upon the notion and nature of splitting and loss of self as I experienced it, its bearing on the role I was playing and the implications of this for the actor engaged in the sometimes risky but mystical world of theatre and performance. As a clinician I am also aware that there are implications here for dramatherapy and the use of role and embodiment in clinical practice to which the therapist needs to give careful thought and consideration.

There is a book entitled *Fear the Fear and Do it Anyway*. What I believe the director did at that moment in the rehearsal I have described – and therefore enabled me to do – was just that; to feel the fear, but more importantly to know and name the fear as partly Carol's as well as belonging to me. The tension was skilfully held between the dramatic process and the here and now experience of the actor; there was a meeting place between the internal world of both Carol and I, a letting go, a stepping through the barrier into a place where, for a few seconds I felt I had nothing to grasp onto, but in which I discovered much – a surrendering to the moment.

(Jessica Williams-Saunders)

This time in the rehearsal process I remember well as director. It is one which helped me to feel even more convinced that dramatherapy has much to offer those involved in the making of theatre. It was also a living example of how close Stanislavski's ideas are to the dramatherapist's way of working, for the 'moment of truth in the theatre' of which the actor speaks here took me straight back to Stanislavksi's words when he speaks of the process of the actor engaging with what he calls his 'creative emotions':

The actor is now coming to his part not through the text, the words of his role, nor by intellectual analysis or other conscious means of knowledge, but through his own sensations, his own real emotions, his own personal life experience.

(Stanislavski 1988: 30)

However, I would go further and say that it was a partnership of the text and the unconscious of the individual actor which were being with one another here in the same moment.

Stanislavski continues:

To do this he must set himself at the very centre of the household, he must be there in person, not seeing himself as an observer. . . . his imagination must be active, not passive. This is the most difficult and important psychological moment in the whole period of preparation. It requires exceptional attention. This moment is what we in actor's jargon call the state of 'I am', it is the point where I begin to feel myself in the thick of things, where I begin to coalesce with all the circumstances suggested by the playwright and by the actor.

(ibid.)

The Stanislavskian immersion in the state of 'I am' in role is the ultimate state of living in the 'as if' of drama. It is where the two realities of inner and outer merge and as such is a very sensitive moment for the actor. At this point he or she is dwelling on the boundary. In order to inhabit this space safely, especially when playing a role such as that of Carol in *Thursday's Child*, it is the director who must also pay 'exceptional attention' but of a different order, for the director must supply 'the observer' who has all but disappeared at that

157

moment for the actor. This must be harnessed while also following the process of the actor with empathy.

It is here that the primary task of the work must always be kept in mind for it provides focus and containment for the director at this point where his or her own unconscious might be being activated. In Chapter 3 I discussed the importance of boundaries and of making a contract. In the rehearsal that Jessica Williams-Saunders has written about, these were crucial to my being able to help her through a very frightening experience. The contract was that we were engaged in a rehearsal process working through the combination of improvisational and script work which was my directing style. The task was theatre, not therapy. I was a director and the actor was an actor. Whilst both of us were also dramatherapists these boundaries were clear. But the issue is also more complicated; underneath that there was my awareness of the actor's stated blocks, her fear of not being able to go far enough and of her wish that she should be challenged in this piece. If I was going to deliver the best piece of theatre I could, I must also take that into account, but – and this is an important but – not by means of being a therapist to her, but solely through my role as director. In any role in our lives we utilize those parts of ourselves and our skills and training which will help that role to be effective and the task to be done as well as possible. Thus, without functioning as a therapist, I could still use the attributes of the therapist in me to help me in my director's role and with my director's task.

Thus when the actor writes that she needed to be 'held' by the director, we are talking about precisely that kind of holding Winnicott described (see Chapter 2). It is the kind of holding where the parent can, in effect, say to the child, 'It's all right. Yes you're frightened and it is frightening but it's all right, I'm here.' The issues of focus on task and containment are crucial, for in this instance it was not clear to me where the terror was coming from. It happened quickly; was the actor projecting part of her terror and feelings of fragmentation into me by means of projective identification so that I would know it and be able to hold it and hand it back in a more manageable form? Could it be, on the other hand, coming from me and she was experiencing a terror of fragmenting of which, sitting there at that moment in that rehearsal, I was consciously quite unaware? Was it coming from the choreographer, or the writer whose lines she was speaking? I could not know the answers to this though the questions were all present in a flash in my mind. All I knew was that, while clearly feeling the fear, I had also to remain separate from it in order to maintain the reality of the rehearsal to which she could return. I, too, in order to play my life role of director had to live in two realities simultaneously.

When discussing this much later she told me that I had helped her to 'get on the horse' again by not bringing her out of the rehearsal or stopping it on the lines of 'We'd better leave it there for today.' I can truly say that that was never an option because the therapist in me knew that the only way we could all stay sane, as it were, in that moment was for me to put the fear back to where it belonged *in the task*, that is in the context of role and script. Telling the actor that she was experiencing the character's feelings and states helped to reassure and ground her. She was an actor in rehearsal who had momentarily got lost in her character, yes it was very frightening, yes there were real feelings and we, in the audience space, could feel them too, but actually it was OK. Carol had got into us all but we could handle her – all these messages needed to be conveyed by looks and words and total attention to the boundaries of the task in hand coupled with an awareness of psychological processes.

In this example the boundaries issue is a particularly important one because Carol is a character whose boundary confusion is a disturbing challenge to both actor and director. Being clear about the boundaries of role and task enabled me to look after my actor in a way which was not like putting sticking plaster on but which acknowledged the experience for what it was and helped her through and out the other side. My keeping in touch with the eventual purpose of directing – to put on a play for an audience – helped to ground me in a potentially overwhelming moment so that I could help her on the road to the realization of that shared aim.

In the more ordinary moments of directing there are many ways in which I use the dramatherapist in me to help me in the task of directing. I shall end this exploration of the theme with some notes I wrote after a rehearsal. In writing them I found myself musing on the relationship between the two roles of therapist and director.

Tonight I told my actor that my ultimate duty was to the audience – it was translated as 'total' this is what the actor heard and consequently felt abandoned. This raises the question of how it is that the director's words are heard – what is heard and how is it heard. Paying attention to this must be part of the director's job; here the therapist in the director is alert, looking at body language – a change, even a flicker in the eyes – pouncing on each of these moments and paying attention to them, either by noting them and linking them with aspects of the play to be stored and used later or by directly exploring or confronting the actor with them. Thus the reality can be teased out for use – the real feeling which is the actor's raw material. 'I felt abandoned and betrayed', paying attention to those feelings, supporting the actor while you do so, then, gently inviting a link, 'Does your character feel like that at any point?' Then the work into the character flows; it doesn't matter if it's not the precise scene of the play you're working on at that moment – seize it while it's there and the real meaning and the real feeling will flow into the character; it won't be lost, it might go underground for a while, but it will emerge when it's needed and will be integrated.

But working in this way means taking risks, trying things out. Sometimes they work, sometimes they do not and sometimes they feed into the themes of the play or are produced by them. An example of this is the use of the actor's chair which I devised in one rehearsal. I suggested this as a place for Jessica to retreat to in improvisation at times when she wanted to come out of Carol and comment on what was happening for her in her struggles with the role. It was intended as a focusing place, a kind of potential space within the rehearsal in which she could voice feelings and difficulties about herself as an actor taking this role, relating to the blocks we had spoken of. It is only with hindsight that I realized that this would have compounded her difficulties, adding yet another character. She had to play Carol, who played Sylvie, and now I was asking her to play another character called an actor! This may well have contributed to the confusion she experienced so violently as she has already described, and had the opposite effect from what was intended. Here, perhaps, the material of the play which is in us all, as the writer reminds us in the passage I quoted at the very beginning of the chapter, found and met those areas of my own identity confusions. Was I then getting the actor to act those out for me? Or as a director with an awareness of the audience was I perhaps finding a way to engage with the dynamic of actor/audience and was not fully focused on the actor? These are the kinds of unconscious mechanisms at work in play production; the congruence of the material of the play and those working on it should not, I believe, be ignored but be speculated upon, contemplated and an attempt at an understanding made. Working with intuition but with the benefit of rigorous analysis of process, as one does as a dramatherapist, exploring the unconscious processes at work, is an exciting and fruitful experience when working within the boundary and task of the theatre as well as in therapy.

In working on this play with the writer we contemplated having a second act which shared some of these issues with the audience but we decided to let Carol and the audience tell each other their own stories every night in the potential space called the theatre. One day these dialogues between actor, writer, choreographer and director might find their way into another play but until that happens I let the curtain of this chapter close with the writer's final words of that 'shadow' play which belongs so well with the themes of this book.

> Tonight we have built a dam across the rivers of love and hate that thunder through our lives; we have captured a still pool – a pool that reflects us and all that's around us. Together you and I have looked into the water.
>
> Yes, just water. Just a part I've played. It was just a make believe shop in a theatre where anyone can walk in and buy a slice of time.
>
> So now, if you want, you can pick up something sharp and hard

and real – a witty word or a stiff drink or a quick intake of breath – and chuck it at the reflections you've seen.

That's the safety of the play. You can always break the reflections.

And that's the danger of it: that it's only the reflections you can break.

(Daphne Thomas, unpublished working draft)

7

THE OPPRESSION OF TABOO
Ghosts by Henrik Ibsen

In *Thursday's Child* we found the private agony of a woman in a small town, taking refuge in the success of her public role of shop owner. This public role helped her to cope for she must be superwoman or die in the attempt. Her final refuge is in psychotic breakdown. An aspect of Carol's life which contributes to who she is and her eventual fate is that she is the victim of taboos within the family. There are rules as to who she can be, what can be talked about, especially with her mother. The greatest taboo is to try to find out who her father is; to have knowledge of her inheritance.

Every culture, every society or family will have its own set of taboo subjects; while some are universal, the degree to which they are taboo may vary. And where a collection of individuals become a group, taboos will form part of the group culture. In the therapy group different group members will bring their own taboos with them from their various family, societal or cultural backgrounds. There will be things that group members feel that they cannot address or talk about, new taboos that become part of the therapy group culture. There are often issues of disloyalty to dead or living members of the family; there is the fear of rejection by the therapist or other group members if the truth of the events of one's life are revealed or if the so-called negative feelings of hatred or anger are displayed. There is the fear that both one's own world and those of the other group members will collapse if painful truths are brought out into the open. There may be fear of ostracization or abandonment. These taboos and fears are often inherited or come from secrecy and lack of knowledge and honesty about one's inheritance. They oppress and stultify. They impede growth.

THE PLAY

Ibsen explores some of these factors in his play, *Ghosts*. It is about many things but above all it is about inheritance in its widest sense.

> MRS ALVING: I'm inclined to think we are all ghosts – all of us, Pastor
> Manders. It isn't just what we have inherited from our father and

mother that walks in us. It's all kinds of dead ideas and all sorts of old and obsolete beliefs. They are not alive in us; but they remain in us none the less, and we can never rid ourselves of them. I only have to take a newspaper and read it, and I see ghosts between the lines. There must be ghosts all over the country. They lie as thick as grains of sand. And we're all so horribly afraid of the light.

(*Ghosts*: 59)

It is to all these countless grains of sand in all our lives that this play speaks. In the therapy group this text can be used to work on the feelings and the fears of bringing into the light those aspects of our inheritance which feel impossible to mention. It is therefore a play which can help us to relate openly to issues of inheritance in its widest sense. Particularly it speaks to those profound areas of taboo in society which are to do with sexuality and with notions of family life and feelings.

Résumé of the play

A three-act play, *Ghosts* charts the misfortunes of a middle-class Norwegian family in the late nineteenth century. The Captain Alving Memorial Children's Home has been built by Mrs Alving and is to be opened in memory of her dead husband. At home for the occasion is her son, Oswald, a painter living abroad. Visiting is Pastor Manders who will make a speech at the opening ceremony. Pastor Manders and Mrs Alving discuss preparations and Manders persuades her not to insure the orphanage buildings in case they should be adversely judged by the community as not trusting in divine providence. During this conversation Manders chides Mrs Alving for having been a bad mother, sending her son away from home as a child, and for having free-thinking ideas. In response to these accusations Mrs Alving reminds Manders that, in the first year of her marriage when she sought refuge with him from her dissolute husband, he persuaded her to return and do her duty as a wife. Pride made her fight to conceal the farce that her marriage proved to be and the memorial building is her final act to ensure Alving's respectability in the public eye. Money from the Alving estates, which she alone was capable of managing, has been used to pay for the orphanage; Mrs Alving wants Oswald to inherit nothing from his father. Act I draws to a dramatic close as Mrs Alving overhears her maid Regina and Oswald laughing together. This evokes the memory of her husband's affair with Regina's mother Joanna, a previous maid, of which Regina is the result. Engstrand, a local carpenter, was given money to marry Joanna. Regina is to work at the orphanage but secretly hopes to go to Paris with Oswald; Engstrand asks her to come and work in a seamen's home which he wants to set up, supported by Manders, who apparently does not realize this is, in reality, a brothel. In Act II Oswald confesses to his mother that he has been diagnosed as having syphilis. Because Mrs

Alving has presented him with an idealized father through her letters, he concludes he has only himself to blame for his condition. Mrs Alving decides to tell both him and Regina the truth but is interrupted by the orphanage going up in flames. Arson is the cause, engineered by Engstrand so that Manders appears – and believes himself to be – at fault. Engstrand is then in a position to blackmail Manders, thus gaining financial support for his 'seamen's home'. Money from the Alving estate will be used for this. Act III concludes with Mrs Alving alone with Oswald, having told him and Regina the truth. Regina, insulted, and disappointed in her hopes, leaves to join Engstrand. Oswald explains that he has come home in the hopes that Regina will marry him and, tiring of looking after him when his final attack strikes, will give him an overdose of the morphine he has accumulated. He extracts a promise from his mother that she will do this last service for him. As the sun comes up for the first time in the play, Oswald's final attack happens and Mrs Alving is left with the decision of whether or not to carry out her promise.

Ghosts was first published in 1881 when Ibsen was living in Rome. He knew that it would create a furore in Scandinavia; so great did this prove to be that thirteen years had to elapse before the first edition was finally sold out. As he awaited publication he wrote:

> *Ghosts* will probably cause alarm in certain circles, but that cannot be helped. If it did not, it would not have been necessary to write it.
>
> (Letter to Hegel, November 1881, quoted in Sprinchorn 1964)

The response of the public of Ibsen's day reminds us of the response to Bond's *Saved* nearly a century later in Britain. The discomfort of facing the unacceptable activates projective mechanisms and the writer is scapegoated. What Ibsen wrote in his play was too unpalatable. It was literally too life-threatening in terms of the life of society and the comfortableness of the establishment. The implications for individual responsibility were too great to bear and must be thrust out upon the writer. The 'filth' of his own society, to use the word of one of his critics, must be projected onto Ibsen. He had dared to speak of what must never be spoken about, he had criticized the ethics of his own society:

> Oswald is branded with disease, not because his father was a beast, but because Mrs Alving had obeyed the immoral dictates of society.
>
> (Koht in Meyer 1971: 299)

Meyer makes the point that an added twist is that syphilis can be inherited from the mother rather than the father, although she may have no knowledge that she has the disease:

In other words, and this is a far more frightening explanation of

Oswald's illness than the usual one, Mrs Alving must have caught syphilis from her husband and passed it on to her son. Ibsen knew more about medicine than some of his critics.

(Meyer 1971: 299)

Ibsen's critics branded him because he wrote openly of syphilis and set it in a middle-class respectable household. Thus they defended themselves from what he was really writing about, which Koht makes clear.

This brings us to a very important aspect of the play and one which is of great relevance to the therapist as well as the actor. The readership's response mirrors the way in which people know at one level what they are talking about but somehow speak as though they do not, partly, in my view, because they do not want to know what they really do know. This is reflected in the dialogue of the text. Meyer points to the way in which Mrs Alving and Manders 'spend much of the time circling round a subject to which they dread referring directly, and at these moments the dialogue is oblique, even opaque.' He goes on:

He knew that when people talk about something concerning which they feel a sense of guilt, they cease to speak directly and instead talk evasively and with circumlocution; and actors, when they are playing these lines, have to speak the text but act the sub-text, the unspoken thoughts between the lines.

(Meyer 1971: 301)

As a therapist I attempt to listen with 'free-floating attention' to what the client is trying to say but finding difficult. I try to discern what the unconscious might be saying through the metaphors of speech and body and my own response to these. When teaching *Ghosts* as a literary text I used to work in a practical way, asking the students in role as Manders and Mrs Alving to move in relation to one another according to what they felt was the sub-text while speaking the words of the written text. This technique inevitably produced a dynamic engagement with the play; if we take this into the realm of dramatherapy it produces an added dimension – a dynamic engagement with how the text speaks for the lives of the role-players. We can then work with the difficulty of what cannot be said and find ways to say it. We can help to find the 'unspoken thoughts between the lines'.

When considering the play for dramatherapy I am particularly interested in two areas, and hope that readers will by the discussion of these be stimulated to find their own. The first is that of working within the role of Mrs Alving, allowing the other characters their space as projected parts of her own personality and inner world. The second is to explore each character for what they hold as representative of the experience of the various group members. Either way we need to understand something of each. So let us look at the different characters in the play and consider their dilemmas. We can then look at the ways in which this text can provide a model of choice and change which can help bring the fear of the light out from the dark closet within the creative setting of the dramatherapy group.

Mrs Alving

Although Mrs Alving and her situation are very different from Carol's in *Thursday's Child*, she is another public woman in another small community living with the unbearable. She too bears an intolerable burden. She too provides the audience with a question mark at the end of the play. Mrs Alving is the flesh and blood of the play. In the review of the 1958 Old Vic production where the role was played by Flora Robson, Phillip Hope-Wallace wrote in the *Manchester Guardian*, 'Here indeed was a wife who, more happily married, could have known the joy of living' (quoted in Meyer 1962: 124). She is a proud and passionate woman; highly intelligent and resourceful, courageous and determined. She is the victim of her society's attitudes, behaviours and role. First she must fulfil her mother's and aunt's requirements of her rather than have a voice of her own. She therefore marries Captain Alving because it is what her family want.

Alving is well off and considered a good match. Here Mrs Alving resembles Nora in *A Doll's House*, who is passed from daughter status to wife status without any sense of being a person who is no man's appendage. She hints that her feelings were for Manders himself in those days but these were not taken into account at all (*Ghosts*: 56). Having married Alving and discovered his character she tries to run away, to Manders, their pastor, for refuge. She is sent back to him, reminded of the duty of a wife. After this attempt a way out seems impossible – she must simply endure,

> To keep him at home in the evenings – and at night – I had to make myself his companion in his secret dissipations up in his room. There I had to sit alone with him, had to clink my glass with his, listen to his obscene and helpless drivelling, had to fight with my fists to haul him into bed.
>
> (ibid.: 51)

She has to collude with him rather than bring her distress out into the open. In other words she colludes with an abusive situation rather than risk the consequences of exposing the truth to the light of day. This is hardly different from many such collusions which seem the only way of dealing with impossibly abusive situations which can drive women to crime or breakdown. In having her plea to Manders rejected and being returned to her duty she forfeits the possibility of her own joy of living ever being realized. As she says to her son Oswald after the burning of the orphanage when she realizes that her attempt to erase all influence of Alving from her life has failed,

> They had taught me about duty and things like that, and I sat here for

166

too long believing in them. In the end everything became a matter of duty – *my* duty, *his* duty –.

(ibid.: 86)

but even as she has this revelation it is as though this too must be interpreted through the concept of duty, for she sees no place for self-forgiveness or fury at her own loss of opportunity for her own life; having previously blamed her husband for being how he was, she now blames herself instead, for the speech concludes, 'and I'm afraid I made his home intolerable for your poor father, Oswald'.

She cannot see it as her tragedy, or even their tragedy, but only as her husband's tragedy for which she alone, through her adherence to her upbringing, is responsible. Mrs Alving's real tragedy is that she still caught in a trap. That even when revelation happens she cannot claim freedom from the tenets of society. She can recognize them enough to have new insights but these insights must still be interpreted in a way that continues to enslave her. Her enslavement at the end of the play is therefore all the more terrifying because there is every indication that she will not have the courage to flaunt yet another enormous taboo, that of euthanasia, which Oswald made her promise she would carry out when the time came for his final and irreversible attack brought on by his inherited syphilis.

It is this ending which gives the play its tragic status. Indeed her hamartia or tragic flaw is that she must be brought low. For she has, in a sense, over-reached herself. By taking on the responsibility for solving the issues of how to maintain her marriage she has taken on the reins that must not be allowed a woman. She has worked Alving's estates, kept the business thriving and effected improvements for which Alving is credited. She has dared to do more than becomes a woman and she must suffer for it. She cannot flout the gods of such a society.

Oswald

Ibsen's delineation of the character of Oswald has little of the substance of Mrs Alving. His situation, however, is also that of a tragic character in the Aristotelian sense, for he falls easily into the category of the man who falls from happiness to misery, in his own eyes at least. He believes that his wonderful life of freedom in Italy and Paris amongst fellow artists has been responsible for his syphilitic condition even though Ibsen is rather obscure about the nature of that life; it appears to be very innocent.

Oswald has a curse on him as surely as Oedipus, the 'sins of the fathers' as the doctors abroad told him; a curse as strong as the family curses of the Greek houses. In that sense he is a tragic figure, yet his presence in the play is overshadowed by his mother. To me therefore he is more of an instrument of the playwright, a metaphoric support to the theme of inheritance in the play.

167

As Meyer, the great Ibsen scholar and translator, suggests, 'Oswald's syphilis may be regarded as a symbol of the dead customs and traditions which stunt and cripple us and lay waste our life' (Meyer 1971). The fact of his being less delineated is also because he is like a reincarnation of his father, 'ghosts – walking again', as Mrs Alving says when she hears him and Regina stifling their intimacy in the dining room. He is there to bring into the life of the play the past as it was experienced by Mrs Alving and therefore to underline the inheritance from which she cannot free herself. But this very cardboardness of the character also emphasizes the fact that the child was in a sense the puppet of the parents. The concern which made Mrs Alving send her son away so that he should not be affected by the reality of home life was her way of dealing with the impossible situation in which she found herself. Oswald was therefore caught in the trap of the marriage, and the irony is that he could not escape the results of that marriage anyway as they sowed the seeds of his death: 'I didn't ask you for life. And what kind of life have you given me? I don't want it. Take it back' (*Ghosts*: 92).

The life she has given him is one in which his death has been sealed from the moment of conception and one in which he must be deprived of family life. It is also a life built on lies as Mrs Alving kept up the pretence of her husband being a pillar of the community. In the absence of truth Oswald has had to blame himself for what has happened. On being diagnosed as having inherited syphilis Oswald showed the doctor the letters his mother sent him full of the fabrications of the worthy Alving. He drew the only conclusion he could:

> And then I learned the truth. The incredible truth! This wonderful happy life with my comrades, I should have abstained from. It had been too much for my strength. In other words I have only myself to blame.
>
> (ibid.: 71)

Mrs Alving used lies intended to save him suffering in his life. She presented an idealized father to him, writing from the safe distance of Norway. She kept him from home so that he should never see the truth of his father's condition and the reality of their marriage. She has thereby unwittingly only compounded a suffering which she had not dreamed he would have to endure. 'If only it was something I'd inherited – something I wasn't to blame for' (ibid.).

Still in ignorance in Act II his words are heavy with tragic irony.

Here Oswald gives a voice to more people and more issues than his own, for it makes the point of children being the hapless inheritors of parental and societal codes and circumstances. He gives a voice to the parts of the individual which is a puppet of the parents.

There is another important aspect to this character which can help us in looking at the taboo areas of sexuality and sexually transmitted diseases. For Oswald has been invisible much of his life; he has been out of his own country, an exile, as it were. He reappears to confront his mother with his situation, little knowing how much of a can of worms he is to open in doing so. His pain becomes intolerable when the doctors tell him that his next attack will reduce him irrevocably to a vegetable-like condition. Until he comes home to tell his mother he has had to carry his pain alone.

In the early days of AIDS gay men lived in terror of being known to be HIV positive. Even with the now widespread awareness of the disease, little has changed in having to cope with the double burden of the stigma of the disease and the horror of enduring the disease itself. Admitting to the disease meant, and still means, for gay men, admitting to being gay in a society in which it is by no means safe to do so. In Britain Clause 28, as it was popularly known, with its farcical ban on material which 'promoted' homosexuality, was introduced by the government at a time when there was increasing concern about AIDS – not because more gay men were dying, but because of the evidence of how widespread the disease was amongst the heterosexual population. Earlier publicity tended to be more along the lines of panic and condemnation of the 'gay plague'. The terror and the horror which Oswald faces echoes that faced today by those coping with HIV and AIDS. The isolation he so vividly evokes and the self-condemnation are easily identified with. The fear, the fury, the guilt – and the pain of realization of his own inheritance; all these are feelings which Oswald gives a voice to; so often for those suffering with AIDS there is neither voice nor listener.

Engstrand, Manders and Regina

Engstrand, Manders and Regina are fundamental in looking at the theme of inheritance in society. Apparently on opposite sides of the fence from one another, they are in fact inseparable and interdependent. They represent the force with which the taboos of society are maintained, not for the health of that society but for its dis-ease. They contribute to the pain and isolation which Mrs Alving and Oswald represent. They stand for the partnership of hypocrisy which continues to drive sexual expression underground with resulting tragic consequences.

Manders represents the hypocrisy which guarantees the status quo. When Mrs Alving comes to him in despair he sends her back to 'do her duty'. To do anything else would mean his having to take responsibility and perhaps to stand out against the crowd. For the man who does not dare to insure the orphanage which is dedicated to Alving because public opinion might doubt his belief in God, this would be an impossibility. He is a man who denounces the free-thinking books he finds on Mrs Alving's table without ever having read them, just as some churchmen in the 1990s denounced the film of *The Last Temptation of Christ* without having seen it. His life is one of appearances and superficiality but one which is poisonous in its effect. Just as his judgements are superficial because he dare not engage with any other reality which might demand anything of him, so his judgements of other people are superficial too. He never visited the Alvings after Mrs Alving's defection from her husband. As Mrs Alving taunts him, 'One can never be too careful with such unprincipled women' (ibid.: 49).

When he accuses her of grossly exaggerating, her reply points to the irrefutable fact of his willingness to form his opinion on 'common gossip'.

It is this man, and countless like him, who force Mrs Alving to go underground with her problems. She therefore colludes with society's hypocrisy for the fear of doing otherwise is too great; that itself is a taboo too hard to break. One of the consequences of this is that she feels compelled to bring her son up on lies, thinking she is doing the best thing possible. The result of this is the confusion and anguish of Oswald who has been led to believe in the near-perfection of his father.

Another aspect of Manders's superficial judgement is illustrated by his attitude to Engstrand. He is perpetually taken in by Engstrand and always believes the carpenter's stories of prayer and contrition. Engstrand makes a virtue of being the scapegoat while at the same time being in reality nothing of the sort. He deliberately lights a fire in the orphanage in order to set Manders up. He makes the Pastor believe he did it himself. This puts Engstrand in the position of being able to take the blame and thus have Manders perpetually indebted to him. Moral blackmail is his business. And for this he can ensure Manders's support for his 'home for seamen' which Ibsen makes clear is to be a brothel. As Engstrand says,

> And the house for wandering sailors is to be called Captain Alving's Home; and if I am allowed to run it according to my ideas, I think I can promise you it'll be a worthy memorial to him, God rest his soul.
>
> (ibid.: 84)

By means of the relationship between Engstrand and Manders the tightness of this sub-plot serves to underline the issue of taboo and inheritance in a way which challenges the society built on Manders's values. Manders and Engstrand can be seen as individual characters in the play. They can also be seen as joint forces which together make such people as Mrs Alving and Oswald, and indeed Alving himself, the ultimate scapegoats of society. Engstrand and Manders will survive and continue to breed a society in which change is not possible. They will drag Regina down with them for her inheritance is that real choice is not possible for her either. As she says, she will take after her mother and what was her mother but a victim of the world where a woman must do her duty, as Mrs Alving so clearly pointed out to Manders. Doing her duty meant not rocking the boat but going along with men's desires whatever that might entail.

Unlike Nora, in Ibsen's earlier play, *A Doll's House*, Mrs Alving does not leave her husband; when she tries to do so Manders sends her home to do her duty, with tragic results. For Regina, leaving Mrs Alving's service means the possibility of freedom, but Ibsen makes it abundantly clear that her future is only another kind of slavery. Ironically if she had married her half-brother Oswald, as Mrs Alving is prepared to condone, she would, as Oswald antici- pates, become fed up with nursing him and either leave him or give him the morphine to enable him to die as he wishes. But the taboo of incest is too great and it is impossible for Regina to see this as a choice. 'I suppose I'm allowed to say Oswald now. But it certainly isn't the way I'd hoped' (ibid.: 87).

Regina is also a vital link in the metaphor of disease being inherited since she goes with Engstrand and Manders in the full knowledge that what she is to become is a prostitute. She will be therefore, in terms of being a possible carrier of infection from her father, Alving, or her mother form part of the chain of continuity of inherited disease.

In dramatherapy the concept of repetition is important as I discussed in Chapter 2. The tragedy of all of the characters in *Ghosts* is that they are doomed to repeat, not to change. They rehearse nothing. Mrs Alving put all the money she received in dowry from Alving into the orphanage, 'to make sure that my own son, Oswald, should not inherit anything whatever from his father' (ibid.: 52).

The irony of this is crudely obvious but none the less effective, for Mrs Alving at this stage of the play has no idea that Oswald is suffering from in- herited syphilis. Mrs Alving has worked hard to create the orphanage; she has tried to change history by providing a home for children with her husband's name on it. She has tried to create wish-fulfilment in reality, as though she can somehow create an upright, kindly, responsible, father-figure from her husband's ashes, such as he never was in life. The reality of his father as Oswald remembers him, with agonizing irony for the audience, is, 'I don't remember anything about him, except that once he made me sick' (ibid.: 89).

Mrs Alving, like Manders, believes that appearances can be the reality. But there is a greater reality, which is that the orphanage has to burn and at Eng- strand's hands. For it is Engstrand who is really in touch with reality in a soci- ety where everything is hypocritical. All that can come of Alving's memory is that Mrs Alving has to live with her son in an even worse condition than his father, enduring the days and nights of Alving's real bequest. Therefore she is doomed to repeat; she cannot rewrite history though she has tried to control it.

It is here that the link with dramatherapy emerges, for in a psychodynamic therapeutic process the past must be unravelled before change can take place. Mrs Alving tries to exercise control, as does Oswald in his plans to marry Regina. They both wish to move against the pattern which is set down for them in the past. Where this play can be useful in the therapeutic process is that it offers an opportunity for going back into the past, for reconnecting with past pain and constraints through the analagous situation which the text provides. The feelings can then be engaged with and worked through. Al- though in the therapeutic process we cannot change society, we can look at what we have inculcated of society's values in an undigested form and at what we have projected either into or onto others in order to remain in the same position. At least working on change from within is then possible.

IN PRACTICE

I am going to suggest two ways of working on this play, though the reader may think of others more suited to a particular purpose. The first is to use the play as a mirror in working towards change for an individual in a group context. The second is to use the play as a holding environment for those affected by HIV and AIDS whether directly or in terms of being close to those who have it. This is a more directly cathartic approach where the characters may be used to provide a voice for the difficult and painful feelings of the group members in a safe, witnessing environment. It is important to add that this second approach is a tentative suggestion for I have not yet worked in this context with the play; those working in the field of HIV and AIDS might wish to consider its possibilities. My focus is therefore at this stage of my work on this play on the first of these suggestions.

Ghosts as mirror for client and therapist

The client group

If we concentrate on the character of Mrs Alving we can find that many of the other characters live in her. Another way of putting this is to say that the parts she has split off, repressed, denied or misplaced are found in the other characters. As the play proceeds she begins to find some of those parts of herself as she starts to look at her life in ways prompted by the events of the play – the dedication of the orphanage and Oswald's return. One of the reasons why the other characters seem less complex than her is that they are in some ways more like aspects of Mrs Alving than fully formed characters in their own right. We see parts of each of them in Mrs Alving herself and the remainder of those parts are left to be enacted by the other characters. In dramatherapy we can make use of this feature of Ibsen's character construction very effectively.

Pastor Manders in Mrs Alving is that part of her which is the voice of society. It is the voice within herself that says she must do her duty. We can see how Ibsen identifies that voice and that pressure in her by creating the role of Pastor to speak aloud those 'thou shalts and thou shalt nots' that hem in Mrs Alving and all women of that society. We can empathize with her and her pain when he says to her, prior to her revelations of the actuality of her whole married life, 'And that I persuaded you to bow to the call of duty and obedience, has that not proved a blessing which will surely enrich the remainder of your days?' (ibid.: 47).

He is the internalized voice of her upbringing. He is also, of course, the representation of the pastors who abounded in the society of which Ibsen wrote, but he is also the voice which has been drummed into her from a child, a voice with which the Church spoke to society and helped to form and maintain its repressive and hypocritical values.

It is precisely because he is that mixture of her internal super-ego voice and a representation of the societal super-ego that we can work so directly with that part of Mrs Alving in dramatherapy. A helpful technique here is that of role and role-reversal. Within this structure the group member can take on the role of Mrs Alving and either address an empty chair which represents Manders, or have another group member play that role for her. From this position the individual can then focus on those aspects of her super-ego which have become overdeveloped to the point of damage to herself. She can both talk *to* Manders and talk *as* Manders. In doing so she can find an external form which can help her to shift an internal position which has remained stuck. The engagement with the role through the mechanism of aesthetic distance can allow changes to take place in the intra-psychic relationships of the role-player.

Mrs Alving herself gains some relief in the play by putting Manders right. Even working at that level, of reading the play and finding it possible to find a voice, through the character, for that part of oneself which has always bowed to the super-ego or to external pressure to do what one ought rather than what one wants, can bring some relief, especially if the individual is ready to reflect on what they have done and how the character relates to their own life. Mrs Alving stands up to Manders and in doing so she provides a role-model for the individual which she might never have had before. Mrs Alving's tragedy is that her revelations to Manders come too late for her to change her life. At this point the group member may wish to move into another character to express other aspects of herself or her feelings, for example, Regina.

Regina in Mrs Alving represents that part of her which wants freedom; the young, vital, sexual woman whom she has denied. It is this part of her which she can eventually recognize when she says, 'And I didn't bring any sunshine into his [Alving's] home' (ibid.: 86). Mrs Alving says yes to duty, to repression, to denial of the real self. She builds up a false self based on the notions of her family. She never develops a self which is different except in secret and private rebellion in relation to her husband. It is this Mrs Alving who can speak Regina's lines in the dramatherapy context and begin to explore what having that voice in herself feels like. 'No, I'm not going to stay out here in the country and wear myself out looking after invalids' (ibid.: 87).

This is what she could have said to her husband, but did not, because of the Manders voice in her which colluded with the actual voice of Manders when she tried to leave Alving. Even to think of a possibility other than staying and 'enduring', as she puts it, becomes impossible.

The Regina voice in Mrs Alving has never been awakened, the voice which is aware of her own sexuality and joy of living. The repression of this has caused her to have few resources to fight with for her own independence. Regina stands for the right to choose sexuality. The person playing the role of Mrs Alving and discovering the Regina voice in her can engage in exploring her relationship with that voice. This might lead to the possibility of exploring new avenues, or of mourning the loss of what she did not have. An acceptance of the past is an important part of freeing up the future.

Having engaged with the repression through the character of Manders, and finding a part which has been repressed through the character of Regina, the actor is then free to move into the role of Engstrand.

The Engstrand in Mrs Alving is the scapegoat, the one who colludes. To allow herself to take the entire blame for what has happened to her husband is the function of the scapegoat in herself. The scapegoat, the one who takes the blame for another's sins, is represented by Engstrand. (Although Engstrand does this consciously and to his own advantage he still provides that role in the play.) Mrs Alving even sees part of herself in Engstrand when she likens her marriage to Alving for his money to Engstrand being paid to marry Regina's mother. For the actor, to work with the Engstrand character while in role as Mrs Alving can enable an exploration of that part of herself which finds that collusion with being the scapegoat was a function. To integrate that part can also be healing, for while remaining unconscious but active in the individual's behaviour it serves only to maintain the personality's defensive splitting rather than effecting change through integration.

Having moved through acknowledging the repression and super-ego functions of Manders, the unrealized sexuality and life force represented by Regina, and the collusion with scapegoat characteristics of Engstrand, the actor is now ready to face the hardest role, that of Oswald.

The Oswald in Mrs Alving represents that part of her which is trapped by her inheritance. It is the part of her which is doomed to die, to be burnt out, to be infected irrevocably. It represents the horror and pain of approaching death which Oswald carries within him, of knowing his life is over. All the creativity which Mrs Alving has shown in dealing with her situation by managing to make Alving's estates thrive, is like Oswald's talents as a painter being killed by his illness. Mrs Alving has to face her own horror at the end of the play when she has to take in her son's final collapse. This is different from the implications for her own loss of power which the voice of Oswald can give her. This is the voice of the Mrs Alving who, at last apparently freed of her husband's legacy with the burning of the orphanage, finds the full horror of that legacy enfolding and trapping her for ever, either as the full-time carer of Oswald or as the woman who must live with the inheritance of having enabled her son to die.

To work with the character of Mrs Alving, using the voices of the other characters in the play, is an opportunity for integration. But this is not likely to be achieved through role-reversal alone. Having worked with the characters in whatever order is appropriate the actor can then do what the characters in the play cannot; she can look at the future in terms of change. What change is possible now that the different voices have been able to be expressed? The next stage would be to rework the characters. A method I have used with this play at this stage is to have chairs labelled for all the characters. The protagonist in the dramatherapy can then go to each chair and speak from it. The words which now come are those which result from the shifts made by having engaged with those parts of the self which have been represented by the various characters. By beginning to integrate these the individual is then in a position to add reflection. The exercise of speaking from each chair allows the person to refocus on implications for change and future possibilities. Thus a decision might be to allow the collusive scapegoat less of a voice, or to engage in the external world differently in relation to the voices of the super-ego, be they those of parent or internalized parent. The focus might be to find a new perspective on an intolerable situation which, like Oswald's illness, is not going to go away, and strengthen parts of the personality to cope with those. Whatever is the outcome of the engagement with the role, the group will have provided a containing context for the individual's journey. Its members will have been present as active witnesses, either in role-taking or silently supporting the individual actor's process.

Another way in which the play might be used is to allow for the discharge of emotions which are too hard to bear. The finding of a voice and the sharing of an identity with the character can enable the individual to express intolerable feelings in the presence of group members whose function it is to provide a supportive audience.

The therapist

In approaching a play one must never discount the effect of the material on oneself as a therapist. Some of this will of course remain unconscious for we can never have access to all our own resonances. However, we must stay with the play and what it awakens in us long enough to be able to tease out the effect it has on us as far as we can. While attempting to write this chapter I was struggling with events in my own external life which had repercussions in my internal world. My struggle in writing it was that I felt that I could not use my own experience openly in my writing. I then realized that this was because I felt blocked by issues which I had internalized as taboos. The first of these was that as a therapist I should not reveal too much about my own particular experience. Secondly I felt inhibited from using an example of an important event in my life because it in itself was surrounded by taboos. The prohibition was strong in spite of the fact that this particular experience was the very thing that enabled me to make some of my most vital connections with the play. I was left in a dilemma; how could I either write the chapter or not write the chapter?

I then realized that what I was experiencing mirrored Mrs Alving's problem both at the end of the play and throughout her life. It was the thing that made her, in a different sense from her son, 'worm-eaten from birth'. For Mrs Alving was worm-eaten by society's restrictions and the feelings that she had no choice. One of the reasons that Mrs Alving had no choice, and had to keep silent, was that the behaviour of her husband was in society's terms unmentionable. As we leave her at the end of the play, this is repeated for so is the nature of Oswald's illness. What was left to her was silently to do her 'duty'. This is probably what she will continue to do – or is it? Surely this must remain one of the great questions a character leaves an audience with in the canon of European dramatic literature.

What became clear to me was that I was being eaten up by the difficulty that faced me, which was to do with what I had internalized as the 'duty' of a therapist and the taboo of a situation I was in. This latter was a twentieth-century version of the sexual taboo of this nineteenth-century Norwegian play. A member of my family had died of AIDS and I was stuck with all the taboos about sexuality and sexually transmitted diseases which still lie not far from the surface of this terrible illness. These restrictions were part of my social inheritance.

Aspects of my dilemma mirrored that of Mrs Alving and my own situation. This led me to a more profound sympathy with the character than I had ever had before. Until I had made the connection for myself with my own material I could not shift the block that was stopping me from writing the chapter. It is the same, I believe, in the therapy process whether the block is that of the therapist or the client – that which blocks the character can help one to uncover one's own block; this can be done only through finding the links between the character's material and one's own. This is often done through creative engagement with the unconscious, a kind of Winnicottian playing and it proved to be so in this instance. It was a recognition which fed directly through unconscious creative processes which led me to my understanding that I and the play were so linked at this moment that I could not see the wood for the trees.

The previous day I had painted a picture which I had called 'Forest Fires'. Although I could make connections to my own processes and also to the reality of these fires in the landscape around me at the time of writing, it was not until the next day that I suddenly found myself saying out loud for no apparent reason, 'Everything is burning, we too shall burn.' Instantly I realized I was echoing Oswald's line, 'Everything will burn. . . . I too am burning' (ibid.: 84). It was at that moment that I realized how deeply the play was living inside me. My realization came from the creative and unconscious engagement with the play which had been quietly going on underneath my conscious struggle with it. After a period of living through the blocks and chaos in relation to the play, the text had finally reasserted itself and released me from the thrall in which I had been held. It is at this point that the unconscious can become conscious and the play move into its healing mode. The play and the individual can move apart though they are still linked. The merger of the text and the person enables a relationship to form but the individual cannot move away and use the text for learning unless there is a separation. Then choice becomes possible. In this instance either I could choose, like Mrs Alving, to remain locked in taboos and silence or I could choose to challenge those. My engagement with the play had given me that choice and like all choices it was a risk, a step into the unknown.

This example of the therapist's process is analagous to what can often happen in a therapy group working with a dramatic text; it is therefore an important part of the therapist's personal work with the text as part of his or her own preparation or internal supervision during work-in-progress. The chaos and the stuckness must be respected as part of the process while the group or individual must continually keep their own creative process going, as I did by my painting. At such times sometimes, particularly in an ongoing group, it is the therapist who must 'hold' that part when the clients are in the place of despair. Eventually the reassertion of the text will come and its landscape will be revealed as one known all along but with features which surprise and challenge. Then we are in a better position to be able fully to use the play to rehearse rather than repeat, to go over old ground and lay the seeds for growth.

8

WALLS WITHIN WALLS –
SOCIETY, FAMILY
AND THE INDIVIDUAL
A Shaft of Sunlight by Abhijat Joshi

In this play we move from nineteenth-century Norway to twentieth-century India to explore a different aspect of the relationship between family and society. Although there is a death at the end here too, there is hope and and a restatement of living. In writing about *A Shaft of Sunlight* I concentrate on the theme of division.

THE PLAY

The setting of the play is a society where riots are endemic and the division is echoed in the family. Any civil dispute can be seen as the division of the self, of a society against its own self, a house divided against itself. In his statement in the programme of the play's production by Tamasha Theatre Company and the Birmingham Repertory Company (1994), the author says:

> Time has come for the Indian society to stop shifting blame of the situation onto manipulative politicians and financial giants, and realize their own responsibility. The play attempts to trace the subtle but deeply ingrained prejudice in a generation which has the advantage of both education and a distance in time from the terrible events at partition.

Résumé of the play

Bimal, who is Hindu, is married to Safeena, who is Muslim. They have one daughter, Roona, of about 11. When the play opens Roona is answering the telephone and we learn that there are riots on the other side of the river. Bimal and Safeena return from a function at the college where he teaches; Safeena is upset and angry at the anti-Muslim remarks made by some of Bimal's colleagues. There is evidence of further conflict between Safeena and Shanta, her mother-in-law, who lives upstairs. Thus mirrored in the family are the conflicts in society. Currently these focus on an old wall which both Muslims and Hindus are claiming for their own as an ancient religious site. Into the warring household comes Altaaf, an old childhood friend of Safeena's, seeking refuge having just blown up the wall. He remains with the family during the ensuing six days of curfew, making friends with Roona and urging a reparation between Safeena and Shanta which he helps to effect. As a result of Shanta's fury at the destruction of her religious symbol, Altaaf tells how his father was killed in the riots of the 1960s and of his wish to stop people destroying each other. From Kamla, who is employed by Bimal and Safeena to clean, we learn of the social conditions, corruption and oppression of the poorer sectors of the community and the way the dispute over the wall is used to exploit them further. Soon it is clear that Altaaf's hiding-place is known. In order to protect the family Altaaf devises a plan in which he will pretend to be holding Roona hostage thus clearing the family of any suspicion that he is there with their complicity. He refuses to let Bimal help him to try and escape. Bimal reluctantly agrees to the plan and the important relationship of trust and understanding which Roona has built up with Altaaf enables her to go through with it. The play ends with the family beginning to communicate with one another again after Altaaf's death and with an important message about love and survival.

My own reading of the play leads me see how it illustrates the need to withdraw projections if the responsibility of which Joshi speaks is to be realized; it explores issues of growth and maturation as it illustrates a society, which, like so many others where rioting takes place, takes refuge in paranoid-schizoid mechanisms rather than moving on to the depressive position in which loss can be mourned and what 'is' must be recognized so that relationship and reponsibility are both possible; the individual and society can move on. In *A Shaft of Sunlight* both of these positions are manifest, the paranoid-schizoid by the by adult members of the family and the depressive by Roona, the child, and by Altaaf who destroys the wall which is the site under dispute.

Whilst there are many questions raised in this play, one of the most fundamental the audience is left with is if and how divisions can be healed. What interests me as a dramatherapist is the way in which what I call a 'lived understanding of metaphor and creativity' are shown as a way forward in healing deep rifts in societies. It is by these means, as I hope to show, that a 'shaft of sunlight' can penetrate the barred windows of prejudice and hatred. An awareness of the need to withdraw projected aspects of ourselves in order to take responsibility for our own lives and actions, rather than hide behind blaming the other, is set out in this play.

It is by attention to metaphor and to the child within that the play indicates moments of reparation, moments of coming together, the possibilities of the healing of rifts and the chance of hope. It exemplifies my belief in the efficacy of creative engagement with metaphor which is central to dramatherapy.

These ideas are borne out by the discussion of a workshop on the play at the end of the chapter.

The use of imagery is one of the play's strengths, for it can operate like poetry, creating many layers of meaning which reverberate in the different themes and relationships with which the play is concerned. In the workshop which I shall refer to later, one woman had both heard the original radio play and seen the theatre production; she said that in the stage version she needed to close her eyes and listen to it, for it worked better that way for her; I found this an interesting comment for it emphasizes the poetic quality of the writing which creates its own visual impact on the listening audience.

As soon as we think of imagery in this play we are faced with the central image of the wall around which the whole play revolves. A Muslim friend to whom I showed the play said, 'They couldn't have chosen a better image'. It functions superbly as a metaphor for division. Metaphor is therefore at the heart of the play, its importance reflected in the title and operating throughout in the motif of the wall. Let us therefore explore the wall, what it stands for and how it can help us in our reflections on the relationships in the play, on the inner worlds of the characters, and on the message of the play as a whole.

The wall and society

The wall acts like a backcloth to the interpersonal relationships within the play upon which is printed the symbols of economic oppression and exploitation. Altaaf, who blows up the wall, reveals this clearly:

> When I came here I thought there was just one union and then I realized there were two factions. I went to the Hindu muzdoors. They weren't concerned about their wages. They had been bought by the contractor – to rebuild the temple at the site of the wall. They were given knives. Then I went to the Muslims – they had guns, bombs. The bootleggers had bought them to build a mosque on the same site on the same day. The site would have become a battlefield. . . . imagine thousands of them having these weapons. Angry, humiliated men out of work for a couple of years. Some of them have seen their wives street walking, their kids begging. They're a pushover for anyone who wants to use them.

> (Scene 3)

By providing another focus and target for the feelings evoked by poverty and injustice, those responsible for paying the men divert the aggression which would otherwise come their way and save themselves money at the expense of the lowest paid sector of society. Feelings about the wall, which result in rioting, are therefore built on a lie. The wall itself is built on a lie. It is literally built up in the minds and imaginations of people until it becomes a temple or a mosque onto which they can project all their aggression and hatred as either Muslim or Hindu. In reality the wall is not a symbol of religion but of dishonesty and opportunism. It is a pile of stones which can become whatever those with the most eye to the main chance can make it. It is an object onto which anything can be projected which happens to suit the needs of any social group or individual who wishes to gain from it, either in terms of economic power or personal power, or as a way of resisting change.

As an object onto which the proof that change is undesirable or impossible is projected we can look at the grandmother, Shanta's response. She believes unshakeably that the wall is a holy wall; she accuses Altaaf of shattering the 'symbol of my faith into fragments'. When Altaaf explains to her his reasons for blowing up the wall and lays bare the hypocrisy and hatred which the wall symbolizes through his moving account of his own childhood experience of a riot in which his father was killed, she can only shut her ears: 'I must go. It is too late to change my concept of God. This is not the age to make changes' (Scene 10).

In another section of society the wall seems to be recognized as a container of lies, corruption, brutality and injustice. The servant to this middle-class household, Kamla, is fully aware of how the wall is used as an excuse for the exploitation of the people on a daily basis and as such she sees it as of no more significance than all the other tools of oppression. The playwright gives his audience a lot of important information about the social context in which the dispute over the wall takes place by means of the following dialogue between Safeena, Kamla and Bimal:

SAFEENA: Things all right at the basti? You have adequate police protection?

KAMLA: What protection, behenji? It is the police we fear the most.

SAFEENA: Why?

KAMLA: They can't catch the real rogues . . . or don't maybe. But they must show that they have caught someone. So our sons are picked up as the spoils of the day, put in the jail for a week. And if they resist it is four weeks plus beating.

SAFEENA: I can't believe this.

KAMLA: And the vultures in uniform . . . they demand tea and coffee from us as if rivers of them flow through the basti. But the boys give them gladly. Don't ask me what they mix into that tea.

SAFEENA: This should not be encouraged. You can't hold grudges against the police. They are overworked . . . underpaid.

KAMLA: And our men? They have no work. They are underfed. Ah, behenji, you should see them, how restless they get . . . and to top it all, that sahukaar comes every day to suck their blood.

SAFEENA: The money lender? But how can he come to you during the curfew?

KAMLA: He bribes the police. He knows that curfew is the best time to plague people. You can't say, 'My husband has gone out, come tomorrow.' He takes it out on our husbands and our husbands take it out on us at night. They become bulls. Animals I tell you, (*laughing*). That is why the radiowallahs do the wise thing. After every news about riots they remind us 'Tin tin tin – have only one kid – tin tin tin.'

(*Safeena laughs. Bimal returns.*)

BIMAL: What happened?

SAFEENA: Kamla just showed me the silver lining of the curfew.

KAMLA: And for six days they didn't have the booze. So they went on a betting spree.

SAFEENA: Betting?

KAMLA: When would the curfew be lifted? Would the blowing of the wall stop the riots? Would they call in the army? How many people got killed? How many Hindus? How many Muslims?

BIMAL: How can anyone be flippant about the riots.

KAMLA: Sahib, I am in the riots I can be flippant. This man, Altaaf Niyazi – is a real boon for the bookies. Is he alive or dead? Is he hiding in the city or has he fled? And above all – who is going to catch and lynch him – the Hindus – the Muslims or the police.

(Scene 6)

The wall seems to be part of the cycle of events that attend one upon the other; the police begin and end her tale and in between we see the layers of oppression, lies, opportunism and brutality. We see, in other words, wall after wall after wall erected to keep the least fortunate in society caged into their continuing oppression. The religious significance of the wall has little relevance for Kamla:

> Who cares if they build a temple or a mosque. Would my husband stop beating me? I still have to clean this floor. I still have to clean the latrine.
>
> (Scene 6)

If we compare the words with those of Shanta earlier we are clearly shown that for the old lady's class the religious significance of the wall is a luxury which those of Kamla's cannot afford. In this context the metaphor of the wall therefore serves as a reminder of the gap between the educated middle classes and the poor who may work for them – if they have the chance to work at all. The fact that Safeena is so unacquainted with the everyday reality of Kamla's life reinforces the playwright's presentation of the wall which exists between them.

The wall, therefore, is an effective symbol for social divisions: rich and poor, educated and non-educated, men and women, those in uniform and those without, employer and employed.

The wall and the family

In exploring how the wall serves as a metaphor for division within the family I shall look at four relationships – Shanta and Safeena; Safeena and Bimal; Shanta and Bimal, and finally Roona and her parents. Here we shall see how divisions are created by individuals, yet their foundations lie in the religious and cultural heritage and previous experience of division for which they, individually, may not be directly responsible. In this section I focus on the wall; later we shall look at ways in which the walls in these relationships can be taken down.

Shanta and Safeena

Almost from the start of the play we are aware of the hostility between Shanta, Bimal's Hindu mother, and Safeena, her Muslim daughter-in-law. The image of the wall serves to illustrate the barrier between them, but it is more than that, for both Safeena and Shanta have come to experience each other as a wall, a barrier which prevents them from reaching Bimal and indeed one another. There is a double layer to the metaphor here. In the row which Bimal and Safeena have in the first scene this is already clear.

> SAFEENA: So that's what you think . . . that I am jealous of her. Jealous of HER. You are mad. It is she who is jealous of me. Can't you see that? Can't you see? She can't bear the fact that I would survive her and move around in her son's house, her cluster of keys clicking at my saari. She thinks that I have snatched away her son so she is out to snatch my daughter.
>
> (Scene 1)

Shanta for her part blames Safeena for alienating her son. When she begs Bimal to take her to see the wall so that she can make an offering, she immediately assumes that Safeena is behind his refusal. Bimal is bemused:

> BIMAL: How does she come into this? Safeena never said you cannot go to see the wall.
> SHANTA: The Queen doesn't say things. It is up to the courtiers to know what she wishes.
> BIMAL: She is not a queen, she is Safeena.
> SHANTA: They ruled this country once. They were the victors. They haven't forgotten it.

Here Safeena becomes for Shanta the wall not only of the present but also of the past, dividing her son and herself, echoing the divisions seen so often in India's history. She continues, 'They capture the country first, then the house, and then the heart.'

Both women project onto one another the hatred inherited from historical events and relationships. In doing so they move further apart from one another and further towards a paranoid position in which reality testing becomes impossible. The vendetta between them becomes manifest in many apparently small gestures of punishment and revenge in the context of which the audience is given hints that the situation between the two women has been so bad only during the last twelve months. It is only towards the end of the play that the reason for this is disclosed. When it comes it shows how easily, when there is a history of mistrust in the wider society, actions within the family can be misinterpreted. The resulting feelings are then slotted into boxes which are placed on either side of a wall which seems to be built instantly and out of nothing unless we see its historical and cultural context.

In the first attempts at taking down this wall we see how flimsy was its fabrication but how firmly that became set over the previous year. When her father died Safeena visted her home for the first time since her marriage. What happened that night reveals a misunderstanding which Safeena has carefully nurtured over the ensuing months, building up a wall which divides her from Shanta, firm in her belief that its first stones were laid by her mother-in-law.

> SAFEENA: I can't forgive you. I won't forgive you. That night you accompanied me to my papa's house. I thought you would be a comfort to me – you knew how I was feeling – being called home after twelve years. I had to go in secret, still a taint on the family. You loved it – having accepted me you were able to show that you were better than them. Papa was commanded by the biradaari to sever all ties with me. My sisters would remain unmarried if the family continued to see me. Papa didn't have the courage to go against them. That night he just wanted to say good-bye. Do you remember the advice he gave me – 'Beta – you've burned your bridges – now you are on that side of the river in the hands of those Hindus. Keep them happy – you don't know how they can make you suffer' – how you relished those words. And then you laughed at him – you laughed at my Papa.
>
> (Scene 12)

We can imagine Safeena's distress, re-visiting her original home after years of what amounted to exile, paying the price for religious, cultural and filial disobedience. In this context it is easy to see how such walls based on assumptions and attendant hasty judgements can begin to be built. For if we follow the scene further, we find what is on the other side of the wall.

> SHANTA: No, Safeena.
> SAFEENA: You did. I saw it – I saw the satisfaction on your face.
> SHANTA: No.

184

SAFEENA: Oh yes – you laughed at an arrogant Muslim brought to his knees ... a Muslim who had finally seen the light ... who had to accept the supremacy of your sect.

SHANTA: Oh my poor child.

SAFEENA: Don't touch me.

SHANTA: I didn't laugh at your father, I smiled.

SAFEENA: What's the difference.

SHANTA: All the difference. When he said the Hindus will make you suffer there was an irony in his words. When I was widowed after only one month of marriage it was the Hindus that made me suffer. Yes – my people, not outsiders. My father was told that if I remarried all my sisters would die spinsters. Does that threat sound familiar? Just like yours my father obeyed. They came to cut off my hair – I had long hair – Safeena – it almost reached my feet. They cut it till I was almost bald. Then they wrapped up my belongings in this white saari, and put me in a corner to grow old. Safeena, that night when your father spoke of suffering, all this was in my mind. His people cut him off from his dearest daughter ... my people ruined me and yet, we spent a life hating each other. And so I smiled.

(Scene 12)

What has been projected onto the outsider is the aggressor within her own society. What Safeena suffered at the hands of her own culture, especially its dictates as executed by the loved father, is displaced onto the mother-in-law from the opposing culture. Shanta becomes the recipient for her hurt and anger; she becomes the enemy. It is convenient then for Safeena to see slights where none were intentioned and to ignore the possibility of finding commonality with her mother-in-law.

Yet the experience of the two women is remarkably similar. Shanta herself has also displaced feelings in the sense that her acceptance of a Muslim daughter-in-law is tangled up with feelings towards her own family at whose hands she has suffered so appallingly.

SHANTA: I was defying my people. They had stripped me of all my dignity and so thirty years later I graciously accepted a Muslim daughter-in-law. And so I got my revenge.

(Scene 12)

She too has built her own wall, a wall of dishonesty of motive never shared until this moment. It is in this relationship that we can see how feelings generated within the family of origin get carried forward into the family the individual marries into; how history is relived projectively and how hate and mistrust are thereby perpetuated. As we look now at the relationship between Safeena and Bimal this becomes apparent.

Safeena and Bimal

From the beginning of the play the wall which exists between husband and wife is seen to be strong and growing bigger every day. It is a wall which clearly is related to the events which we have just heard Safeena describe in the previous section. Part of the wall is constituted from the non-communication of Safeena's pain and hurt. This has largely contributed to the wall's existence. We see how quickly the wall can grow in these circumstances. In this relationship my image of the wall is that its destructiveness lies in its thickness. It is as though Bimal and Safeena can still see over it but are moving further and further away from each other. Practically every move of Bimal is interpreted as an attack on herself by Safeena. Bimal's survival tactics are to extend his secularist liberalism to his personal relationships where it does not always work. In this way both husband and wife build up the thickness of the wall and are consequently pushed by this further and further away from each other and into positions of loneliness in the relationship. We can see this in their opening row in which the bigger wall of Muslim–Hindu relations looms and shadows their personal relationship and strengthens the wall between them. Having returned from a function at the college where Bimal teaches, Safeena explodes:

SAFEENA: I'm sick of talking things over.

BIMAL: You must give me a chance to explain.

SAFEENA: Explain it to your friends.

BIMAL: My colleagues didn't deliberately insult you. Feelings are running high. They were just expressing their opinions.

SAFEENA: Opinions! You call those gross stinking statements opinions. 'Muslims try to have a hoard of children to outnumber the Hindus and take over the country! They teach their kids to use weapons. If they demand anything they should be thrown out' – you call these opinions!

BIMAL: But those chaps have been recently transferred to my college. They didn't know that you are a Muslim, Safeena.

SAFEENA: How would they know? A Muslim doesn't have four arms or three legs. There is just one way of distinguishing a Muslim – the name. And how did you introduce me? This is my wife – your wife doesn't have a name?

BIMAL: Safeena.

SAFEENA: It's customary practice to introduce people by their name? For a second you forgot who I was?

BIMAL: Safeena it's not like that. This is my wife – that's how you make introductions. Are you going to jump down my throat for every little thing?

SAFEENA: It's not little thing. It's big thing. You've got into the habit of pretending because you're afraid.

BIMAL: Afraid.

SAFEENA: Yes. And today you were afraid that even after knowing that they had a Muslim in their midst they would continue and then it would become a personal affront and you would have to take sides. Why have friction with your colleagues, right?

This dialogue illustrates that the mixed marriage inevitably constitutes a wall in the characters' social and professional environment. We are shown how easily this helps both to create and reinforce a wall between the partners concerned. Safeena's experience of her husband's social and educational context is a painful one for her. It is also one fraught with dilemmas for her husband, presenting him with unacceptable choices which lead to compromise solutions which do nothing but exacerbate either the personal or the professional situation or both.

Another factor in the relationship is the way Shanta is used by both Bimal and Safeena to fuel their difficulties with one another. She becomes another wall between them. They quarrel about Roona, their daughter, having access to her grandmother, and over smaller matters we see Bimal desperately trying to avoid confrontation and Safeena ready to pounce on him for paying his mother attention and not being open about it with his wife. The bickering and tension of the relationship is evident in this extract from Scene 6.

SAFEENA: Going out?

BIMAL: After six days of curfew it will be good to stretch my legs.

SAFEENA: Where are you going?

BIMAL: To the paan shop.

SAFEENA: How long will you be?

BIMAL: As long as it takes.

SAFEENA: Have you got the prescription?

BIMAL: For the glasses – yes.

SAFEENA: You'll get her specs then.

BIMAL: I thought I might. Maybe some bread as well.

SAFEENA: Makes sense. The optician is opposite the paan shop.

BIMAL: Yes and the bakery is next door.

SAFEENA: Why don't you tell me?

BIMAL: I'm telling you now.

They are interrupted by a commotion outside, otherwise this would doubtless develop into a full-scale row as Bimal tries to hide the fact that he is really going out to collect his mother's glasses and Safeena feels left out. This dialogue is a typical 'brick' in the wall that is rapidly separating husband and wife. It is also an example of how Shanta becomes for Safeena – and for Bimal himself, as we shall see in the next section – a third 'object', a kind of scapegoat, another wall composed of projected feelings. In this Shanta becomes lost. When Safeena asks Bimal if he is going to take his mother to the wall and 'fulfil her dying wish' he asks why it matters so much to her. Safeena's reply is telling, 'It matters to me that you answer me.'

Shanta and Bimal

In the relationship between Bimal and Shanta we see another aspect of the religious question. For Shanta's faith is unshakeable and she clings to her rights to protect it.

> BIMAL: Mother, I don't believe in all this stuff. This temple and all – it means nothing to me.
> SHANTA: But your mother does mean something to you doesn't she. Faith is a very private thing. You said this to me on so many occasions in this very house. But once, just once . . . you don't have to tell Safeena.
>
> (Scene 8)

Just as Shanta is seen as a barrier between Safeena and Bimal, so Safeena is viewed by Shanta as a barrier in her relationship with her son. When she tries to accuse Safeena of preventing him from taking her to the wall (see p. 000) Bimal says, 'Don't bring Muslims into this. She is Safeena your daughter-in-law.' He tries to pretend that the wall between his wife and his mother does not exist and in doing so creates a wall between himself and his mother.

Bimal's secularism is an attempt to avoid emotion. He seems to think that to rationalize will take down the walls between individuals and sections of society. But by ignoring the metaphorical importance of the wall he helps to create another one; in this case between him and his mother. For the actual wall, the significance of which he tries to minimize by intellectual rationalization, has a metaphorical function within his relationship with his mother which he does not recognize. It is the wall which divides youth and age which is irrespective of religion or culture or political opinion.

> SHANTA: . . . I can hear you coughing at night.
> (*Bimal doesn't answer*)
> SHANTA: I know what you are thinking.
> BIMAL: What?
> SHANTA: That my ears are always twitched towards your room. That's how I could hear you coughing.
> BIMAL: For God's sake mother.
> SHANTA: I don't eavesdrop on anybody.
> BIMAL: Who says you do?
> SHANTA: Look at those black circles under your eyes. You are not sleeping well, son.
> BIMAL: Shall we talk about something else.
>
> (Scene 8)

Here we see the irritation of the grown man who is still seen by his mother as the child she must nurture and protect, and the rejection of the old woman who has no role any more in relation to her son. (We need to remember the all-consuming nature of this role for it was the only one allowed her after her husband's death. As such it must have put a great strain on both of them.)

When, in this same scene, Bimal finally tells her that the wall has been blown up and does not exist any more, Shanta reacts by suddenly re-living the moment when she had been forced by the demands of her culture to live a life of seclusion, following the death of her husband after four months of marriage. The past becomes the present as she screams: 'Not my hair, not my hair. I don't need ugliness to protect my virtue. . . . not my hair, not my hair, not my hair' (Scene 8).

It is as though with the news of the destruction of the wall the long intervening years have been blown apart too. Shanta feels again the real wall in the shadow of which she has had to live for so long – the wall which prevented her from marrying again and living a fuller life in the world. We shall look at the significance of this moment in the play in the way it affects the relationships within the household. Before that there is another wall to explore.

Roona and her parents

The fourth wall is that which is built up between Roona and her parents. It can exist only because the other three are already in place. At the very beginning Roona answers the telephone. We do not know who the caller is, though later there is a hint that it might have been Altaaf. What is relevant to this discussion is that Roona tells the caller to ring back in an hour even though she hears her parents arriving home at that moment. On putting down the telephone she gathers her school books and rushes out. What we infer from this is that Roona is used to the perpetual quarrels of her parents; she knows that it will take them at least an hour to move into another gear. She also does not want to be around when they come in, and have to witness yet another row or argument between her parents. This is borne out when she later says to Altaaf, 'Can you try to bring people in this house together?' (Scene 5).

When the caller on the end of the line shows concern for her welfare, she says she is not afraid because 'the riots are on the other side of the river'. The irony in this is that the riots on the other side of the river are reflected in the home and that in those riots Roona is a victim. Whilst the Muslim and Hindu factions continue the public warring, the private warring in her parents' mixed marriage is carried out in her home. This psychological irony heightens the dramatic irony of the conflict on the other side of the river, soon to come right into their home, and prepares the audience for Roona's vital part in the denouement of the play. At the beginning of the play, then, we see Roona having to look after her parents, in a sense. Her management of the phone call indicates this. We also see how this role is something she does not want, as she rushes out of the room as soon as they enter, engaged in what we can safely assume is one of their perpetual fights.

Roona is depicted as a child whose experiences are little understood by the adults around her. There is a wall between her and her mother. Looking at a picture her daughter is drawing Safeena asks her what it depicts. 'People,' Roona answers shortly. 'Who are they?' pursues the mother, 'People in the playground?' Roona replies in the negative but offers no further explanation. The gap between mother and daughter is clear.

Although close to her grandmother, Roona provides an object onto which the old woman can project her lost girlhood and youth. She stresses the importance of Roona having long hair, for example, perhaps in an attempt to ease her pain of the trauma of having her own hair cut off all those years ago. But Roona's own experience of the world and what is important to her are not really understood by Shanta whose life is ruled by how things should be done; tradition and even superstition are powerful allies to her in her lonely ageing.

Roona's father, Bimal, has very little contact with his daughter until the very end of the play. We see him fiercely opposing Altaaf's plan to use Roona as a pretend hostage to prevent the family being killed. He talks of Roona's smile being one of his sources of greatest happiness but the play shows us little evidence that they spend much time together.

This isolation is particularly important to highlight the relationship she develops with her mother's childhood friend, Altaaf, who comes to seek refuge after blowing up the wall.

Metaphors of connection: Roona and Altaaf

From an understanding of divisions we can now begin to look at connections. In the first meeting between Altaaf and Roona we are shown the immediate connectedness which exists between them. They are looking at one of Roona's pictures; unlike the scene with her mother which immediately precedes this one, we see Altaaf tuning in immediately to the child. The scene opens in mid-conversation:

ROONA: What do they look like?
ALTAAF: They remind me of the eyes of a cat.
ROONA: Yes, that's right Altaaf Uncle. They're the eyes of my cat. Not his real eyes. He died.
ALTAAF: What was his name?
ROONA: Rustom. Daddy said he'd get me another one. But I don't want one.
ALTAAF: Why?
ROONA: Because he'd die as well.

190

ALTAAF: I used to have a cat. I found it in the streets. The other kids
were throwing stones at it so I brought it home.
ROONA: Did he die?
ALTAAF: No. I lost him. One day I came back from school and he was
gone. I suppose you lose things in life.
ROONA: At times I feel so bad. I wish I never had him.

(Scene 5)

Here we witness a rapport which is clearly missing in Roona's relationships
with mother, father and grandmother. In this conversation the cat becomes a
shared metaphor for loving and losing. A bond is created between the adult
and the child, for both can share the same kind of experience empathetically;
Altaaf is readily in touch with his childhood memories and feelings. It is because of this relationship that it is possible for Roona to provide an effective
foil for Altaaf at the end of the play when he allows himself to be killed but in
a way which saves the family who sheltered him. It is not, however, as though
child and adult merge. They clearly have their own perspectives on life. From
the passage just quoted Altaaf goes on to give another perspective on loss
which I believe is important in helping Roona take on Altaaf's message of
hope at the end. He continues:

Don't say that, Beta. If you are going to feel bad like that . . . I won't be
able to make friends with you. Look, Roona . . . there are friendships,
which are like . . . sand castles on the beach . . . you know they won't
last, and yet you make them . . . and then remember them for a while
with joy, not regret.

In this short conversation we see the way in which child and adult communicate, through images and metaphors. The child has drawn her cat's
eyes – she uses her creativity to try to come to terms with her loss. The adult
makes contact with her by sharing his memory of a similar loss; he remembers in detail the finding of a little animal, befriending it and losing it.
In this way he links with the child's world. Then he gives another view of
relationship by connecting with an image a child would know about, sandcastles; 'you know they won't last and yet you make them.' He does not
just say that some relationships are like sandcastles, he takes her right into
the activity of play and creativity remembered, the actual building of the
sandcastle. His own creativity finds the way to tap into her play and her
experience of the need to create even if the work one has created is
impermanent. He then reminds her of the feelings of joy that creativity
engenders. This image of impermanence is like the transitoriness of drama
and his sandcastles remind me of Shakespeare's 'We are such stuff as
dreams are made on', and of Everyman who has to understand that a condition of mortality is to accept 'how transitory we be all day'. Yet the joy of
living and creating, of being in relation, we could say, to life itself, is also

191

evoked by Altaaf's description of the building of the sandcastles in the full knowledge that they will be washed away. The fact that Altaaf is speaking with the awareness of the likelihood of his own approaching death adds both weight and poignancy to the words. With hindsight we know that he was also gently preparing Roona at the beginning of their relationship for the end of it.

This scene closes with Roona and Altaaf discussing the wall and why he blew it up. The directness of Roona and the respect with which Altaaf treats her questions allow other images to surface which reverberate far beyond the end of the scene itself.

ROONA: Isn't it bad to break things?
ALTAAF: Most of the time it is bad to break things. But there are times when it's not bad. The sparrows and the parrots that you love so much . . . they have to break out of the eggs to be born, right? You have to break the earth to plant a tree, break the rock to chisel a statue. It is bad to break things out of hate, or jealousy, or anger. Do you understand? Sometimes you have to break things and that wall was dividing people.
ROONA: The Hindus and the Muslims?
ALTAAF: Yes, it stood between me and them so I broke it.
ROONA: And will they be together now?
ALTAAF: If they really want to.
ROONA: Altaaf Uncle . . .
ALTAAF: Yes.
ROONA: Can you try and bring people in this house together? Things were not like this before. . . . Will you try? You can break anything of mine – my piggy bank . . . or . . . or even my doll's house – it has four walls. Will you try?

(Scene 5)

There is a complexity in Roona's response to Altaaf's definition of breaking. She hears him explain the importance of breaking in order to release, rather than breaking solely in order to destroy. What he is trying to tell her is that creation can come from destruction; the shell must be broken for the bird to be born, the earth to create a space in which a tree can grow and the rock for the work of art to be created from it. Roona's association with this is with the things that are important to her personally, so to Altaaf's list she adds her own, offering them as a sacrifice. She offers two objects which are very clearly containers, the piggy bank which contains money and the doll's house which contains people, her symbolic object for that which contains the family. Her offering of her doll's house, her object, which is an extension of herself, can therefore be seen as an offering of herself, for Roona's containing function is clear in the way the play begins and ends with her. The action is folded between Roona's opening and closing dialogue. The aptness of what she offers

192

to break, her own savings and her own image of the family provides a dramatic tension as we wonder whether Roona herself will be sacrificed in this conflict which enters right into the home with the blowing up of the wall.

In this notion of sacrifice Roona is allied to Altaaf. He sacrifices himself, destroys and breaks himself, in order for something new to become possible. Roona seems instinctively to understand this by producing her offerings which can be broken and sacrificed, even though as yet she does not know what will soon happen. Perhaps she instinctively understands this because she is already being sacrificed, for she is being split between the demands of mother and grandmother with little hope of rescue from her clearly caring but ineffectual father. The simplicity and intensity of her need to bring people together is no less in its way than Altaaf's. Whilst he wants the two factions of society to come together, she wants the two factions of her family to do so too. They are at war because of those very same reasons which engendered the social conflict. The forcefulness of her desire is expressed in her description of the doll's house – 'it has four walls'. The doll's house is a complex image. It shows her child's logic that if blowing up one wall is not enough then perhaps four would do it. It also emphasizes the container aspect of the four walls which must be broken in order for something to be born. Yet again it is perhaps an echo of the four walls which exist in the relationships within the family which need to be broken down for a new connectedness to exist. As the doll's house belongs to Roona it underlines her as someone who is being sacrificed in the family because of its warring. It acts for her like a transitional object, perhaps, in that it is something to contain her feelings; her risking its destruction is the psychic equivalent of Altaaf's risking his life, for it is a vital part of her own growing identity.

Later we learn that for Altaaf the wall is a memory of where he used to play improvised cricket as a child, a memory of good times, joy, those moments of living with which he is so clearly in touch. Like a doll's house for Roona, the wall for Altaaf was an object of childhood pleasure. He sacrifices that. Both Altaaf and Roona understand the importance of playing and dying, loving and losing. Because of this she can bring her parents one step closer to each other with his help at the end of the play. Both characters serve in the play as symbols of hope.

The possibility of change

Altaaf does not die for nothing. Even though change on a societal level seems, perhaps, as far away as ever, by his blowing up of the wall Altaaf forces the family members to reassess the positions they have taken up in relation to one another. Such a re-positioning of personal relationships within the family of the mixed marriage is offered as a way, perhaps the only way, to work towards wider change. The effect of Altaaf on Roona is the way in which the two contexts are united at the end of the play and it is with some thoughts on this that I shall end my discussion of the text. Meanwhile the ways in which Altaaf's presence and actual interventions influence Bimal, Safeena and Shanta need some attention.

From the moment Altaaf seeks refuge in Bimal's and Safeena's home his presence is influential in the changes that begin to be wrought within the family. He forces everyone to reassess their actions and their attitudes. An old childhood friend of Safeena who knows her well, he enables her to understand the importance of telling Shanta about the hurt and pain she experienced on the night of her father's death. He helps her make the vital step towards communication and away from silence. She has told neither Shanta nor Bimal the source of her anger and bitterness; Altaaf is crucial in effecting a change in Safeena which means that projections are able to be withdrawn. Both women begin to recognize that they have projected feelings of anger and hurt onto one another which rightly belong to their own fathers and cultures.

This comes about partly because of Altaaf's relationship with Roona which, in Scene 7, links to Safeena, his old childhood friend. Altaaf asks Safeena for ribbons, flippantly and as we see with tragic irony, telling her they are for committing sucide. They are in fact to make tails for Roona's kites so that they will have 'the most spectacular tails' on the kite-flying day, Sankranti. Safeena tells him of her father's death on that very day a year before and that consequently she hates it. He responds:

ALTAAF: You shouldn't hate Sankranti. Your Papa loved kites. 'Altaaf, look at this. A piece of paper. So fragile. But there comes one moment in its life when it flies. Find out, son, which way the wind blows. Then pull . . . and let go. It is life, son. The more you let go, the higher it soars.'

But Safeena greets this with bitterness, saying that her father 'had a metaphor for everything but didn't know which way the wind was blowing'. She is referring to his not having left India at the time of partition and his sudden loss of prestige as a result. After Altaaf's gentle remonstration with her she falls silent and then expresses a wish that he will influence Roona away from her grandmother; this leads to her saying that she feels like 'a minority in my own house'. It is in this conversation that she begins to confide in Altaaf which enables him to urge her to talk with her mother-in-law. The link between what she feels about her own father and what she projects onto Shanta begins to be made here. Roona has already a strong and loving relationship with her paternal grandmother. What Altaaf does is to enable her to have a relationship with her maternal grandfather through the symbolic quality of the gift of the kite-tails, thus strengthening her affectional bonds to both sides of the mixed marriage inheritance.

Where Shanta is concerned, Altaaf's blowing up of the wall shakes the old lady into an acceptance of reality; it literally brings her out of her room from

which she has said she cannot move. In fury at his having destroyed her illu-
sions she has to hear Altaaf's explanation for his blowing up of the wall: 'I
blew it up because human blood was being shed for it – human blood. It
would surely make god unhappy.'

He then goes on to describe in vivid detail a complex event in the riots of
1966 in which his father was thrown into the fire alive when he, a terrified little
boy, had innocently called out to his father, 'Abba!', thereby giving away to
the Hindu rioters that they were Muslim. He then talks about his rage and
'impotent anger', his murderous fantasies which finally became manifest in
his destroying, not his felllow human beings, but the wall. He tries to explain
to Shanta:

> The next few years were ones of impotent anger. The punishments that
> I dreamt of inflicting on those . . . no not only on those murderers but
> on all Hindus! It took thousands of small mercies to lift me from this
> mire of crude, cynical generalization. But not everybody is so lucky,
> Madam. They go on destroying people, not the dogma. I had to do it,
> believe me. I had to destroy the wall.
>
> (Scene 7)

Even if she cannot change, Shanta cannot hide any more. As for Safeena,
maybe she recognizes in herself the mire of 'crude, cynical generalizations', for
the next time we see her it is with Shanta in the scene where they uncover the
events of the night of Safeena's father's death and some form of reconciliation seems possible as greater honesty is achieved and a redistribution of
what fcclings bclong whcrc.

Bimal, too, cannot escape Altaaf's influence. Bimal, who operates on the
principle of 'anything for peace sake', finds himself making an impassioned
speech in an attempt to reach Safeena; in it he lays himself bare:

BIMAL: Do you know why I welcomed Altaaf here. . . . Because I understand him. I understand for what he is pledging his life. He is trying to
touch the hearts of the likes of you – people who are not malicious,
but who are fanatical.

SAFEENA: Me . . . a fanatic!

BIMAL: Yes – a fanatic. There is a lot of pain – I know – a lot of pain.
But what do you do with that pain? You polish it every day and keep it
bright. Roll your sorrows into a ball and juggle with it. It's unnatural
Safeena. Unnatural to reject the healing touch of time. It is the likes of
you that Altaaf is trying to touch – people who refuse to forget. People
who behave terribly because their cause gives them the moral sanction,
because that is the only thing that is sacred, and nothing else. The likes
of you. And do you know who he is fighting? The likes of me. People
like me. People who are extremely adaptable. People who adapt to anything to survive. People who are happy to pass by a stinking gutter and

195

not lodge a complaint so long as they have a handkerchief to hold to their nose.

(Scene 9)

In his understanding of Altaaf he owns that part of himself which Altaaf lives out for him; he owns his own inability to take the path which Altaaf takes. Altaaf himself shows that he has something within him which is akin to Bimal. Having urged Safeena to go and patch up her quarrel with Shanta he adds, 'We are a country that survives by patching up. We are a people of temporary separations' (Scene 12). While it is not Bimal's avoidance which Altaaf exhibits, neither is it the sort of thing that a destroyer of walls might be expected to say.

In the presentation of these two men, one Hindu, one Muslim, who both have the aim of peace in their hearts however differently they choose to attempt to bring it about, we see two parts of the same coin. But we also see that without Altaaf and what he stands for Bimal's way of dealing with things is unlikely to have much impact. Although he works in education where one might think the seeds of change could be sown, the opening dialogue between himself and Safeena showed both the intransigence of some of his colleagues and that Bimal's evasion is tantamount to non-action and therefore stalemate.

The lasting impact of Altaaf lies in his legacy to Bimal's daughter. For finally Bimal cannot withstand the logic of Altaaf's plan to save the family who will surely otherwise be killed for harbouring him. Altaaf proposes to pretend to hold Roona hostage, thus giving the impression that the family are sheltering him against their will and under the threat of violence. Bimal says he cannot allow it to happen, yet he cannot prevent it. He wants to try and get Altaaf away and in so doing prevent both his martyrdom and Roona's ordeal, but Altaaf will have none of it. By not being able to do this he has to be affected by the consequence of Altaaf's death and the manner of it. The most important consequence is the relationship between his daughter and Altaaf and the symbol of hope which enters the family as a result of this. This takes us to the final scene of the play.

It opens with a news bulletin which reveals that the death of Altaaf, following his destruction of the wall, has sparked off the activites of Muslim and Hindu rival factions; the former's plans to hold a 'sabha' in respect for Altaaf is threatened to be sabotaged by a group of Hindu fundamentalists. The proceedings are to go ahead and 'police presence around the polo ground is high as clashes between rival groups are expected'.

Listening to this are Bimal, Safeena, Shanta and Roona. For the first time in the play we see them all together. Juxtaposed, therefore, is the image of continued destructiveness on a societal level and the possibility of creative change in the family context. The bulletin evokes three significant responses from the adults listening:

BIMAL: God – it will be awful if they start fighting in Altaaf's name.

SAFEENA: They need a wall, Bimal.

SHANTA: They won't change overnight.

BIMAL: What did he gain? Did he die for this? First they'll fight and then they'll make a statue of him for pigeons to shit on.

Here it is Bimal who is angry and bitter. Yet, although it looks as though the world outside their house will use Altaaf's sacrifice only to fuel its ongoing dissensions, in their own lives things have changed; all the members of the family are together in the same room for the first time in a year. Again the juxtaposition of change and no-change is clearly implied. In this atmosphere, where the walls which have formed such barriers in the home are seen to be crumbling, the final metaphor which is Altaaf's gift to the future is brought alive in the final words of the play.

ROONA: Did you get it, Mum?

BIMAL: What is it?

SAFEENA: A map of the world. They must have asked for it at school.

BIMAL: What do you want to see, Roona?

ROONA: A mountain called Vesuvius. Near a city called Naples. Altaaf Uncle wanted me to go there.

BIMAL: Why?

ROONA: To see human figures. They died centuries ago because of the lava. When the lava came, they held hands with each other, or they embraced, and they are preserved like that. But they held hands, you see?

BIMAL: Yes, we do. What else did he say.

ROONA: He asked me if I trusted him and I said 'Yes.' Then he said, 'Well, you must run when I tell you.'

SAFEENA: And then?

ROONA: And then the people were coming nearer and I think he was afraid?

SAFEENA: He was afraid?

ROONA: His hand shook. And he asked me. 'Are you afraid my little one?' I said 'No', although I was. And he said, 'Let's see how wildly your little heart beats. So he put his hand here and began to listen. And then do you know what happened? His hand stopped trembling as he listened. He closed his eyes and listened and listened as if there was no other sound in the world. For a moment I thought he was asleep but th . . . slowly a smile came on his face. His eyes were closed, and he was listening to my heart beats and there was a smile on his face. Then you shouted and I ran. But last night when I woke up, and looked into Rustom's eyes, do you know what happened? I also saw that smile. Right between Rustom's green eyes, I saw his smile.

(*She takes the map*)

I'll hang it in my room.

Here is a reconciliation between life and death. Earlier we saw Roona telling Altaaf she would never have a cat again because it was too painful to love something and lose it. Now Altaaf's smile becomes integrated with the cat's eyes in her picture. Roona has discovered, at a level which can be communicated only by metaphor, the ability to face loss and still go on. As for Altaaf, he has understood her plea to 'bring the people in this house together' and, by his influence on their lives and by his death, he has enabled that process of reconciliation to begin. He knows that she will understand the story of Pompeii as a metaphor for how that beginning must continue.

On a societal level Altaaf's death may seem a waste; Bimal told him that the country had too many martyrs already; Kamla talked of him being an object of speculation which lined the bookies' pockets; for some he may become a hero or even a god and thus an excuse for more warring to defend another dogma. On the level of interpersonal relationships, however, he left his mark. Each family of a society makes up that society. Through his influence on Roona we are left with hope that every such contact can make a contribution to the possibility of change in the succeeding generation.

Altaaf becomes a projective object for both Hindus and Muslims; he can become, after his death, whatever they want him to be. We could be cynical and say that he simply takes on himself the role of the wall played as a projective object. But this would, I believe, be untrue to the play. For a wall is a wall is a wall, but a human being can grow and learn and change and take responsibility for action as Altaaf does. The difference in Altaaf allowing himself to become a projective object is that he can touch people and influence them as he has touched this household in a way no wall can ever do. As such he is a symbol of unity as opposed to division.

I have said that Altaaf represents the depressive position. One of the features of this developmental stage is the ability to feel loss and mourn, to feel guilt for one's murderousness and make reparation. 'It is only when the loss has been acknowledged and the mourning experienced that re-creation can take place' (Segal 1955: 190). Altaaf takes upon himself this role for society; he does its mourning for it and can therefore re-create. He does this for society through the symbolic function of his action; he does it for the family through what he gives to Roona which nourishes her ability to move beyond mourning. He reinforces the value of metaphor and symbol through his conversations with her, his giving her the kite-tails redolent with symbolism, and his final gift of the image of Pompeii. He thereby celebrates creativity and new life.

His society asks him to do what it cannot do for itself, to take on the living-through of the depressive position.

The memory of the good situation, where the infant's ego contained the whole loved object and the realization that it has been lost through his own attacks, gives rise to an intense feeling of loss and guilt, and the wish to restore and re-create the lost loved object outside and within the ego. This wish to restore and re-create is the basis of later sublimation and creativity.

(ibid: 187)

Safeena provides an example of what happens when the depressive position is not moved through successfully whenever our life circumstances present us with visiting it again. Instead of mourning the loss of her father, her way of dealing with his death is to resort to the splitting mechanisms of the paranoid-schizoid position. It would seem likely that she would, at his death, experience a return of the feelings of loss and anger at being exiled from home when she married Bimal, just as Shanta relives her comparable experience when she hears of the wall's destruction. But Safeena's response is not to feel loss and anger it would seem; it is to become depressed, which is very different from allowing herself the healing but painful feelings which re-entering the depressive postion would mean. (Bimal, in Scene 1, says she lies on her bed and stares at the ceiling.) She maintains a position of projected anger and hatred and in so doing cannot move. She is in denial. Instead of truly mourning, feeling guilt and love, she has, as Bimal tells her, turned her father into an institution, a dogma; this is a form of defence. In this she mirrors the wider society with their continual riots in which Hindus continue to project their own disowned parts onto Muslims and vice versa.

But we must not forget to see Altaaf as an individual character as well as a kind of dramatic and psychological Mr Fix-it. For a question we must be bound to ask is what effect the blowing up of the wall has on Altaaf himself; what happens to Altaaf in those six days between his action and his death? Here again his reparative actions and his bonding with Roona seem to me to echo the resolution of the depressive position. The wall was a place of childhood pleasure for Altaaf. He played cricket there with his father; more than that, he *made* it into his own personal cricket-ground by drawing the wicket stumps on it. It was his memory of perfect happiness. And he has destroyed it. This destruction may even repeat the destruction of his father for which he may feel responsible. In the six days following the blowing up of the wall he engages on reparative work with Roona's family. He mourns the loss of his own past, perhaps the loss of innocence too. He is faced with the persecutory responce and potential destruction. But the complexity is that these mechanisms cannot remain simply internal persecutors with which Altaaf can deal as he has done in the past, for he is living in a society which operates in a paranoid-schizoid way. The persecutors are out there in the external world and they come for him. To avoid them would be to bring sure destruction onto the family who has sheltered him. Emerging from the depressive position means taking responsibility. Altaaf takes responsibility. He chooses death.

The creativity which can be the result of successfully working through the depressive position manifests itself in two ways. One is Altaaf's death, which I see as his final creative act; the other is his legacy to Roona. Listening to her heart beat he can face his death safe in the assurance that through her he can continue to be a creative force in the society he cares so passionately about.

Conclusion

Like Altaaf I do not espouse dogma. But religion is a haunting thing. I am reminded of a phrase from the religion of my own background, 'Except . . . ye become as little children ye shall not enter into the kingdom of heaven' (*The Gospel According to St Matthew* 18: 3). If I do have a dogma it would be that the kingdom of any heaven, be it Hindu, Muslim, Christian or any other, is one where love overcomes hate; where peace rather than war is espoused. For me the hope in this play lies in the very fact that it is a play, a creative work. As such it puts us in touch with the child within in ways which for me exemplify and are exemplifed by two concepts from psychoanalytic writing.

First it draws upon those early infant mechanisms we looked at in Chapter 2. In the context of this chapter my reference point is Segal's propositions concerning a work of art, both in terms of its creator and its audience. Speaking of tragedy – though she later expands her argument to the wider field of aesthetic experience – she proposes that the work of art is a working through of the writer's depressive anxieties which finds expression in the creative work, the 'harmonious whole'. The reader, and I would say the audience, can identify with the process the writer has undergone through experiencing the play and in so doing, 'experience a successful mourning', and a reintegration of the objects of his or her internal world. I find this particularly relevant to *A Shaft of Sunlight* where the writing so clearly demonstrates the relationship betweeen the mechanisms of both the paranoid-schizoid and depressive positions.

Second the play speaks of the importance of staying in touch with the creative child within, that part of us which can play with ideas and feelings and metaphors in the way that Winnicott (1971) suggests is the basis for adult creative activity. Herein lies the possibility for the integration of opposite feelings and therefore for growth. For Roona this is the uniting of loss and living again, for Altaaf the acceptance of his own hate which he can unite with a greater love of humankind.

'Those who would die well and those who would create well are people who must be capable of being open and available to both the life forces and the death forces' (Gordon 1978). Whilst not everyone can be or wishes to be an Altaaf or would want to go through the trauma that Roona experiences, the play offers us a metaphor for healing. It reminds us of the importance of facing what we feel, owning and taking responsibility for our feelings and actions, however painful that might be, for that is the only way to live creatively. I see these two characters as central to the play and to the way in which this play can serve as a projective object itself for exploration of division and creative reparation. As such it is a valuable text for dramatherapy work.

IN PRACTICE

An account of a workshop

In a workshop on *A Shaft of Sunlight* some of these themes were movingly and realistically brought out. 'Light shining through the prison bars.' 'Light streaming in through the window in the morning – I hate the darkness.' 'I don't feel it's very optimistic really, it's only a *shaft* of sunlight.' 'Oh no, to me it suggests hope.'

These are some of the responses to being invited to comment on this play's title at the beginning of a workshop with a group of women from a wide variety of backgrounds; Sikhs, Hindus, those from a mixed marriage of both those two Indian religions, a woman whose parents were from what used to be East Germany and Yugoslavia, a woman from the north of England whose parents were West Indian but who had never herself been to the Caribbean, a woman from East Africa of Hindu religion who went increasingly back to India where she had never lived but where she felt connected. And, as I reflected afterwards, the workshop was led by me, a Welsh woman brought up in England whose parents spoke Welsh in addition to English, a language to which I had no access (they spent much of their forty-year sojourn in England feeling, in some fundamental way, alien). In all of us working on this play, therefore, there were experiences of divisions, of alienation, and inner and outer conflicts which culture, language, religion and history engendered. What we discovered by the end of the workshop was that the shaft of sunlight was what was experienced in that workshop, the taking of responsibility to own our ability to reach out across the differences.

For all of us involved there were apprehensions. The participants had been invited by an Asian drama community worker. I was worried I would make some blunder through my lack of a full-enough knowledge of what the issues in the play might spark off. Would I be rejected by the group or individual members of it? Did I have the right to be working on a play from a culture very different from mine? Would I be allowed to learn or would I be 'punished' for not knowing? These were some of my fantasies and projections. For their part I came from yet a different culture again, which caused the participants some apprehension – the culture of dramatherapy.

What emerged strongly from the workshop was how much the play highlighted the importance of creativity in working towards harmony. Hand in hand with this came an awareness of the centrality of the child within who has access to imagery and symbolism and the ability to play. These points manifested themselves in unexpected ways and subsequently reinforced and deepened my thinking about the play which has emerged in the discussion of the text above. I was left feeling how much we could work on if this group were to continue; how much we could use the play as a containing object to explore the painful issues which I suspected lay not too far from the surface, and more fully engage with some reworking of those early mechanisms I have discussed above.

After the usual introductions and contract making I asked the group to warm up into the space which was the studio of a London Youth Theatre. One of the things I asked them to do was to find a place which they particularly liked and to show it to other members of the workshop. They all ended up in the gallery, a dusty muddle of theatre paraphernalia, a cosy place of mysteries. When they returned to the circle of chairs in the main body of the studio I asked them where they would like to read the play. With one accord they decided on the gallery. Up we all trooped and found somewhere to squash up, relatively physically uncomfortable, yet clearly for the group the resulting snugness was important. While we read I allowed my mind to ponder this unexpected decision. Suddenly it came to me that it was like Roona's attic room which she shares with Altaaf and in which their important discussions take place. In fact another unconscious echo of the text found its way in, for it was also like Shanta's upstairs room where Roona would so often go, a place of respite from her warring parents. This became clear to me when one participant arrived well after we had begun the reading of the play. She wandered around downstairs for some moments. Whilst I knew there were other people in the building and that some of them might have strayed into our space by mistake, I also somehow knew that this woman was looking for the workshop and was not an intruder. I was therefore astonished to find myself for a split second almost ignoring her. I quickly recovered myself and went down to meet her. It was only later that I realized that, apart from any annoyance I felt at her lateness, what was happening was a replay of the play, for it was totally alien to the kind of reaction I normally have to anyone entering a workshop space, as I tend to be quite lion-like in its defence and would normally have immediately checked out who the newcomer was – friend or foe as it were. What the group, and I by my uncharacteristic behaviour, had been re-enacting was the trick that Roona plays on her grandmother in Scene 2. She allows her grandmother to ring the bell (which always annoys Safeena) letting her think she is alone when all the time she is hiding under the bed. I also wondered if we were creating a doll's house, a small snug place. This part of the workshop was an excellent example of the reflection process at work, 'the here-and-now reflecting the then-and-there' (Hawkins and Shohet 1989) of the play which I find is a frequent phenomenon in text work in dramatherapy. Like Roona this mirror effect sneaks up and plays tricks, which can offer considerable insight and illumination on both the play and the group's and facilitator's unconscious response to it.

In this instance my interpretation was clarified by the group's response near the end of the workshop. I asked them to de-role the reading space we had used in the morning. From a very serious adult mode of de-roling from the characters they had played in the afternoon in a series of sculpts, the group members became children in an instant. With whoops of delight they rushed back up to the gallery. They noticed things they had not noticed in the morning, even though the earlier exercise had been one which gave time and opportunity to do so. Downstairs in the studio, 'holding' the other space for them while they de-roled the gallery, I experienced one of those moments of delight where creative engagement seems more like magic than anything else. It was when I heard a shout of discovery, 'Oh look, here's some silver slippers.' In my discussion of the play I said that Roona begins and ends it. Unconsciously the group played Roona doing just this, finding something special at the end of the journey in the upstairs room.

The afternoon workshop began with my passing round a wooden egg. While holding it each person said what they would like their focus for discovery to be in the course of the afternoon. Though chosen by me, I felt that the egg resembled a transitional object for the group, something safe to hold on to as they began to move out into practical engagement with the play. It could also symbolize that something could be born even in a short while in a newly constituted group with a facilitator they had never met before. The egg is one of Altaaf's examples to Roona of creating and it seemed a fitting object to choose. By speaking, witnessing and being witnessed in relation to the symbol, they could give themselves a containing focus for the session. We would return to the egg at the end.

Each group member spoke and was witnessed. Then we moved straight into discovering and owning the characters. In the sculpts which formed the centre-piece of the afternoon's session much emerged which showed the play working deeply on the participants' response to having read it in the morning. Each moved around the room thinking about one character at a time, finding that character in movement, words and feeling until all the workshop members had touched base with all the characters. Then we formed a circle to mark the enactment space. I invited people to come in and take up the role of a character they wanted to explore further. They could then invite another character into the circle whom they would like to engage with.

Here there is not space to describe the whole session in detail; I shall highlight some moments. Again the movement and themes of the play were reflected unconsciously, this time by the order in which the group took turns in the enactment space. Shanta began. She wanted to meet Roona. The image in the centre showed the strength of the relationship between the two which had come across to the group from the reading of the text. Roona lay with her head in her grandmother's lap and a real connection was felt across the generations. The way that it was portrayed, the loneliness experienced by both characters in relation to the family was clearly felt by those of us watching. These audience responses were articulated by the audience giving a word or phrase which the sculptors simply heard. After leaving the enactment space they commented on what had been projected onto them and returned to de-role further if necessary. Most comments seemed to feel remarkably accurate to the players. In this way deeper understanding of the play was possible.

Two sculpts/improvisations in particular I shall comment on more fully because they reflected the issues of both the family and the wider society. The latter came first. Kamla came into the middle. She showed a mixture of the coarseness and humour and harsh realism which we find in Scene 6. She presented as a survivor. But the pain of her life was mirrored gesturally where she held a hand to her back. Altaaf went in. Immediately Kamla began to drop to the floor as the servant character would have done in real life. Altaaf, in one quick gesture, prevented her. It was a powerful moment as Kamla stared in amazement at Altaaf's acknowledgement of her equality with him. 'We are equals in oppression' was the comment of the person playing the role of Altaaf.

The other sculpt showed the group's response to the relationship between Safeena and Bimal. In the text Safeena is more and more resistant to Bimal's attempts at reconciliation. The evasion game was beautifully played out in a sculpt which moved into a silent improvisation in the centre. We saw another side to the husband and wife, for where in the text Safeena is forever trying to get hold of Bimal and pin him down, here, in a setting which depended solely on relating through space and body, we saw, I reflected later, the Bimal who tells his mother to make friends with loneliness; his isolation in relation to his wife was pointed up by her continual rejection of him as she turned away and away and away. It showed a side of Bimal which tries to communicate but is blocked by his wife. It showed, too, that by her hatred and anger she cuts herself off from his attempts to relate. Husband and wife moved emotionally further and further apart. Roona then came into the circle. Here both the preoccupation of the parents and the resulting isolation of Roona became obvious. When they eventually noticed her they moved across to where she was standing, outside, looking on, waiting, hoping. She took their hands and after a minute they took one another's. I asked Roona how she felt at this point. She said that the truce did not feel real, that they were holding hands only because of her. I asked her to say Roona's lines at the end of the play about the volcano. She improvised the essence of the text and as she spoke the energy of her words seemed to make her draw them physically closer to her and therefore to each other. Afterwards the two players taking the roles of Bimal and Safeena said that they had felt the impulse to draw closer. The resulting embrace had softened them but they both felt there was a long way for the characters to go. This, we reflected, was perhaps the *shaft* of sunlight.

And so we ended our exploration of the relationships and moved into finding out a little about the wall and how that could take us further. 'Make whatever wall is there for you now', I said. The result was a circular wall. At first it felt a safe, strong wall, which they enjoyed experiencing, supporting one another, looking inwards, aware of each other. It was, in the context of the workshop, an expression of bonding, for the group was working well together. It seemed to me as though it was an act of consolidation, as though the group was creating its own history, and each part of the workshop had been the building bricks which could now be formed into a metaphorical structure.

In terms of it representing a wall in the play it produced some interesting material. I asked each person to adopt a character and to allow that character to become a brick in the wall. One person said that, playing Altaaf, it helped her to be aware of the enormous strength of this character. Thinking of him as part of the wall helped her to get in touch with that. It was interesting, in the light of the relationship between Roona and Altaaf, that this person had read the part of Roona in the morning and in the afternoon had also played her in the piece I have just described. She therefore moved from introjecting Roona to introjecting Altaaf, thus unconsciously following what happens to Roona in the play.

Another person spoke of her experience of standing in the wall as one in which an important realization had come feelingly to her. Suddenly she realized that this close-knit inwards-looking wall meant that nothing could penetrate it from outside. It was at the point when I was side-coaching the group to feel the wall in their backs. 'I realized I wasn't letting anything in', she said later.

After revisiting the characters in the way they had done at the beginning, through finding their relationship to space, their physical selves and their words, reflecting on how they saw those characters in this second visitation, they de-roled themselves from them individually both physically and verbally. Then I invited them to de-role the gallery space as I have described, after which we returned to the original circle of chairs where we had begun and ended the morning and resumed at the beginning of the afternoon. I placed the first egg and another egg beside it in the centre of the circle and invited people to think back to their aims for the afternoon. What had been given birth to in their work on *A Shaft of Sunlight*? Several had spoken about barriers at the beginning; now they said that they felt that they had been in touch with that and realized how by creatively engaging with one another they had modelled ways in which barriers could be broken down. None of these women had been involved in dramatherapy before. By risk taking and by trusting and sharing, by reaching out into the unknown, new insights could come.

One person spoke of the need not to underestimate the legacy of history, and as she spoke I was reminded of *Cloud Nine*. For the woman whose parents were from old East Germany and former Yugoslavia the work on the wall had been particularly resonant. It was she who had spoken of not letting anything in while being part of an inwards-looking wall. Another, whose first egg had represented her wish to gain some insight into her difficult relationship with her mother, picked up the second egg and said,'I know now that I must make the first move towards my mother.' By working through a creative dramatic engagement with the play she was able to move a step forward in thinking about her relationship with her mother in terms of reconcilation. The play was therefore working for her in her own life in the way that the writer suggests it should, by helping this woman look at issues of responsibility in relationship.

Conclusion

The play itself serves as a metaphor for both divisions and healing in that it is a play about one particular culture which reaches out to all who experience division. In that very reaching across there is a healing of division and a withdrawal of projections. Just as Altaaf looks to ancient Roman civilization for a metaphor to give Roona, so we can take this play, whatever our culture, to help us with issues which are akin to those of the India represented in *A Shaft of Sunlight*, for they are in us all. Whilst everyone in this particular workshop felt that the characters in the play had far to go and that we, in our contemporary British society have as well, they felt that such work as they had done that day was a step forward in personal understanding, both feelingly and in thought. Such experiences must, they felt, precede societal change. It only went to show, they said, how much we need such work. In our modest workshop I felt that *A Shaft of Sunlight* had done what its writer intended, 'to provide not only an aesthetic but humanizing experience'.

In the shimmering city of Ahmedabad, riots have become an annual feature. Not to be affected by them would not only be impossible but irresponsible. A play is one of the many ways in which an individual can voice his or her protest. It is also a way of thanking and saluting the frequent sparks of unbelievable courage and unselfishness in the midst of absolute cruelty, chaos and corruption.

(Abhijat Joshi)

9

DEATH AND ACCEPTANCE
Riders to the Sea by J. M. Synge

It has been said that all therapy could be seen as being about mourning, of one kind or another. Life is a constant flow of leavetaking and moving on, but how well we deal with this and truly accept loss and so become free to gain is another matter. This is the case in therapy; we are faced with patterns which, though they might have impeded us, are known and safe, whereas the unknown is an uncharted place. Even the maps provided by others' experience cannot truly tell us our own way. It is often a frightening time when inner chaos attends the process of change.

All separations remind us of the final separation which we must prepare for. All endings are mini-endings reminding us of the deaths of those near to us, whether past or to come. All deaths remind us of our own eventual fate. This dynamic therefore is ever present in the therapy situation and in that context few things bring up the feelings about death more than the ending of a therapy group. This stage is marked by the complex feelings which actual deaths generate, particularly fear, anger, guilt, denial and grief. It is the therapist's role to enable the group to be in touch with as many of their true feelings as they can bear (Malan 1979). A group in denial of death and ending may take refuge in anger; this may be anger which is part of the ending process. But it may also be a less painful emotion than the grief or despair which the thought of ending may provoke at an unconscious level. Working at a deep level the dramatherapist can use the containment provided by dramatic enactment to enable the group to move through the various emotions, finding dramatic form to synthesize and integrate the clients' experience and feelings.

In early enactment of scenes involving death and grief group members might find themselves in a state of underdistance, where the overwhelming loss which happened last month, last year, or even many years ago, but which has lain buried and not properly mourned, floods over them as freshly as if it had just happened. But if the therapist trusts the dramatic structure and the holding environment provided by this and by the therapist and the group, then this release of emotion can be a positive revisiting, a step in the process of integration of the stages of grief. Whilst a state of underdistance cannot in itself create change, as I suggested in Chapter 1, the revisiting of an experience of the death of someone close can provide a context for the free release of these feelings.

I remember the courage of a woman who had dealt insufficiently with the death of a very dear friend finding her own ritual for expressing this, using the enactment space and creating a beautifully formed piece of drama. In this her tears were those she had long needed to shed, with a witness to validate her experience and support her. In the actual funeral she had had to take an official role and had thus not had the space to be simply in the role of mourner. Now she re-created this funeral in a symbolic ritual. Knowing the importance of staying within the form, which I knew would eventually enable her to move through the mixture of feelings she needed to visit, I and the group sat and witnessed her piece through to its conclusion; she returned to the group space (which during the enactment was always clearly defined and apart from the enactment space), and invited her to talk and share whatever she wanted of her experience which had been so powerfully evoked in the drama. This she did, and others who were deeply touched by her piece and by her grief found the space to share some of their stories of bereavement and unfinished mourning. This group was coming to the end of its time together. Initially at this stage anger, though truly felt, was being used as a defence against the deeper anxiety of facing grief and all it might bring up. The woman in question asked the others if they would play the role of mourners in her enactment in the form of a dramatic chorus. In doing so they too became deeply touched by the song which she asked them to sing which had particular cultural resonances for them, with very specific painful associations for some people. Each of these re-lived mournings strengthened and healed the group in their grief. At the final performance it was the turn of the audience to be deeply moved. By this stage the mechanism of rehearsal and repetition had allowed the group to move into a truly contained piece of theatre. Seeing the audience moved, they found the final stage of this particular part of their therapeutic journey – integration and reconciliation. The audience's validation of their feelings and experience was the final witnessing which related the world of the group and its intimate sharing with the world 'out there' – the universal experience of one of the most profound aspects of the human condition.

Working with dramatic text which deals with these matters is another tool which the dramatherapist can use. In *A Shaft of Sunlight* we saw a society in which loss was a daily occurrence, life was cheap as riots destroyed and maimed. The image of Pompeii with which we were left put human life in the perspective of natural disaster. To embrace and face the end, however terrible, is eventually the best we can do. In the play that I focus on in this chapter, we move to Ireland to a tiny community which constantly faces another natural force, not a volcano but the sea. In *Riders to the Sea*, the emphasis is one of moving through the experiences surrounding death and dying, to reconciliation and acceptance.

THE PLAY

In order to find the structure for the group to work with, we must first put ourselves in touch with the structure of the play, pay attention to the fine tuning of this beautifully crafted piece. At times of great upheaval in life small detail is often important, as it is here. If we are to find the possibilities in the play for healing, we must pay attention to the detail that the group members offer us of their own experience and to the detail of the play, in order to find a fitting match in the preparation work. Finally the play will carry the participants through, just as in the biographical piece I have just discussed.

Résumé of the play

This short one-act play is set on an island off the west coast of Ireland – one of the Aran Islands. It opens with two young women of the fishing community concealing from their elderly mother the bundle of clothes thought to belong to their missing brother, which has been brought to them by the priest. The mother enters; her talk is all of waiting for Michael to be washed up. We are introduced to a second strand in the story, which is that her one remaining son, Bartley, is planning to take the pony to sell at Galway fair on the mainland and she is fearful that he will die too for the weather is worsening. He enters and confirms his decision; she turns her back on him and he goes, giving but not receiving a blessing. His sisters realize they have forgotten to give him the bread they were baking and send their mother down to the well past which Bartley will go with the horses on his way to the boat. While she is out they take down the bundle of clothes and by counting the stiches on the stocking are able to identify them as indeed belonging to Michael. Maurya, the mother, comes back, keening and at first unable to communicate what is the matter. She says she has seen Bartley on his horse and Michael arrayed in fine clothes following on the pony. She knows this is a message of the death of both her sons. The daughters confirm to her that Michael is dead, and has been given burial in the far north. As she starts to recall the previous deaths of her husband, her husband's father and four other sons, Bartley's body is brought in attended by women of the village, keening. Maurya anoints the clothes of Michael and the body of Bartley with the last of the holy water. The bearers of the body begin to build the coffin and the play ends on a note of poetic and dignified acceptance of the lot of the human condition.

Therapist's initial preparation

Before discussing the text itself, a note on how I approach the play as a drama-therapist. After reading it several times I allow myself to free associate for a while. What emerges is firstly pictures – rocks, grey driving rain, wind, high white waves moving in a froth. Then sounds; I hear the sounds of the sea and with it the sound of the language in the play – 'when the surf is in the east and the surf is in the west'. Words come unbidden into this picture – 'roaring', 'crying', 'lamenting', 'when the tide's turned to the wind', 'it's a long time we'll be and the two of us crying'.

The howling of the elements and the howling of the women who lose their menfolk to these elements. The play becomes elemental; I see an old woman, Maurya, picking her way over the wet stones to the well, clutching the bread to give a blessing to her son, Bartley, walking with the stick given to her by her son, Michael; it is these two deaths which the play uses as its focus. I see the tiny local environment, remember my visit to the Aran islands, arrive in the landscape and seascape and soundscape. Suddenly I see the procession at the end of the play – the women coming in at the door, keening, the men following bearing the body of Bartley, just as Maurya is telling how the bodies of her other sons were brought home. Suddenly the ritual, the dignity of the play comes home to me. This is a play which lends itself to dramatherapy. It is a play of balance, archetypal and elemental, yet down to earth – a play about ordinary people yet of extraordinary stature. So, as a dramatherapist, I am beginning to see still pictures, tableaux, then moments of ritual coupled with moments of ordinariness.

Now from these impressions I need to explore it more fully, get to know its components, so that I can draw upon them. What I take with me into my next more focused reading of the play is the imaginative engagement of this free association which, as in analytic free association, will allow me access to 'far other worlds and other seas' which will help me eventually to hone my insight and empathy, the tools of the therapist, when working on the play.

Discussion of the text

Riders to the Sea is an extraordinary gem, a tiny one-act jewel that has all the stature of a Greek tragedy. James Joyce pronounced that its twenty minutes made it too short for tragedy, but many other critics have not found it wanting when weighed in the scales of tragedy. A renowned authority on Irish literature, Tom Henn (1972), suggests that 'perhaps it is the only complete one-act tragedy in any literature, for it requires no space to develop its characteristic momentum'. It moves inexorably to its conclusion, its tragic tone being set from the very start as we shall see. Its brevity is of advantage to the dramatherapist, who can work with it in its entirety in a short time, yet it is large enough to encompass the great theme of mortality. In order to appreciate what it has to offer we need to explore the tight relationship between the dramatic and symbolic function of the components of its structure. We need to look at how the world of the play is built up by reference to objects and the natural environment. It is not a world of ideas but one where life is reflected, lived and explained by action. Yet the details of action also serve on a symbolic level to lay bare the feeling world of the characters and allow our identification with them. Let us look therefore at the setting, the characters and the dramatic devices which Synge employs and then at how an understanding of the ways in which these form the whole can help the dramatherapist to make this play available as a vehicle for work on death, ending and acceptance. In particular I shall look at ways in which he uses everyday objects as both symbolic and dramatic devices.

The setting

The opening stage directions give us a world which is as timeless and elemental as those of myth:

> Cottage kitchen, with nets, oilskins, spinning wheel, some new boards standing by the wall etc. Cathleen, a girl of about twenty, finishes kneading cake, and puts it down in the pot-oven by the fire; then wipes her hands, and begins to spin at the wheel.
>
> (*Riders to the Sea*: 73)

It is almost the scene of fairy-tale and as such immediately takes us into those places in our interior world which myths inhabit. It prepares us for the meeting of conscious and unconscious worlds where symbol and metaphor can both nurture us and expand our experience. The action takes place entirely in this cottage with events which take place outside it reported within the dialogue in the cottage. That we are on an small island surrounded by a fierce coastline is clear from numerous references. The island is brought alive through the language and the exterior world is as present as the interior of the cottage. The fact that it is present through language rather than as a set on stage serves an important purpose in terms of the dual worlds of actual and symbolic space, for the resonance of the island and the sea can enter us at a deeper and less conscious level. An awareness of this is vital to finding the appropriate dramatic structure when working with the play therapeutically. For the island itself is spoken of by Maurya as a place apart.

> In the big world the old people do be leaving things after them for their sons and children but in this place it is the young men do be leaving things behind for them that do be old.
>
> (ibid.: 77)

These lines help the island to become available to us as a place set apart in which grief can be contemplated. It is a world in which we can focus on the phenomenon of bereavement, and where the grief-stricken can be comforted by finding their experience validated. The setting of the play becomes therefore a metaphor for grief itself, and for the experience of bereavement, where we so often feel alone, marooned on an island in a topsy-turvy world where things feel upside down, where contact with the mainland seems beset by

211

mountainous waves and the crossing feels at times impossible. The setting therefore gives back to the audience validation of the experience of grief in this metaphorical way. We learn of the howling of the winds and feel them as an accompaniment to the keening of the women. The harmony of the natural setting and the inner human experience is one of the most powerful aspects of the play.

The group dramatherapy setting is similarly an island in the world of everyday experience. Holding on to this parallel can intensify the way the play can work for those wanting to find expression for the experience of grief and the healing made possible by the transformational power of dramatic aesthetic work.

The characters

The characters are not only central characters but also chorus, for they both comment on and participate in the action of the play. In so far as there is a tragic hero it is Bartley, the youngest son, who determines to go the fair because he has heard it is a particularly good one for horse prices. If he waits for the rising weather to calm he will not be able to get another boat for two weeks and thus will miss the opportunity for a good sale. A quiet hubris of a humble life. No great pretensions to be a king, no seeking for revenge, just a daring of the fates in the service of easing poverty.

The protagonist is undoubtedly Maurya, a woman who has reared six sons and who is about to lose the last and youngest of them. She is like a Cassandra, doomed not to be believed by proud and headstrong men and at the same time she is totally herself, an old woman exhausted by grief and travail.

> MAURYA: (*Turning round to the fire, and putting her shawl on her head*)
> Isn't it a hard and cruel man won't hear a word from an old woman, and she holding him from the sea. . . . He's gone now, God spare us, and we'll not see him again. He's gone now, and when the black night is falling I'll have no son left me in the world.
>
> (ibid.: 76)

As the play proceeds Maurya becomes almost an archetypal figure, one who speaks for the grief of all women who have served husbands and borne sons. At the end of the play there are two pictures of her, one which her daughters see, of an old woman exhausted by grief, and one which she herself shows us, the audience, which is a woman of dignity and stature having travelled beyond the point of being broken. She assumes a priestly status as she takes the holy water and blesses Bartley's body and the remains of Michael's clothing and prays for her sons, continuing 'And may he have mercy on my soul, Nora, and on the soul of everyone left living in the world' (ibid.: 84).

In speaking Nora's name it is as though she passes the mantle of woman and priestess to her youngest daughter. In doing this she reinforces the function of this role in human life and the part it plays in acceptance of the inter-relationship between life and death.

In Maurya the essence of Mother and Sea are inextricably related. Errol Durbach in his essay entitled 'Synge's Tragic Vision of the Old Woman and the Sea' (1972) draws attention to Synge's stage directions when Maurya returns from her mission to take bread and blessing to Bartley, having been unable to do either. He points out that Synge tells us that 'her shawl falls back from her head and shows her white tossed hair. Maurya here is like the sea, with its white tossing waves.' 'If, like the sea, she is the womb of life, she is also, like the sea, the natural source of her children's death as well.' From this point on, he argues, Maurya moves towards the acceptance of her role as Universal Mother with its inevitable concomitant acceptance of that of Sorrowing Mother in the face of Necessity. This aspect of the feminine feeling function presented through Maurya is one of great importance when working on this play, for working in the role of Maurya provides an access to the unconscious which must be engaged in the course of bereavement.

The two daughters, Nora and Cathleen, play a vital part in the dramatic structure of the play but it is important to note that they have very different characters even though their main function is to underline the tragedy of loss and to be the agents of the action's movement.

Nora has an eagerness which suits her role as the youngest, a brightness and curiosity which, while it serves to give her a choric function of anticipating the next piece of action, makes her totally credible as a character. She contrasts with Cathleen, who already feels and shows the burden of managing the household in which her mother is depicted as old and becoming burdensome, and which has sustained the loss of father and brothers. There is an anxiety and irritability about Cathleen. Where Nora is involved in action, Cathleen sees the relationship between action and feelings states.

> Put these things away before she'll come in. Maybe it's easier she'll be after giving her blessing to Bartley, and we won't let on we've heard anything the time he's on the sea.

> (*Riders to the Sea*: 79)

Cathleen has to manage relationships and feelings and throughout we feel her dread of the coming disaster. It will be left to her to manage everything and we feel the burden of her imminent lot.

A character of great importance in the play is that of the priest, always referred to as the 'young priest' and with reason. The priest is a link between human life and God's design and as such an authority. But he is also a human being and therefore by definition flawed; he in a sense suffers from hubris too and others are brought down into suffering by his limited sight and his assumptions to know the mind of God – in other words his pride. There is confusion between his temporal and his non-temporal powers. The priest has provided Nora with the bundle of clothes which were 'got off a drowned man

213

in Donegal'. Cathleen's disbelief that her brother's body could have floated as far away as 'the far north' is countered by Nora's asssertion of the priest's knowledge of communities and happenings far beyond the tiny island which is all they know:

> NORA: The young priest says he's known the like of it. 'If it's Michael's they are,' says he, 'you can tell herself he's got a clean burial, by the grace of God.'
>
> (ibid.: 73)

The priest as authority in this matter is different, however, from the authority that he assumes in the affairs of the living in relation to God's will:

> CATHLEEN: (*Looking out anxiously*) Did you ask him would he stop Bartley going this day with the horses to the Galway fair?
> NORA: 'I won't stop hin,' says he; 'but let you not be afraid. Herself does be saying prayers half through the night and the Almighty God won't leave her destitute with no son living.'
>
> (ibid.: 74)

The young priest is proved wrong, however, which only serves to add to the picture of the frailty of human life and the need to accept it. We are asked to accept the final limitation which constitutes the condition of mortality; using the priest to express this is an important dramatic tool which Synge deploys. Even as Nora repeats these words of the priest we know that Bartley will drown; the tone of tragic irony is set; the next words confirm this sense as one sister asks the other how the sea is and concludes, 'And it's worse it'll be getting when the tide's turned to the wind' (ibid.: 74).

The priest is powerless. He is young and has not yet learned humility in the face not perhaps of the God of the Catholic Church but of the ancient Celtic gods, the elemental gods of the natural world.

The characters of the women who accompany the body of Bartley and the men who bear him and make his coffin, perform the choric function of bearing witness to the bereavement of a member of the community. They identify with the family for their lot is the same, and in doing so they mirror the experience of all men and women faced with the fact of death.

Dramatic structure

At the very beginning of the play dramatic tension is immediately provided and audience attention secured by the opening action and line. Nora, Cathleen's younger sister, 'puts her head in at the door' and says, 'in a low voice' 'Where is she?' We know there is a secret. Immediately we are introduced to the community as Nora produces the bundle of clothes from under her shawl and the two sisters talk. Essential components of this community are the sea and the priest; the sea means both livelihood and death. The feeling of dread of the revelation of death is continually brought in by the sisters' need to hide from the mother the clothes which the priest has brought in. The tension is provided by this simple dramatic device.

The essence of the dramatic structure is that two threads or plots are working simultaneously. One is the issue of the identification of the clothes as Michael's or not, and the other that of whether or not Bartley will go to Galway in dangerous conditions. The two sisters hold this dramatic tension: they act as the link between the two plots. We know through them that the clothes have been found and probably belong to Michael, yet we wait with them in suspense for the moment when they can examine the bundle without their mother seeing. We know through them that the priest has not attempted to dissuade Bartley from going to Galway; we know through them, therefore, the impending final tragedy. We, the audience, understand implicitly the function of tragic irony. We know what they do not know, but we know it only because of what they know. Their knowing and our knowing therefore serve to heighten our empathy with Maurya, who is to make the two discoveries of the certain deaths of both her sons. The poetic climax of revelation therefore, when she sees the vision of her remaining son with behind him her dead one is of fitting proportions. The two are brought together in an ecstasy of tragic revelation:

MAURYA: I seen Michael himself.

CATHLEEN: (*speaking softly*) You did not, mother. It wasn't Michael you seen, for his body is after being found in the far north, and he's got a clean burial, by the grace of God.

MAURYA: (*a little defiantly*) I'm after seeing him this day, and he riding and galloping. Bartley came first on the red mare, and I tried to say 'God speed you', but something choked the words in my throat. He went by quickly: and 'the blessing of God on you,' says he, and I could say nothing. I looked up then, and I crying, at the grey pony, and there was Michael upon it – with fine clothes on him, and new shoes on his feet.

CATHLEEN: (*begins to keen*) It's destroyed we are from this day. It's destroyed surely.

NORA: Didn't the young priest say the Almighty God won't leave her destitute with no son living?

MAURYA: It's little the likes of him knows of the sea. . . . I've had a husband and a husband's father and six sons in this house – six fine men, though it was a hard birth with every one of them and they coming into the world . . . but they're gone now the lot of them.

(ibid.: 80–1)

Women united in the reality of their lot, united in abandonment in a world in which the authority of the priest is fallible and the women's capacity for learning the truth is through a combination of practical activity and vision-ary revelation. This moment is the turning point in the play and marks the transition towards the final acceptance with which the play ends.

Maurya speaks of the deaths of three generations of men, so simply, yet with such grandeur we could be listening to a tale of heroic proportions such as the woes of the women of Troy. For their woes are as great as those depicted in any Greek heroic tale and we are allowed to perceive and feel its stature through the cadence of the language: 'And some of them were found and some of them were not found but they're gone now the lot of them' (ibid.: 81).

What difference is there between the fate of these men and women of the Aran islands and those of the Greeks so long ago? I am reminded of the words of the chorus in *Oedipus Rex*, 'things old as the circling year'. For the fate of human beings in all time and all place is ultimately the same and each generation comes round to face that it is as inevitable as the seasons.

One of the most interesting ways in which Synge weaves the fabric of this short play bears some relation to the craft of the short story, where no detail can afford to be redundant. Part of the dramatic structure which I want to explore here is the use of objects, for in this there is much to help the drama-therapist. I shall explore just three – the bundle of clothes, the bread, and the white boards. All have a practical function in the lives of the characters, all have a function within the dramatic structure and all have a symbolic func-tion in relation to the events of the play which give the action weight and allow deep emotional resonances in the audience.

The bundle of clothes has a very straightforward dramatic function, for the two young women can inspect it only when Maurya is out of the house. This dilemma serves to heighten the dramatic tension in the play and to carry us forward to the final revelation. The bundle itself thus contributes to the play's tragic status. But more than that it is a major device to make available to us the emotional content and universal application of a play which is about the relationship between life and death, and the experience of mortality as lived by ordinary human beings. Synge does this through the careful positioning of references to the bundle and the language which the characters use in relation to it. Let us look at this more closely.

The bundle of clothes represents the objects of the living. When it is first referred to, Nora says, 'It's a shirt and a plain stocking were got off a drowned man in Donegal' (ibid.: 73).

Not only does this serve as immediate information that the drowned man must have something to do with this household, but it creates a sense of a real living human being, thus enabling the audience to empathize with the women whose bereavement is subsequently confirmed. When next it is referred to, it is as 'it', the bundle; it is as though it is already becoming an inanimate object. When the girls succeed in being on their own to inspect the bundle, Cathleen asks Nora for a knife because 'the string's perished with the salt water, and there's a black knot on it you wouldn't loosen in a week' (ibid.: 78).

The clothes have assumed the identity of the dead; just as Michael has been in the sea for several days, the bundle of clothes echoes this. We move from an awareness of life to an awareness of death. The stiffness of a dead body is echoed by the 'black knot you wouldn't loosen in a week'. The string perished with salt water is a reminder of the putrefaction of the body at the hands of the sea. The very word 'perished' evokes the perished man whose thread of life has perished like the string. The symbol of the living thus moves into a symbol of the dead. Yet the 'black knot' simultaneously creates a suggestion of the grip of the hand of death and the grip of the tenacity of human life so appropriate to this island community. As Cathleen cuts the string Nora ponders on how long it would take for a man to float to Donegal as opposed to walk – the phenomenon of the living and the dead are juxtaposed at the moment when the string is cut and the dead man's clothes are revealed. This is intensified and taken further by the link with the living man soon to die, Bartley, and the once-living man soon to be established as dead, Michael. For the sisters, looking for Michael's other shirt to identify the material of the one in the bundle, remember, 'Bartley put it on him in the morning for his own shirt was heavy with the salt in it' (ibid.: 78).

It is as though Bartley has identified himself with his dead brother, in his wearing of Michael's shirt, and the detail of his own shirt being 'heavy with the salt' prepares us for Bartley's imminent death. There is added power in the metaphorical content of the language, where the phrase 'heavy with the salt' evokes echoes of grief and tears. It is at this point that life and death are inextricably linked in the play as surely as the stocking is knitted. The conclusive evidence that Michael has been drowned comes from Nora's inspection of the stocking which has four dropped stitches in it. Any Aran islander will tell you that the individual patterns of sweaters originated in a need to have a means to identify drowned fishermen. Here the simplicity of the four stitches has echoes of the loss, the gap in relationship. Nora made the stockings for her brother, and did it with care and attention to detail; she knows exactly which pair it is of the three she made him. It is a symbol of relationship maintained and lost. Having identified the stocking and therefore her brother she cries out against the terrible truth of mortality: 'And isn't it a pitiful thing when there is nothing left of a man who was a great rower and fisher but a bit of old shirt and a plain stocking?' (ibid.: 79). Her words not only are words of personal grief, but also speak for the human condition, as this play itself does.

The second object I want to explore is the pair of white boards. The white boards are there throughout the play. They are introduced almost carelessly in those initial stage directions. They are part of a list of essential objects for a fisherman's cottage; they are followed by 'etc.' as though the list could go on and the boards are simply part of it. It is almost as though Synge himself was

217

not aware of their significance, yet knew it unconsciously because they are placed at the end of the list. In his 'Ode to Autumn' Keats personifies the season of dying and ending 'sitting careless on a granary floor'. The boards are like this, carelessly placed on the list, equal with all the objects of survival, the fishing nets, oilskins and spinning wheel yet significantly placed at the end, and juxtaposed to the information that Cathleen is kneading cake; again the juxtaposition of life and death as with the treatment of the bundle of clothes. It announces the play as one in which the relationship between life and death will be explored and reconciled.

So there the boards are, set at the beginning, in preparation for death. At the end they are used, not for the expected death but for the unexpected death. This reflects one of the great factors of death and why it is so feared, the fact that we normally have no control over it, its timing or its manner. It is ever-present, waiting for us, from the moment we are conceived, yet we 'know not the hour'.

The presence of the boards also signifies the possibility of preparation for death. They are the focus of Maurya's final speech. As writers on death have repeatedly said, preparation for death and our own mortality rather than a denial of it, can help us be reconciled with the inevitability that our lives will end.

> Bartley will have a fine coffin out of the white boards, and a deep grave surely. What more can we want than that? No man at all can be living forever and we must be satisified.
>
> (ibid.: 84)

Maurya's acceptance of the human condition at the end is expressed through the most tangible means – the coffin and the deep grave. The white boards have served as transforming objects. They signify a quiet act of transformation as the play moves to its end – 'a fine coffin out of the white boards'. How different if Maurya had said only 'a fine coffin and deep grave surely'. Instead she marks the transformation from the presence of death, ever waiting in our lives and homes like the white boards, to the finality of death and an acceptance of that. The boards are about to be made into a coffin. Just as they contain the body of Bartley so do they act as a container in the therapeutic sense, containing the feelings surrounding death and making them manageable for the characters and therefore for us at the end of this play. All the agitation of the earlier part of the play, the turmoil, fear, uncertainty are gone; the final speech is given in a context of silence as the keening 'sinks away'. There is a sense of completion.

The last object we shall look at is the cake or bread. It is an example of the tightness of the structure and the way in which the linking of objects holds the fabric of the play together. It is also of considerable symbolic significance as we shall see.

At the outset of the play Cathleen is finishing kneading the bread, an everyday action, an action which also places Cathleen in context, that of a woman in a simple household, in traditional role. It places her in a context of life, rather than of death. Bread enables living and therefore continuity. Synge tells us that she 'finishes kneading cake'. There is a sense of preparation – something has been completed and with this a sense of something to come. The dramatic function of the bread has therefore already begun. It also serves a practical purpose in being linked to the necessity of keeping the turf fire alive in order that the bread should be baked. This allows Cathleen to bring up the subject of Bartley's trip to Connemara in front of Maurya and provides an opening for the old woman to voice her fears. The bread is also an excuse to fetch more turf from the loft, an action which serves to disguise the hiding of the bundle of clothes from Maurya. The bread as a symbol of life and the clothes as a symbol of death, brought together in the dramatic structure in this way, intensify the attention we may pay as audience to the relationship between life and death which runs through the play. It is worth noting here that the turf must be kept alight. Maurya in her despair at having no control over Bartley's leaving

> *Takes up the tongs and begins raking the fire aimlessly*
> NORA: (*turning towards her*) You're taking away the turf from the cake.
>
> (ibid.: 77)

It is Nora who sees this, Nora, the youngest, who by this simple intervention underlines her role as the one who carrries the torch of the future; the fire must be kept alight and the bread baked. The bread is the symbol of continuity of the people. In the end it is not Bartley who eats it but the men who make his coffin.

> CATHLEEN: Maybe yourself and Eamon would make a coffin when the sun rises . . . and I have a new cake you can eat while you'll be working.
>
> (ibid.: 83)

One man may die but others must live.

This sense of the bread binding the living and the dead, holding the essence of mortality, unites in the centre of the play's dramatic structure also. Bartley goes, without his mother's blessing. Maurya aimlessly rakes the fire thereby almost letting it out. The action denotes Maurya's despair, her giving up, as she knows instinctively that her remaining son will die. Nora, the youngest, rescues the fire as we have seen and that in turn gives Cathleen the opportunity to find a way to get Maurya out of the house in order for the two girls to inspect the bundle of clothes.

> CATHLEEN: The Son of God forgive us, Nora, we're after forgetting his bit of bread . . . . (*Cutting some of the bread and rolling it in a cloth; to*

Maurya) let you go down now to the spring well and give him this and
he passing.

(ibid.: 77)

But even as she enables the inspection of the bundle to be consequent upon
this action, she also provides the opportunity for Maurya to make good her
having let her son go without a blessing. It is this little journey to the spring
well from which Maurya returns having seen the vision of her sons' deaths;
and it is the bread which takes the action on to allow that revelation to the
sisters.

> *Maurya comes in very slowly without looking at the girls ... the cloth
> with the bread is still in her hands. The girls look at each other, and Nora
> points to the bundle of bread.*

(ibid.: 79)

The bread takes her to the spring well, takes her, as it were, to the source of
life, but what she meets is a vision of death. Here the play's tragic tone is
supreme. Dead men have no use for bread and Maurya has no use for life.
'My heart is broken from this day' (ibid.: 10).

Here the tone of the old Celtic myths is evoked and we move deeply
into that world with Maurya's vision. Cathleen has cried out, 'The Son of
God forgive us, Nora, we're after forgetting his bit of bread.' In doing so
she has contextualized the characters and events firmly in Christianity in
general and Roman Catholicism in particular. (There is almost a sense that
it is the Son of God's bread that has been forgotten, the syntax being
ambiguous.) But with Maurya we move further back. The spring well has
connotations far older than those of Christianity, and sure enough it is to
these that Maurya turns to find a metaphor strong enough to describe her
experience.

> MAURYA: (*speaking very slowly*): I've seen the fearfullest thing any
> person has seen since the day Bride Dara seen the dead man with the
> child in his arms.

(ibid.: 80)

The bread and Maurya are joined in a relationship which not only creates
dramatic tension and supports tragic irony but also provides echoes to a collective unconscious which recognizes the fundamental importance of the
mother and feeding in the infant's struggle to survive.

The border between life and death is conveyed through the use of the bread
in the play and reminds us of the true hardship of the life led on those islands
where survival is always an issue. In doing so it provides a metaphor for the
struggle within us all of the survival of life over death, of hope over despair.
Maurya's eventual acceptance of her lot and of mortality, 'No man at all can
be living forever and we must be satisfied' (ibid.: 84), is said in the context of the

bread having been given to the old man to eat 'while you'll be working' at making the coffin for the young one.

The bread is an everyday object, making it part of the women's everyday work, yet it is also a deeply symbolic object which is used here to bind together some of the most profound themes of the play.

IN PRACTICE

Second preparation

By exploring the play in this way I can become more aware of its texture and its central themes. The waters which drown the men are also the source of life. In working with the play the interdependence of these ultimate opposites of life and death is crucial to ponder. Initial preparation, the musing which I shared with the reader earlier, now takes on body, moves into more concrete thinking but without losing its contact with the symbolic. I hold on to the idea of the centrality of opposites.

I now know for sure that I want to link ritual, text and objects. I want to link doing and being; we have seen that the men and women of the play 'do' and Maurya 'is'; there is movement, tension, anxiety and there is supreme stillness. Within the supportive atmosphere created both by group members and the activity of 'making', objects used in the play can be prepared and its world gradually created in the studio.

I am left with the image of the boards. I move with seeing where it leads me. The boards simply 'are'. Purchased by Maurya they wait quietly, boldly stark upon the set yet part of the everyday clutter. Then they are fashioned into a coffin by the men. These boards may evoke memories of seeing relatives or friends just after death or laid in the coffin prior to burial or cremation. They may also provide contact with feelings about death as it touches everyone. With some groups the actual making of symbolic boards, talking together whilst they do so, could be a helpful way to share and open up material for work on death and mourning. Slade's (1954) 'absorption' of projective play could provide expression and containment for feelings here.

This leads me to the possibility of the creation of the set, an enactment space to hold the play for both reading and improvisational work, peopled with the objects the group has made or assembled. As I have discussed only three objects in particular here, those are the ones that I shall continue to focus on.

First the bread: my exploration of the text has led me to appreciate how tightly the relationship between life and death is woven in this play. To make the bread out of clay would be a way to echo and support this theme. The idea of clay as the earth to which we must return; the memories of burials with the wet soil surrounding a grave, are evoked by working with clay in the context of this particular play. To therefore make loaves of clay, allows that image to be transformed into a symbol of life and continuity. If a kiln is available and the time span long enough, to bake the 'loaves' will add to that, as the transforming element of fire is introduced. This would echo the importance of the turf fire in the play which is always kept alight and used for baking the bread. By working with clay to make bread the essential opposites can co-exist and be balanced here.

I began by looking at the bundle of clothes. What my exploration of that has given me is thoughts about the thread of life spun on a string. For the string binds and holds and yet 'perishes'. I think of the spinning wheel on the set. Suddenly I remember a ritual devised by James Roose-Evans (1994: 74) where group members weave a tapestry by each throwing a ball of wool of a chosen colour across the circle to another. Each ball represents someone who has died who was known to that particular member of the group. I feel that this activity could reinforce the themes of life and death as the living remember the dead by means of this ritual.

Now some structures have begun to present themselves to me it is time to go back to the text. I think again about the power of the language, the way it rises and falls, the way the play moves towards its climaxes and ebbs away again, surging forward like the sea and sliding away. I know that I want people to have access to all this. Reading the play aloud will be important. In doing this we shall find all this and the characters too. I said earlier that it is a play about ordinary people yet of extraordinary stature. This is another balance I must try to help people to find.

A workshop

Designing an individual workshop means taking the overall preparatory thoughts and moulding them, allowing them to grow new shoots of possibility while keeping them with me as roots. These roots feed the creativity needed to adapt to the aim of a particular workshop both in planning and in execution.

Here I describe a workshop which in the event was, as my work usually is, a combination of a planned design and redesigning as I go along. The nature of the redesigning depends on two things; first, what I am picking up from the group and discerning its needs to be, and, second, allowing the play and all my encounters with it to work on me afresh in the 'now' of the session. In this particular workshop many of my preparation thoughts were not used, though some were used indirectly.

In this example I am sharing my methods with peers; all have come knowing the theme and some have read the play. Here I shall list the events of the workshop, putting them up on a screen for the reader to re-create the workshop in the mind's eye. Afterwards I shall comment briefly on aspects of the design and share resonances afforded by the subsequent writings of two of the participants.

222

1 Gathering together in a circle, clarification of aim, task and contract. Making contact then moving away to 'discover' the room, walking around and focusing on it as the space for the day's workshop.
2 Choosing an object from seashore objects provided; these were to be kept throughout the day.
3 Private time with the object; silent reflections on why each person had decided to come to this particular workshop, free associations, what they wanted to get out of it, etc.
4 Sharing some of these thoughts and feelings, and object choice if wished, with a partner.
5 Saying the play's title out loud all together, then finding sounds and holding hands in the circle. This led into swaying and evocation of the sea.
6 In two groups a reading of the text – actors on the inside circle and audience on the outside circle.
7 Second reading of the play without discussion in between but with a ritual for handing over the role and for exchanging actor role for audience role.
8 All turning in towards the circle and saying the title 'Riders to the Sea' aloud together, then outwards towards the 'world out there' area and repeating it.
9 Whole group talking and sharing; time for personal reflection with the object again and the option of retaining it in a safe place or putting it back in the basket over lunchtime.

BREAK FOR LUNCH

10 Reconnecting with objects in whole group, sharing thoughts and feelings if wished.
11 In a circle a movement which the play evoked for each person. Then a sound.
12 Two groups, each group having had two improvisation tasks:

   (a) Devise an enactment of what the play means to you as a group – feelings, themes, personal echoes etc.
   (b) Devise a dramatic collage of your interpretation of the play.

13 Sharing these through enactment; the other group and myself comprised the audience.
14 Feedback and sharing in relation to the enactments.
15 Returning object to the basket, taking time over this.
16 Final discussion and leavetaking of the workshop.

In this workshop my focus on objects in the play became translated into offering the group shells, stones, small pieces of driftwood. Particularly in day-workshops such objects help to focus and contain as I suggested in Chapter 2. The individual can 'create' them in his or her own image. In a workshop on this particular play where issues of separation are so central, the transitional

223

quality of the object is bound to be evident in group members' responses to it for the transitional object is the beginning of the infant's process of separation. If the workshop has been a 'good breast' then the object will be important in helping participants to move away from the workshop at the end, to be 'weaned'. For some this will feel premature and time needs to be given to the letting go of the object. Although the transitional object is not mourned but rather 'loses meaning' as Winnicott says, an object in such a workshop as this might be used partly in its transitional function and partly as projective object. Time needs to be given towards the end of the session for the individual to take back what has been held projectively by the object. Space needs to be given for the expression of any feelings that are evoked by the dramatherapist taking away something that has been lent to the group.

In this workshop one member said she was angry and felt she wanted to throw her stone. Spending time allowing her the space for the possibility that she might be angry with me enabled her to get in touch with being angry with herself for not having given herself the opportunity to read the part she had been ambivalent about taking. At the moment of feeling deprived in the session, i.e. at the time of giving back the objects, she could get in touch with another aspect, the way in which she had deprived herself. In the two passages which end this account of the workshop the writers clearly show that working with objects can evoke feelings; the first shows that the process of returning it is not easy. Here time must be given for this object is to be mourned, the 'death' of the relationship the person has to it is premature. In the second the transitional quality of the object is clear; it is invested with great meaning early on, stands in for the 'good breast' and, its purpose having helped the individual to involve herself through playing and using other objects in a symbolic way, it is de-cathected; handing it back is surprisingly easy.

On this occasion I never used the idea I might have adapted from Roose-Evans (1994). I did not need to; one of the groups did a powerful improvisation involving thick rope-like wool which they had found amongst the props of the dramatherapy studio. As the facilitator I felt a deep sense of satisfaction at seeing the play work on the group; my thoughts on the string and the thread of life were there in the group too because they were generated by the text itself. The group found its own way of engaging with them, serving their purpose much better than mine could have done. I had the feeling, every time I thought of introducing this idea, that it was not right, and stopped myself. I am convinced that the preparatory work on the text contributes greatly to my being able to have hunches and respect them in the session itself. It is essential to my being able to hold back, knowing that the group may well come up with its own version of an idea I might have had, as in this instance.

Any work on this text can be enhanced only by respecting the ritual quality of the play. The ritual of daily life mingles with the rituals of death and mourning. The ritual of moving in and out, respecting the boundary of actor and audience yet allowing relation between them, is an important part of allowing the play as mirror of the human condition. The idea of people silently handing over actor and audience roles to each other came to me in the session as I felt and witnessed the quality of the absorption of the group's engagement with the play as both reader and audience. Again my preparatory work on the text helped me here, for the ritual *in situ* I realized would be fitting echoed the handing on of the mantle from Maurya to Nora and the continuity of life, the ever-returning cycle of life and death.

Two participants reflect

It was a difficult journey that day.
Foggy, cold.
At the beginning of the workshop we formed the circle.
We stretched out our arms and touched one another's finger-tips.
We looked inward.
We turned and looked outward.
And so we would continue throughout the day.
Looking inward.
Then, externalizing our internal experiences through performance.
Through movement, mime, dance, sounds and words.
We chose an object to keep, to return to, safely
take care of. At the end we gave it back.
Not easily.

The colours of the play were dark.
Brooding greys, greens and darkest blue.
Only the waiting boards were stripped of colour.

The women in the cottage waited, hiding the clothes.
Losing sons, brothers.
The abiding loss of fatherhood.

I brought feelings of vulnerability, an anticipation of loss.
I became in close contact with old losses;
Of my mother my father and my sister.
Within the group we glimpsed, were aware of each other
Re-experiencing separation, grief and mourning.

Through the characters in the play
And through the contact of the group working together
I felt held and healed by the symbolism of the actions and the words
and sounds expressed.

I chose an object from a box. It was a vertebra, washed and bleached smooth by the sea. I found my space in the room and sat with my

225

object, lay with it, wrapped myself around it, rested it on my spine. Thought about connections, about support. Felt strangely connected and strengthened. In hindsight I realised how much I needed this in order to later allow myself to feel loss and pain and to express my life-long lonely motto – 'It's not fair!' I felt strangely attached to this piece of skeleton and hated Marina (aptly named) prematurely for taking it away from me at the end of the session. I felt that it would be almost impossible for me to let it go.

We read the play aloud and I took the part of Nora. The younger sister. When my group came to improvise I found myself tangled up in rope crying, 'I'm only a girl', 'It's not my fault.' I had reached back into my past, to the death of my mother, and to the feeling that I had been too young.

We sat in a circle and shared our experiences. I cried as I described the connections that I had made. And also felt a great relief both at having felt it and expressed it. I had been too young, and it hadn't been fair, but denying that I'd ever had a mother was not the way to heal myself. It was easy, then, to put the vertebra back in the box.

It feels important to say two more things. One is that at the time of this workshop I was discovering in my personal therapy the extent to which I had cut myself off from my past and that the deaths of my parents acted as a sort of watershed in this, as though there had been two lives, one before and one after. The other is that my parents were Irish and my mother, in particular, had a love of Irish literature, especially of the theatre. And the west of Ireland is a special place to me.

Conclusion

The final word in this chapter must surely go to what I might call the unconscious of the space. A shared lunch had been eaten and the food still lay on a long table at the side of the room. At the beginning of the afternoon session, the group discussed whether or not it should be cleared away before we began work. They decided to leave it but not use that area for enactment. As we worked on issues of death it seemed to me that the food perhaps needed to stay there, within sight, a reminder of life. In working in the presence of the food and drink, the plates and cups, the knives and forks, we seemed to have unconsciously created the set of *Riders to the Sea* and found the essence of the play. The bread, as it were, lay upon the board.

226

10

THE EPILOGUE

What we call the beginning is often the end
And to make an end is to make a beginning.
The end is where we start from . . .
Every phrase and every sentence is an end and a beginning.
(T. S. Eliot, 'Little Gidding' in Four Quartets)

I began this book with a discussion of a text in which a group of people exiled from their home country find the possibility of growth through putting on a play. Through this text we were able to explore some of the basic properties of dramatherapy. Then we moved on to look at how some of the contributions of psychoanalysis can help us to understand and work with dramatherapy processes. Notions of projection and introjection, potential space and the relationship between illusion and reality have been explored in different ways throughout these pages. Always the 'me' and 'not-me' and the 'as if' of drama have been found in many guises. So let us end by looking at the place where the two worlds of illusion and reality both meet and part company in the theatre in a single dramatic form – that of Shakespeare's epilogues. Shakespeare helps us to begin to let go, to separate from the play by means of the epilogue which is an intermediate place. It lies between the world of the play and the world 'out there'. It is a gentle way of reminding us that the reality principle exists. What is special about Shakespeare's epilogues is that he brings the paradox of art right into focus; he states it, makes us engage with it. He tells us that the play is an illusion, but he does it from within the play which in itself belongs to the world of illusion. Shakespeare reminds us of the illusory quality of the theatre in his famous lines spoken by Prospero after the masque in Act IV of *The Tempest*.

> Our revels now are ended. These our actors,
> As I foretold you, were all spirits, and
> Are melted into air, into thin air:
> And, like the baseless fabric of this vision,
> The cloud-capp'd towers, the gorgeous palaces,
> The solemn temples, the great globe itself,

> Yea, all which it inherit, shall dissolve,
> And, like this insubstantial pageant faded,
> Leave not a rack behind. We are such stuff
> As dreams are made on; and our little life
> Is rounded with a sleep . . .
>
> *(The Tempest* Act IV, Scene 1: 148–58)

Here Shakespeare speaks of the illusory quality of both the theatre and human life itself. He reassures us that the ending of the play is not the ending of life, yet reminds us that it mirrors that aspect of the human condition. And he does this by means of a character in a play, an illusion. So how do we find our way home? Shakespeare frequently helps us make the transition from the theatre and the world of the play by means of an epilogue. In *As You Like It* he reminds us of who we are in 'real' life, as for example in the epilogue spoken by Rosalind in which he invites the audience to think about their concerns and ways of being in the world, their familiar life constructs:

> I charge you, O Women for the love you bear to men. . . . And I charge you, O men for the love you bear to women . . .
>
> *(As You Like It* Act V, Scene 4: 220)

And he also speaks directly to the audience, appealing to another part of its members' reality by reminding them of their role in the theatre.

> If we shadows have offended,
> Think but this and all is mended:
> That you have but slumbered here
> While these visions did appear.
> And this weak and idle theme,
> No more yielding but a dream,
> Gentles, do not reprehend.
> If you pardon, we will mend.
>
> *(A Midsummer Night's Dream* Act V, Scene 1: 413)

Of all the epilogues, it is that with which he ends *The Tempest* which is most relevant to the themes of this book. Indeed *The Tempest* has been present, by direct reference, analogy or quiet implication throughout. At the end of this play, commonly believed to be Shakespeare's last, and his farewell to the theatre, Prospero, the protagonist, prepares to leave the island on which he has spent the last twelve years in exile, having been usurped by his brother from his role as Duke of Milan. Here he has learned to face his shadow, find his feeling-function and his creative imagination with the help of the indigenous Caliban, his daughter Miranda and the spirit Ariel. His work on the island is analogous to the work of therapy as I have discussed elsewhere (Jenkyns 1988). What will concern us here is the epilogue to the play.

In this play the island is a place of illusion. It is a potential space full of transitional phenomena where it is not clear what is real or not real, where reality is an illusion and illusion is reality. It is a wonderful shifting, sliding, magical place which can slip through our fingers like the water which surrounds it and yet is hard and solid as the rocks on which the ship founders and yet is made whole again. Through omnipotent control of his 'art', his 'playing', Prospero brought the court of Naples and Milan to the island, yet the court was on its way anyway. He created it but it was there, sailing on the waters all the time; just as the baby 'creates' the breast and the transitional object is there waiting to provide nourishment and comfort.

This experience is repeated in the theatre. The writer creates this play for us by his writing, but we, the audience, create it for ourselves. At the end of any play the character, the actor and the audience have to find the means to separate from one another and go their separate ways. In our different ways we all have to de-role. Some do it through the rituals of the curtain call and applause, others as they walk out into the foyer or the street begin to discuss the play or silently share a drink, still others move through the illuminated darkness of the trees bordering a Greek amphitheatre. The character slips back between the pages of the text as the stage manager organizes the clearing of the set. Like Prospero we must all return to our mainland to take up our roles again.

It is by means of the epilogue that Shakespeare enables the character, the actor, and us the audience to make this transition. Let us therefore explore some of the complexity of the epilogue to *The Tempest*.

> Now my charms are all o'erthrown,
> And what strength I have's mine own,
> Which is most faint: now 'tis true,
> I must be here confined by you,
> Or sent to Naples. Let me not,
> Since I have my dukedom got,
> And pardoned the deceiver, dwell
> In this bare island by your spell;
> But release me from my bands
> With the help of your good hands:
>
> (*The Tempest* Epilogue: 1–10)

The opening lines show Prospero having rejected magical omnipotence. He is 'most faint' because he has ended his role as master-minder of the plot, for the culmination of Act V is behind him. He is now in an in-between place, for he has not left the play, neither is he in it. He is, in essence, 'but a bare fork'd animal' (*King Lear*) and thus a man like any other; the epilogue invites us see him as being like anyone in the audience. Thus Shakespeare, by weaning Prospero of his omnipotence, begins to lessen the gap between Prospero and ourselves.

In doing this, the relationship between the space of illusion and reality is

229

brought more into consciousness for the audience. Prospero acknowledges himself to be the creation of the audience; they have the power to retain him on the island and the power to release him from it. The audience is given omnipotence here. In these lines we are being invited to reach out our hands across the stage but – and this is crucial – metaphorically, not actually. We must preserve the roles of actor and audience and the boundary between them or we are in chaos, not nourished and contained by the art form. As Kermode points out (Notes to Arden edition of *The Tempest*, 1964), the 'good hands' of the audience are for clapping. The quality of being so near and yet so far, the fine boundary line between the actor and audience is created here, for to literally leap upon the stage and free the actor would be to cross the line between illusion and reality and break it. The actor is still Prospero. He may not be de-roled yet. 'That way madness lies' (*King Lear*). But what is happening is a kind of handing over.

Shakespeare does not allow us omnipotence but Prospero allows us the illusion of omnipotence,

> Gentle breath of yours my sails
> Must fill, or else my project fails,
> Which was to please. . . .
>
> (*The Tempest* Epilogue: 11–13)

With these lines we move into another layer of the reflective process. To whom did the task of pleasing belong – Prospero or Shakespeare? Here it is the playwright who begins to emerge into the picture and in doing so takes the audience a little further on the road to the world 'out there'; we become a little more conscious – did we like the play or not, we are invited to consider – oh then it was a play we have been watching, not reality. So now we can begin to leave. But Shakespeare has not finished with us yet.

> Now I want
> Spirits to enforce, Art to enchant;
> And my ending is despair,
> Unless I be reliev'd by prayer,
> Which pierces so, that it assaults
> Mercy itself and frees all faults.
>
> (ibid.: 13–18)

Shakespeare's use of 'want' is used here in the sense of lack, and Prospero on one level seems to invite us to contemplate a world without imagination, without art. One which is desolate indeed. He has broken his magic staff and drowned his magic book. Momentarily he seems to have forgotten that they were only tools which helped towards the resolution of his past; towards love. He has forgiven his enemies and is ready to return to take up his role fully as Duke on the mainland. He seems to have forgotten, too, that he found within him greater powers to move on from this place – the functions of Caliban,

230

Miranda and Ariel. But Prospero is on the brink of the unknown – he is leaving the island. He is experiencing the anxiety inherent in that intermediate place, the place of separation. At the moment preceding this leavetaking therefore, he plunges into near-despair, a state so often preceding the final stages of creativity. Like an infant he panics. The re-construction of himself which has taken twelve years on the island cannot be completed without the audience's blessing; their goodwill is necessary for him to individuate, as the mother's is for the child to separate, and the therapist's for the client. The epilogue here serves to mirror those experiences to us; Prospero stands in for them as we too prepare to leave.

Shakespeare's lines are firmly rooted in the framework of the moral universe of his own place and time, Christianity. The power of prayer is evoked and the efficacy of mercy. Yet Shakespeare, whose personal moral universe is surely not confined to a particular doctrine, ends the play on a note which crosses all cultures and religions, the relationship of one human being to another,

> As you from crimes would pardon'd be
> Let your indulgence set me free.
>
> (ibid.: 19–20)

Here, in this last couplet, the epilogue rests in perfect balance between illusion and reality. The stage is the stage, the character is the character, the actor is the actor and the audience is the audience. And in the shadows is the playwright and perhaps his farewell. All are still in their places. But the partnership is clear. Omniscience is no one's prerogative. We are all, whatever our role has been in this theatrical encounter, in need of giving and receiving love, having an awareness of guilt and the need to make reparation. Finally we, the members of the audience or participants in dramatherapy, must withdraw our projections from Prospero, re-introject what he has held for us and sail back to our mainland for 'no man is an island'. Prospero can live his individuated life on the mainland and we can be released into our worlds, enriched by the power of imagination which Prospero has held for us and mirrored to us. Only by letting go of the island can Prospero, paradoxically, take it with him to support him in his mainland life. And so it is for us. Only by letting go of Prospero, by means of the epilogue, can we take with us what the playwright has given us, the island of illusion and reality which is the play.

BIBLIOGRAPHY

Andersen-Warren, M. (1991) 'The Revenger's Tragedy: From Spectators to Partici-
pants', Dramatherapy: Journal of the British Association for Dramatherapists
(BADth) 14(2).
Aristotle (1920) On the Art of Poetry, trans. I. Bywater, Oxford: Oxford University
Press.
Baker Miller, J. (1976) Toward a New Psychology of Women, Harmondsworth:
Penguin.
Bates, B. (1986) The Way of the Actor, London: Jessica Kingsley.
Beckett, S. (1955, 1965) Waiting for Godot, London: Faber & Faber.
Berkhoff, S. (1988) Greek, London: Rosica Colin.
Bion, W. R. (1961) Experiences in Groups, London: Tavistock.
—— (1963) Elements of Psycho-analysis, London: Karnac.
Boal, A. (1979) Theater of the Oppressed, trans. C. A. and Maria-Odila Leal McBride,
London: Pluto.
—— (1992) Games for Actors and Non-Actors, London: Routledge.
Bollas, C. (1987) The Shadow of the Object: Psychoanalysis of the Unthought Known,
London: Free Association.
Bond, E. (1965) Saved, London: Methuen.
Brook, P. (1968) The Empty Space, Harmondsworth: Penguin.
—— (1987) The Shifting Point, London: Methuen.
Brown, D. and Pedder, J. (1979, 1991) Introduction to Psychotherapy: An Outline of
Psychodynamic Principles and Practice, London: Routledge.
Casement, P. (1985) On Learning from the Patient, London: Tavistock.
—— (1990) Further Learning from the Patient, London: Tavistock.
Chodorow, N. J. (1978) Reproduction of Mothering, Berkeley: University of California
Press.
—— (1989) Feminism and Psychoanalytic Theory, Cambridge: Polity.
Churchill, C. (1980) Cloud Nine, London: Pluto Press/Joint Stock Theatre Group.
—— (1983) 'Introduction to Cloud Nine', in Churchill Plays: One, London:
Methuen.
Cobb, N. (1984) Prospero's Island: The Secret Alchemy at the Heart of The Tempest,
London: Coventure.
Coleman, A. D. and Bexton, W. H. (1975) Group Relations Reader 1, Washington DC:
A. K. Rice Institute.
Coleridge, S. (1950) Selected Prose and Poetry, ed. S. Potter, London: Nonesuch.
Corti, P. (1993/4) 'Bearing Witness', Dramatherapy: Journal of BADth 15 (3).
Cox, M. (1978a) Structuring the Therapeutic Process: Compromise with Chaos,
Oxford: Pergamon.

—— (1978b) *Coding the Therapeutic Process: Emblems of Encounter*, Oxford: Pergamon.

—— ed. (1992) *Shakespeare Comes to Broadmoor: The Performance of Tragedy in a Secure Psychiatric Hospital*, London: Jessica Kingsley.

—— (1994) *Shakespeare as Prompter: The Amending Imagination and the Therapeutic Process*, London: Jessica Kingsley.

Cox, M. and Theilgaard, A. (1987) *Mutative Metaphors in Psychotherapy: The Aeolian Mode*, London: Tavistock.

Davis, M. and Wallbridge, D. (1981) *Boundary and Space: An Introduction to the Work of D. W. Winnicott*, Harmondsworth: Penguin.

De Board, R. (1978) *The Psychoanalysis of Organisations*, London: Tavistock.

Durbach, E. (1972) 'Synge's Tragic Vision of the Old Mother and the Sea', in R. Ayling (ed.) (1992) *J. M. Synge: Four Plays*, London: Macmillan.

Edgar, D. (1987) *Mary Barnes*, in *Edgar Plays: One*, London: Methuen.

Ehrenzweig, A. (1967) *The Hidden Order of Art*, Berkeley: University of California Press.

Eichenbaum, L. and Orbach, S. (1982) *Outside In . . . Inside Out: Women's Psychology; A Feminist Psychoanalytic Approach*, Harmondsworth: Penguin.

—— (1983) *Understanding Women*, Harmondsworth: Penguin.

Eliaz, E. (1992) 'The Concept of Dramatic Transference', *The Arts in Psychotherapy* 19 (5): 333–46.

Eliot, T. S. (1944) *Four Quartets*, London: Faber & Faber.

Emunah, R. and Read Johnson, D. (1983) 'The Impact of Theatrical Peformance on the Self-images of Psychiatric Patients', *The Arts in Psychotherapy* 10: 233–9.

Erikson, E. H. (1977) *Childhood and Society*, London: Triad Granada.

—— (1980) *Identity and the Life Cycle*, New York: W. W. Norton.

—— (1982) *The Life Cycle Completed*, New York: W. W. Norton.

Ernst, S. and Maguire, M. (eds) (1987) *Living with the Sphinx: Papers from the Women's Therapy Centre*, London: Women's Press.

Farquhar, G. (1988) *The Recruiting Officer*, London: Methuen.

Fink, S. O. (1990) 'Approaches to Emotion in Psychotherapy and Theatre: Implications for Dramatherapy', *The Arts in Psychotherapy* 17: 5–18.

Freud, S. (1973a) *Introductory Lectures on Psychoanalysis*, trans. J. Strachey (1962) ed. A. Richards, Harmondsworth: Penguin.

—— (1973b) *New Introductory Lectures on Psychoanalysis*, trans. J. Strachey (1962) ed. A. Richards, Harmondsworth: Penguin.

Friday, N. (1977) *My Mother My Self*, London: Fontana.

Genet, J. (1972) *Reflections on the Theatre*, London: Faber & Faber.

Gersie, A. (1991) *Storymaking in Bereavement: Dragons Fight in the Meadow*, London: Jessica Kingsley.

Gordon, R. (1978) *Dying and Creating: A Search for Meaning*, London: Society of Analytical Psychology.

Grainger, R. (1990) *Drama and Healing: The Roots of Dramatherapy*, London: Jessica Kingsley.

Hawkes, T. (ed.) (1959) *Coleridge and Shakespeare*, Harmondsworth: Penguin.

Hawkins, P. and Shohet, R. (1989) *Supervision in the Helping Professions*, Milton Keynes: Open University Press.

Heimann, P. (1950) 'On Counter-transference', *International Journal of Psychoanalysis* 31.

Henn, T. R. (1972) ' Images, Symbols and Literary Echoes', in R. Ayling (ed.) (1992) *J. M. Synge: Four Plays*, London: Macmillan.

Hinshelwood, R. D. (1989) *A Dictionary of Kleinian Thought*, London: Free Association.

BIBLIOGRAPHY

Holmes, P. (1992) *The Inner World Outside: Object Relations Theory and Psycho-drama*, London: Routledge.
Howe Kritzer, A. (1991) *The Plays of Caryl Churchill: The Theatre of Empowerment*, London: Macmillan.
Ibsen, H. (1962) *Ghosts*, trans. M. Meyer, London: Rupert Hart-Davis.
Isaacs, S. (1948) 'The Nature and Function of Phantasy', *International Journal of Psychoanalysis* 29.
Jenkyns, M. (1988) 'Time for Change or Prospero's Journey', *Dramatherapy. Journal of BADth* 11 (1)
—— (1990) '"Bless Thee! Thou art translated": An Exploration of the Theme of Body and Image in *A Midsummer Night's Dream*', *Dramatherapy: Journal of BADth* 13.
Jennings, S. (ed.) (1987) *Dramatherapy, Theory and Practice for Teachers and Clinicians*, London: Routledge.
—— (1990) *Dramatherapy with Families, Groups and Individuals*, London: Jessica Kingsley.
—— (1991) 'Theatre Art: The Heart of Dramatherapy', *Dramatherapy: Journal of BADth* 14 (1).
—— (1992) *Dramatherapy, Theory and Practice 2*, London: Routledge.
—— (ed.) (1995) *Dramatherapy with Children and Adolescents*, London: Routledge.
Jennings, S., Cattanach, A., Mitchell, A., Chesner, A. and Meldrum, B. (1994) *The Handbook of Dramatherapy*, London: Routledge.
Jones, P. (1991) 'Dramatherapy: Five Core Processes', *Dramatherapy: Journal of BADth* 14 (1).
Joshi, A. (1994a) *A Shaft of Sunlight*, unpublished playscript.
—— (1994b) Notes in programme for *A Shaft of Sunlight*, Birmingham Repertory Theatre.
Keats, J. (1956) *Poetical Works*, London: Oxford University Press.
Keneally, T. (1987) *The Playmaker*, London: Hodder & Stoughton.
Klein, M. (1988a) *Love, Guilt and Reparation*, London: Virago.
—— (1988b) *Envy and Gratitude*, London: Virago.
Landy, R. J. (1986) *Dramatherapy: Concepts and Practice*, Springfield, Ill.: Charles C. Thomas.
—— (1990) 'Role as a Primary Bridge between Theatre and Drama Therapy', *Dramatherapy: Journal of BADth* 13 (1).
—— (1993) *Persona and Performance*, London: Jessica Kingsley.
Laplanche, J. and Pontalis, J.-B. (1973) *The Language of Psycho-analysis*, London: Hogarth.
Little, M. (1951) 'Counter-transference and the Patient's Response to It', *International Journal of Psychoanalysis* 32.
McDougall, J. (1985) *Theatres of the Mind*, London: Free Association Books.
McGuire, W. and Hull, R. F. C. (1977) *C. G. Jung Speaking*, London: Picador.
Maguire, M. (1987) 'Casting the Evil Eye: Women and Envy', in Ernst and Maguire (eds).
Malan, D. H. (1979) *Individual Psychotherapy and the Science of Psychodynamics*, London: Butterworth.
Marowitz, C., Milne, T. and Hale, O. (eds) (1965) *The Encore Reader*, London: Methuen.
Meyer, M. (1971) *Henrik Ibsen: The Farewell to Poetry*, London: Rupert Hart-Davis.
Miller, A. (1983) *The Drama of Being a Child*, London: Virago.
Milner, M. (1958) 'Psycho-Analysis and Art', in D. W. Winnicott *et al.*, *Psychoanalysis and Contemporary Thought*, ed. J. Sutherland, International Psychoanalysis Library 53, London: Hogarth.

BIBLIOGRAPHY

Mitchell, S. (1990) 'The Theatre of Peter Brook as a Model for Dramatherapy', *Dramatherapy: Journal of BADth* 13 (1).

Mollon, P. (1993) *The Fragile Self: The Structure of Narcissistic Disturbance*, London: Wurr.

Obholzer, A. and Zagier-Roberts, V. (eds) (1994) *The Unconscious at Work: Individual and Organizational Stress in the Human Services*, London: Routledge.

O'Connor, N. and Ryan, J. (1993) *Wild Desires and Mistaken Identities: Lesbianism and Psychoanalysis*, London: Virago.

Ogden, T. H. (1992) *Projective Identification and Psychotherapeutic Technique*, London: Karnac.

Payne, H. (ed) (1993) *Handbook of Inquiry in the Arts Therapies*, London: Jessica Kingsley.

Pirandello, L. (1979) *Six Characters in Search of an Author*, trans. J. Lindstrom, London: Eyre Methuen.

Racker, H. (1968) *Transference and Countertransference*, London: Maresfield Library.

Read Johnson, D. (1994) 'Representation of the Internal World in Catatonic Schizophrenia', *Psychiatry* 47.

Rice, A. K. (1965) *Learning for Leadership*, London: Tavistock.

Roose-Evans, J. (1994) *Passages of the Soul: Ritual Today*, Shaftesbury: Element.

Rowan, J. (1983) *The Reality Game: A Guide to Humanistic Counselling and Therapy*, London: Routledge & Kegan Paul.

Roy, A. (1994) 'The Hindu–Muslim Relationship: A Historic Perspective', notes in programme for performance of *A Shaft of Sunlight*, Birmingham Repertory Theatre.

Rycroft, C. (1968a) *A Critical Dictionary of Psychoanalysis*, Harmondsworth: Penguin.

—— (1968b) *Imagination and Reality*. London: Maresfield Library.

Samuels, A., Shorter, B. and Plaut, F. (1986) *A Critical Dictionary of Jungian Analysis*, London: Routledge.

Sandler, J. (ed.) (1987) *Projection, Identification, Projective Identification*, London: Karnac.

Sandler, J., Dare, C. and Holder, A. (1973) *The Patient and the Analyst*, London: Allen & Unwin.

Scheff, T. J. (1979) *Catharsis in Healing, Ritual and Drama*, Berkeley: University of California Press.

Segal, H. (ed.) (1955) M. Klein: *New Directions in Psycho-Analysis*, London: Tavistock.

—— (1964, 1973) *Introduction to the Works of Melanie Klein*, London: Karnac/Institute of Psychoanalysis.

—— (1979) *Klein*, London: Karnac/Institute of Psychoanalysis.

Shakespeare, W. (1963) *Hamlet*, New York: Signet Classics.

—— (1964) *The Tempest*, London: Methuen.

—— (1965) *Othello*, London: Methuen.

—— (1965) *King Henry V*, London: Methuen.

—— (1967) *As You Like It*, London: Methuen.

—— (1967) *A Midsummer Night's Dream*, Harmondsworth: Penguin.

Slade, P. (1954) *Child Drama*, London: University of London Press.

Sophocles (1947) *The Theban Plays*, trans. E. F. Watling, Harmondsworth: Penguin.

Spencer, J. S. (1992) *Dramatic Strategies in the Plays of Edward Bond*, Cambridge: Cambridge University Press.

Sprinchorn, E. (ed.) (1964) *Ibsen: Letters and Speeches*, New York: Hill & Wang.

Stanislavski, C. (1968) *Creating a Role*, trans. E. R. Hapgood, London: Mentor.

Storr, A. (ed.) (1983) *Jung: Selected Writings*, London: Fontana.

Suleri, S. (1989) *Meatless Days*, London: Collins.

Synge, J. M. (1961) *Riders to the Sea*, Oxford: Heinemann.

—— (1961) *Playboy of the Western World*, London: New English Library.

Thomas, Daphne (1995) *Thursday's Child*, unpublished playscript.

Thomas, Dylan (1954) *Under Milk Wood*, London: Dent.

Ussher, J. and Nicholson, P. (1992) *Gender Issues in Clinical Psychology*, London: Routledge.

Wagner, B. J. (1976) *Dorothy Heathcote: Drama as a Learning Medium*, Washington DC: National Education Association.

Webster, J. (1933) *The Duchess of Malfi* in *Webster and Ford: Selected Plays*, London: Dent.

Welldon, E. V. (1988) *Mother, Madonna, Whore*, London: Free Association.

Wertenbaker, T. (1988) *Our Country's Good*, London: Methuen.

Wesker, A. (1959) *Roots*, in *The Wesker Trilogy*, Harmondsworth: Penguin.

Wilshire, B. (1982) *Role Playing and Identity: The Limits of Theater as Metaphor*, Bloomington: Indiana University Press.

Winnicott, C., Shepherd, R. and Davis, M. (comps and eds) (1968) *D. W. Winnicott: Home is Where We Start From: Essays by a Psychoanalyst*, Harmondsworth: Penguin.

Winnicott, D. W. (1965) *The Maturational Process and the Facilitating Environment*, The International Psychoanalysis Library 64, London: Hogarth.

—— (1971) *Playing and Reality*, Harmondsworth: Penguin.

Witkin, R. W. (1974) *The Intelligence of Feeling*, London: Heinemann.

Worral, J. and Remer, P. (1992) *Feminist Perspectives in Therapy*, Chichester: Wiley.

Wright, E. (1984) *Psychoanalytic Criticism*, London: Methuen.

Yalom, I. D. (1975) *The Theory and Practice of Group Psychotherapy*, New York: Basic Books.

Zender, J. F. (1991) 'Projective Identification in Group Psychotherapy', *Group Analysis*, London: SAGE.

INDEX

absorption, projected play and 14–15,
19, 68, 221; ritual of theatre and 70,
225
'actions towards equality', opposition
to 113
actively active audience mode 21–2;
individual role-player and 23; Teacher
in 30
actively passive audience mode 21
actor/audience dynamic, management of
session and 70
actor/audience relationship 10, 19–24
actors, *actively active audience* 22;
authorized by audience 20; 'me'
object and 33; mirror for
audience 22–3; need to be 'held' by
director 158; possession and 153;
validate the audience 22–3
aesthetic distance 10, 68, 173;
audience/actor relationship and 19,
22–3, 100–1; dramatic structures
and 72; *Our Country's Good* and
15–19
aesthetic principle, bearing with the
unbearable 6
AIDS 169, 172, 176
'All the world's a stage', metaphoric
value 6
'an acceptance of the agenda you're born
with' 130
analytic psychotherapy, role of
therapist 50, 52
Ancient Greece, debates in 20
Aristotle 1, 18, 81, 167
'as if', drama and 32, 99, 157, 227
As You Like It 2, 37, 52, 228
audience, actor relationship 10, 19–24;
art form of drama implies 27; as

authorizing witnesses 20–1; director's
ultimate duty to 159; holding function
for actor 23; 'not me' object and 33;
power of 230; Shakespeare's need
for 27; space 70; witness to actor
20–1, 71, 175, 208
Auschwitz 41
authority, of priest in *Riders to the
Sea* 215; of text 17–19, 34; use of role
and 18–19, 21

'bad breast' 35, 37, 41, 43, 96, 113
'bad mother' 137
'bad' parenting 10
Baker Miller, J. 105–6, 108, 112–13, 125,
127
Bates, B. 153
'be' the character 13, 156
Bearing Witness (1993/4) 20
Beckett, S. 74
beginnings 82, 97, 101
Berkhoff, S. 9
Bexton, W.H. 60
Bion, W.R. 46
Boal, A.C.A. 25
Bond, Edward 40–1, 44, 164
boundaries 16–17, 66; audience and
actors and 230; contracts and 60–3;
importance of 158; transitional
objects and 32
boundary confusion, between client and
therapist 55; character of Carol
and 159–60; en-roling and
de-roling 66–7, 69–70, 137, 149
Broadmoor (psychiatric hospital) 2
Brook, Peter 154
bundle of clothes, objects of the
living 216–17, 222

237